Regimes and Repertoires

Regimes and Repertoires

CHARLES TILLY

THE UNIVERSITY OF CHICAGO PRESS > *Chicago and London*

CHARLES TILLY is the Joseph L. Buttenweiser Professor of Social Science at Columbia University. He is the author of numerous books, including *Contention and Democracy in Europe, 1650–2000, Social Movements, 1768–2004,* and *Why?*

The University of Chicago Press, Chicago 60637
The University of Chicago Press, Ltd., London
©2006 by The University of Chicago
All rights reserved. Published 2006
Printed in the United States of America

15 14 13 12 11 10 09 08 07 06   1 2 3 4 5
ISBN-10: 0-226-80350-3 (cloth)
ISBN-13: 978-0-226-800350-0 (cloth)

Several pages on South Africa have been adapted from Charles Tilly, *Durable Inequality* (Berkeley: University of California Press, 1998), 118–23. ©1998 the Regents of the University of California.

 A small portion of chapter 1 has been adapted from "Regimes and Contention," in *The Handbook of Political Sociology,* ed. T. Janoski, R. Alford, A. Hicks, and M. Schwartz (Cambridge: Cambridge University Press, 2005), 423–29. ©Cambridge University Press 2005. Reprinted with the permission of Cambridge University Press.

Library of Congress Cataloging-in-Publication Data

Tilly, Charles.
  Regimes and repertoires / Charles Tilly.
    p. cm.
  Includes bibliographical references and index.
  ISBN 0-226-80350-3 (cloth : alk. paper)
   1. Revolutions. 2. Social movements. 3. Political violence.
  4. Government, Resistance to. I. Title.
  JC491.T53 2006
  322.4—dc22   2006002485

∞ The paper used in this publication meets the minimum requirements of the American National Standard for Information Sciences—Permanence of Paper for Printed Library Materials, ANSI Z39.48-1992.

CONTENTS >>

	PREFACE	vii
1	What Are Regimes?	1
2	How Regimes Work	18
3	Repertoires of Contention	30
4	Repertoires, Meet Regimes	60
5	Trajectories of Change	90
6	Collective Violence	118
7	Revolutions	151
8	Social Movements	179
9	Conclusions	209
	REFERENCES	217
	INDEX	243

PREFACE >>

BEHOLD AN ORPHAN that became a beloved foster child! As Doug McAdam, Sidney Tarrow, and I were writing segments of the manuscript eventually published in 2001 under the title *Dynamics of Contention* (*DOC*), I took special responsibility for analyses of the political regimes within which (and often against which) contentious politics takes place. My drafts of statements on the subject, however, meshed uneasily with the more voluntaristic, actor-centered analyses pursued by my collaborators. What's more, my treatment of regimes added even greater complexity to chapters that already ran the risk of imploding from the weight of their cross-connections. We finally decided to extrude almost all mentions of regimes from our joint book. We made the right decision: that additional dimension would have made *DOC* unreadable. But it separated my essays on regimes from their family.

Orphaned, the child did not die. Regimes figured prominently in most of my later work, including analyses of collective violence, visible political identities, democratization, and social movements. So, for that matter, did repertoires—the limited, familiar, historically created arrays of claim-making performances that under most circumstances greatly circumscribe the means by which people engage in contentious politics. Repertoires kept reappearing in contexts ranging from political boundary activation to intergroup violence. But the siblings—regimes and repertoires—deserved their own vehicle. Students of conflict and collective action have long proposed partial arguments connecting change and variation in contentious *repertoires* to change and variation in *regimes*, whether or not they have used the two principal terms as used here. This book takes relations between the two elements as its central problem.

Instead of seeking to construct general accounts of all regimes, all repertoires, and all interactions between them, however, the book narrows its focus considerably. It doggedly pursues three crucial questions: How do change and variation in regimes affect the forms and contents of contentious politics within those regimes? What explains the substantial differences in contentious politics among different types of regimes? How, in turn, do contentious processes alter regimes?

Those questions exclude others that readily come to mind. Taking "regime variation" chiefly to involve differences with respect to governmental capacity and democracy, this book does not ask what causes variations in capacity and democracy, a question that organizes my earlier books on state transformations, revolutions, and democratization. Nor does it ask what else—economic organization, population dynamics, cultural variation, and more—affects regime-to-regime variation in contentious politics. As a result, it arrives not at total but at partial explanations of variation and change in contentious politics, and at even more partial explanations of differences among regimes. It concentrates deliberately on the interplay of regime organization and qualities of political contention.

The siblings acknowledge their connection to the *DOC* lineage. Fearing another excessively complicated book, I have suppressed the extended discussions of mechanisms, processes, and episodes that *DOC* and later writings provided. Instead, this book shifts its emphasis to larger-scale arguments about interactions between regimes and repertoires without spelling out all the causal connections or demonstrating them by means of systematic comparisons among episodes. Nevertheless, its fundamental assumptions belong to the *DOC* tradition:

▸ When it comes to large-scale political structures and processes, no general laws or sufficient conditions exist.

▸ We might be able to identify necessary conditions for such processes as revolution and democratization.

▸ Correlational analyses and case comparisons can serve well to identify what we have to explain. But they cannot provide the explanations because they trace back variable outcomes to variable conditions without specifying the causal chains between conditions and outcomes.

- Proper explanations require identification of the mechanisms and processes in those causal chains.
- Conditions enter explanations, however, to the extent that they shape combinations and sequences of mechanisms and processes.
- Adequate explanations of large-scale social processes therefore show how variable combinations and sequences of invariant mechanisms produce variable outcomes under different initial conditions.

Instead of drumming away at these points, this book largely takes them for granted. The case for their validity rests on the credibility of the book's analyses concerning the interplay of regimes and contentious politics.

With permission, I have adapted several pages on South Africa from my *Durable Inequality,* and about the same number of pages from "Regimes and Contention." About a tenth of the book's text reproduces or adapts material from my previous publications. In no case, however, have I simply pasted in an old text. Careful readers of my *Politics of Collective Violence,* for example, will find chapter 7's analysis of French demonstrations familiar. Even there, nevertheless, I have updated the description by drawing on Danielle Tartakowsky's 2004 analysis of Parisian demonstrations since 1975. I hope that readers will take pleasure in the continuities with my previous work rather than becoming bored by *déjà vu.*

I am happy to acknowledge advice, criticism, information, and encouragement by Adam Ashforth, Mark Beissinger, Miguel Centeno, Mikael Eriksson, Lotta Harborn, David Laitin, Douglas Mitchell, Sidney Tarrow, Peter Wallensteen, Lesley Wood, Viviana Zelizer, and an anonymous reviewer. David Bemelmans gave me the gift of insightful copyediting. From opposite directions, both Centeno and Tarrow recommended major revisions in the text. Neither one will be satisfied by the modest attempts at clarification I made in response to their critiques. I hope, nevertheless, that the book will give all these helpful colleagues and others some new ideas with which to contend.

CHAPTER ONE >>
What Are Regimes?

PERU, CENTER OF THE INCA EMPIRE, became a jewel of Spain's colonial domains during the sixteenth century. Its silver and gold eventually financed trade as far away as China. Despite its promising background, since Peru's independence in 1824 the country has had a troubled history. Regime succeeded regime and coup followed coup. One faction of military men or another usually ran the country, often with the backing of foreign capitalists. Then, in the late twentieth century, halting democratization began.

It began, however, with a nondemocratic blow. Coming to power by yet another coup in 1968, the regime of General Juan Velasco Alvarado adopted its own variant of the Latin American populist model: it tolerated the formation of labor unions and granted land titles to squatter settlements in an effort to contain them both. Those concessions, however, solidified the opposition and opened the way to precarious democratization (Collier 1999, 115–19; Mason 2004, chap. 9). After two more regime turnovers, in 1980 a sustained period of formally democratic rule began. Even then, intense struggles continued among civilian officials, military leaders, organized workers, indigenous peoples, the urban poor, and organized rebels.

Democratic rule never reached much of the Peruvian countryside. By 1988, highland Peru bled with civil war. A Maoist guerrilla group called Sendero Luminoso (Shining Path) posed the regime's greatest threat. In 1988, Sendero's leader Abimael Guzmán gave a Lima newspaper his first interview in ten years. While he remained silent about the recent capture and arrest of Osman Morote, his deputy and military commander, the venerable *Annual Register* reported:

> [Guzmán] called for a new stage in the struggle. "Our process of the people's war has led us towards the apex," he claimed, adding: "We have to prepare for insurrection, which will be the taking of the cities." In May the discovery of five bodies in an unmarked grave confirmed the reported massacre by soldiers of 28 peasants in Cayará, but President Alan García, who had initially been critical of such excesses, indirectly defended the armed forces, who had been increasingly insistent that he should do so. (*Annual Register* 1988, 80–81)

At the same time, the rival Túpac Amaru Revolutionary Movement was battling the Peruvian army in the mountains. During 1989, Sendero Luminoso was organizing attacks and strikes in the Peruvian capital Lima, where García declared martial law (Burt 1997). Meanwhile, hyperinflation was racking the national economy.

Over the next fifteen years, a spectacular set of regime changes occurred in Peru. The country's struggles from 1989 to 2003 illustrate the questions that are the focus of this book: how do diverse forms of political contention—revolutions, strikes, wars, social movements, coups d'état, and others—interact with shifts from one kind of regime to another? To what extent, and how, do alterations of contentious politics and transformations of regimes cause one another? Does virulent violence, for example, necessarily accompany rapid regime transitions?

These questions loom behind current inquiries into democratization, with their debate between theorists who consider agreements among elites to provide necessary and sufficient conditions for democracy and those who insist that democracy only emerges from the interplay between ruling-class actions and popular struggle. They arise when political analysts ask whether (or under what conditions) social movements promote democracy, and whether stable democracy extinguishes or tames social movements. They appear from another angle in investigations of whether democracies tend to avoid war with one another. At least as context, they loom large in every historical account of popular politics.

The same sorts of questions recur in studies of industrial conflict, where one school of thought declares that strikes represent breakdowns in bargaining pursued more efficiently by other means, another school argues that strikes entail compromises of labor with capital and thereby integrate workers unwittingly into capitalism, while a third view treats strikes as rational, essential means of struggle in competitive capitalism but not elsewhere. They dog every analysis of revolution, which must consider whether certain kinds of contention regularly promote revolutions as well as whether revolutions regularly generate certain kinds of contention.

So far, we have no coherent theory of links between regime change and contentious politics. We have, that is, no widely accepted, logically connected, and empirically defensible account of how prevailing forms of popular struggle vary and change from one sort of political regime to another, much less why such variation and change occur. At least two obstacles bar the path to coherent theory: first, the relationship between regime change and contentious politics is complex, contingent, and variable; second, no codification of variation in regimes or in contentious politics has commanded wide assent.

Regimes and contentious politics clearly connect, but only contingently. Many a relation among political actors operates without open contention, as participants fulfill routine obligations, form coalitions, make deals, share members, and pay each other off. On the other side, contentious politics need not center on governmental agents or major political actors; many strikes, for example, pit workers against employers while enlisting police or officials chiefly as monitors and boundary-setters. Here I seek not to explain all facets of regimes or every aspect of contentious politics. The focus instead is on the zone of their mutual influence.

In order to connect these complex phenomena to each other, furthermore, we must work very selectively. We must concentrate on a few significant variations and causal connections. In meeting this challenge, we have deplorably little systematic analysis to build on. Analysts commonly recognize the concentration of social movements (narrowly defined) in parliamentary democracies, the vulnerability of weakened despotic regimes to revolution, and the greater frequency of coups d'état where military forces exercise great autonomy. Discussions of regimes also retail a miscellany of near-tautologies such as the prevalence of strikes under industrial capitalism or the concentration of peasant revolts in large-landlord systems. But we have no well-established general mapping of variation in the forms and dynamics of contentious politics across the multiple types of governmental regime.

Existing formulations, furthermore, suffer major weaknesses. They offer little insight into two-way interactions between contentious political processes and their social settings, especially into the processes by which contentious politics incited by certain sorts of regime (for example, authoritarian states) in turn transforms those regimes. Nor do they offer a plausible account of interpretation—for example, the interplay between understandings that pervade routine politics and those that inform contentious claims. Much less, then, do we have a dynamic causal account that explains interconnections between regimes and contention.

This book proposes a dynamic causal account of regimes and political contention. Put starkly, its organizing questions run like this:

1. How do political regimes vary and change?

2. How do the means by which people living in various sorts of regimes make consequential collective claims on each other and on their governments—their contentious politics—vary and change?

3. What connections exist—in both directions—between regime change or variation and the character of contentious politics? How much and how do the two influence each other?

Superior answers to these three questions should help us identify the sorts of struggle that occurred in Peru from 1989 to 2003 not simply as expressions of Peru's uniqueness but as consequences of more general regularities in the interplay between regimes and contentious politics.

Back to Peru

Before surveying the analytical tools available for that formidable task, let us reconsider Peru. A closer look will identify some connections between Peruvian regime structures and contentious politics and thus help specify what we must explain. It will also underline the high stakes of our inquiry.

After a decade of relatively democratic civilian government threatened by mounting civil war, Alan García's presidential term ended in 1990. Voters sought change. Out of a large field of candidates emerged two who survived to the runoff: novelist Mario Vargas Llosa and mathematician Alberto Fujimori, rector of Peru's National Agrarian University. Internationally famous Vargas Llosa aligned with the Peruvian elite, while Fujimori identified himself with the masses; his immigrant parents, after all, had been school caretakers. Fujimori opposed Vargas Llosa's free-market program and pledged to resist International Monetary Fund demands for belt-tightening.

In his autobiographical *Fish in the Water,* Vargas Llosa describes his amazement at the late surge in support for Fujimori, and his deep suspicion that García's forces had secretly shifted their support to Fujimori in order to forestall the disaster of a Vargas Llosa victory and the political housecleaning it would produce. Still, up to two weeks before the election he remained confident:

> I thought, however, that the vote for Fujimori—the vote meant to castigate us—couldn't possibly amount to more than 10 percent or

so of the electorate, the most uninformed and uncultured voters. Who else would vote for an unknown, without a team for governing, without any political credentials whatsoever, who had hardly campaigned outside of Lima, who had been jury-rigged overnight to serve as a candidate? No matter what the opinion polls said, it never entered my head that a candidacy so devoid of ideas and with no planning staff could carry weight in the face of the monumental effort we had put in over a period of almost three years of work. (Vargas Llosa 1994, 459)

But Fujimori received 24 percent of the popular vote, second only to Vargas Llosa's 29 percent, both far short of the 50 percent required for a first-round victory. In the runoff, after a grueling campaign, Fujimori was elected by a margin of 57 to 34 percent. The "most uninformed and uncultured voters" had spoken. Despite Fujimori's populist campaign promises, however, once in office he began abolishing governmental subsidies, privatizing public services, and promoting international trade. He also made another move, little noticed at the time, that marked the rest of his tenure as president: he recruited Vladimiro Montesinos as security advisor.

The appointment was no venial incident. Vladimiro Ilyich Montesinos Torres, born to a left-leaning Arequipa family in 1946, owed his name to his parents' admiration for V. I. Lenin. The prodigal son would move away definitively from his communist elders. After military training in Panama and Peru, he entered the Peruvian army as an artillery lieutenant, rapidly becoming personal adjutant to General Mercado Jarrin. When Jarrin became prime minister and commander of the armed forces in 1973, the twenty-seven-year-old Montesinos began his personal collection of compromising information about military officers and political figures. He also launched a career of semi-legal and illegal activity.

In 1976, Montesinos forged a presidential signature, sent himself on a mission to the United States, passed himself off as an official representative of the Peruvian government, then advised the Rand Corporation and the CIA on Peruvian military capabilities. The army riposted sternly: it court-martialed Montesinos, gave him a dishonorable discharge, and sent him to jail for a year. He studied law in prison, bought himself a law degree and admission to the bar, then began legal practice in defense of accused tax evaders and drug dealers. But he also started working closely with the Servicio de Inteligencia Nacional (SIN), the government's domestic security agency.

During the 1990 election campaign, opponents accused Fujimori's wife of tax evasion on a real estate deal. Advised by the director of Peru's secret service, Fujimori took on Montesinos as his legal counselor; the tax evasion charge evaporated. (So, some observers say, did Fujimori's birth certificate, which established that he was born in Japan and was therefore ineligible for the presidency.) In fact if not in name, Montesinos became Fujimori's chief of intelligence. At the time, indeed, U.S. Army intelligence agents wrote a report about relations between the two titled *Who is Controlling Whom?* (National Security Archive 2000). Under Montesinos's guidance, Fujimori soon placed allies in the army's high command, suspended Congress and the courts, packed their successors with more compliant officials, stepped up clandestine action against leftist rebels and their sympathizers, but also—with U.S. support—managed an economic recovery.

By 2000, SIN was receiving 8 to 9 million dollars per month altogether from three sources inside Peru: its official budget, under the table transfers by government agencies, and payments from Montesinos's collaborators in arms deals or other illegal businesses (McMillan and Zoido 2004, 76). Montesinos reportedly also received massive chunks of money from the American CIA for his collaboration in the U.S. war on drugs. Meanwhile, he stashed millions of dollars in his own Swiss bank accounts. No one held him accountable for the huge amounts of cash he handled.

Fujimori and Montesinos engineered a previously forbidden second presidential term in 1995, defeating former UN secretary general Javier Pérez de Cuellar in what seems to have been a fair vote. True to populist tradition, Fujimori's modest origins continued to attract the urban poor and many rural people as well (Panfichi 1997). The elite, however, remained suspicious. Montesinos used a combination of threats and bribes to keep legislators, judges, newspapers, and television stations in line, secretly filming his payoffs as insurance. Fujimori ran an unprecedented third-term campaign in 2000. As the economy faltered, however, a strong opposition formed around Alejandro Toledo, another newcomer. Toledo had grown up in an Indian shantytown but had gone on to study economics in the United States. Both outside observers and domestic opponents declared the vote fraudulent, but Fujimori had himself certified as the winner.

Fujimori hung on until September 2000, when a dissident television station—one of the few not paid off by Montesinos—intervened. Taking a leaf from her master's playbook, Montesinos's bookkeeper and mistress had removed a tape from his collection for her own use. She gave it to opposition politicians, who brought it to the television station. The video showed a former opposition member of parliament accepting a bribe to change his vote. Montesinos fled to Panama with $15 million in "severance pay" from Fujimori, returned to precipitate a political crisis including an attempted army coup, then left for Venezuela. On a November trip to Southeast Asia, Fujimori detoured to Japan. He never returned to Peru.

In 2001, new elections brought Toledo to the presidency in a victory over Alan García. Soon after, Venezuelan and Peruvian agents seized Montesinos in Venezuela and took him back for trial in Peru. Two years later, Switzerland repatriated $77.5 million from bank accounts Montesinos had controlled. But Toledo discovered that Montesinos's institutional legacy lived on; in September 2003, Toledo fired the retired admiral he had appointed to head SIN when it came out that the spy agency had tapped Toledo's telephone and leaked the tape to a scandal-mongering television program.

As Montesinos came to trial, some seven hundred "Vladivideos" surfaced. Reviewing the evidence from videos and state documents, two Stanford economists (McMillan and Zoido 2004, 78–81) showed that payments (typically made in U.S. dollars) to cooperative individuals ran as follows:

Legislators and officials	$10,000–50,000 per month
Judges	$2,500–55,000 per month, graded by rank of court
Newpapers	One-time payments or payments per issue or per (favorable) headline, from $1,000 apiece to a total of 1.5 million for one newspaper
TV channels	$500,000–1,500,000 per month, plus one-time payments

The payment schedule displays a perverse logic. It shows that, at least in Montesinos's estimation, media mattered more than public officials. By the late 1990s, the threat that popular mobilization against the regime would spring from television coverage looked even more salient than the likelihood that officials would defect. In the event, a television broadcast of a video recording a bribe did start the cascade that sent Fujimori into exile and put Montesinos in jail.

Why does this sordid story matter? It matters because Peruvian history after 1988 poses specific versions of our three organizing questions: How should we describe and explain the spectacular changes of regime that Peru underwent during that brief period? What shifts and variations in Peru's popular contention occurred, and why? What connects the dynamics of Peruvian political contention to alterations in its governing regimes? We notice, for example, that Fujimori and Montesinos did not simply return to the authoritarian nondemocratic regimes of their many predecessors; they felt obliged to manipulate the forms of democracy.

How generally, to what extent, and how, does the installation of formally democratic institutions inhibit raw forms of governmental coercion such as simply assassinating members of the opposition?

The story of Peru from 1988 to 2003 also underscores another point that will matter repeatedly throughout the book. Controlling a government gives people major advantages over those who lack that control. It gives them access to information, resources, and coercive means that in most regimes greatly surpass those available to any other organization within the same regime. Holders of governmental power can use the information, resources, and coercive means to their own personal profit, to favor their own segment of the population, to promote causes they espouse, or to advance their visions of the public good. These features help explain why people kill, bribe, lie, conquer, form coalitions, or compete strenuously in elections on their way to securing governmental power. Inevitably, struggles to acquire or retain governmental power involve contentious politics.

Aristotle on Types of Regime

In order to explain how connections between regimes and contention work, we must think more generally and systematically about variations and transitions among political regimes. First, how shall we map regimes? Aristotle made it all seem vividly simple: "The true forms of government . . . are those in which the one, or the few, or the many, govern with a view to the common interest; but governments which rule with a view to the private interest, whether of the one, or of the few, or of the many, are perversions" (Barnes 1984, 2:2030). This reasoning led to a straightforward typology of all governmental forms:

TRUE	PERVERSION
Monarchy	Tyranny
Aristocracy	Oligarchy
Constitutional Government	Democracy

Thus if a single ruler (a monarch) promoted his own self-interest instead of the common good, he became a tyrant; if an aristocracy similarly used governmental power exclusively for its own advantage, the regime became an oligarchy; and if the majority in a constitutional government likewise sought only their own benefit without regard to the commonwealth, their regime became a democracy.

According to Aristotelian principle, proper monarchy rested on rule by the best man, aristocracy on rule by the richest and best men, and constitutional government on rule by free men. (For Aristotle, ineluctable nature condemned women, like slaves, to inferiority.) Since the rich are usually few in number and the free poor many in number, reasoned Aristotle, as a practical matter aristocratic regimes generally mean rule by the few in the common interest, constitutional government rule by the many, likewise in the common interest. Perversions into tyranny, oligarchy, and democracy arise where rulers—one, few, or many—place their own interest above the common good. Democracy's characteristic perversion, in this Aristotelian view, consists of discrimination by the governing poor against both the state's collective interest and the interests of the rich.

To be sure, Aristotle recognized distinctions within his major types of regime—for example, five types of democracy, the fifth of which he described as follows:

> [Not] the law, but the multitude, have the supreme power, and supersede the law by their decrees. This is a state of affairs brought about by the demagogues. For in democracies which are subject to the law the best citizens hold the first place, and there are no demagogues; but where the laws are not supreme, there demagogues spring up. For the people becomes a monarch, and is many in one; and the many have the power in their hand, not as individuals, but collectively . . . this sort of democracy is to other democracies what tyranny is to other forms of monarchy. (Barnes 1984, 2:2050–51)

In these circumstances, furthermore, demagogues often stir up the rabble to attack the rich and thereby seize power for themselves. In this way, democracy turns into tyranny. When he got to details, Aristotle allowed for plenty of transitions and compromises among his three pure types.

Aristotle proceeded repeatedly from ostensibly static categories to dynamic causal processes. In thinking through the effects of different military formats, for example, he offered a shrewd causal account:

> As there are four chief divisions of the common people, farmers, artisans, traders, labourers; so also there are four kinds of military forces—the cavalry, the heavy infantry, the light-armed troops, the navy. When the country is adapted for cavalry, then a strong oligarchy is likely to be established. For the security of the inhabitants depends upon a force of this sort, and only rich men can afford to keep horses. The second form of oligarchy prevails when a country

is adapted to heavy infantry; for this service is better suited to the rich than to the poor. But the light-armed and the naval element are wholly democratic; and nowadays, where they are numerous, if the two parties quarrel, the oligarchy are often worsted by them in the struggle. (Barnes 1984, 2:2096–97)

In the *Politics*, Aristotle confined his systematic discussion of political contention to revolutions, which meant forcible overthrow of regimes by ostensible subjects of those regimes. In passing, however, he also mentioned factional struggles, conspiracies, and collective resistance to governmental demands. In each case, he treated the regime's form as an outgrowth of the balance among social forces (notably among the rich, the middle class, and the poor) tempered by historical circumstance. He then explained contention as a joint outcome of that balance and the regime type, again tempered by historical circumstance.

Without developing his observations at length, Aristotle clearly saw different sorts of regimes as having their own characteristic forms of contention, and changes of regime as resulting largely from political contention. In contrasting regimes, different ruling coalitions pursued distinct strategies of rule, which altered the incentives and capacities of various constituted groups within the state to defend or advance their own interests by acting collectively. Aristotle explained political struggles of his day by combining the perspectives of rationalists and structuralists, millennia before anyone used those labels (for those labels, see Lichbach and Zuckerman 1997).

Principle and History as Bases of Classification

Broadly speaking, recent analysts of relations among regime types, regime transitions, and forms of public politics have arrayed themselves along a continuum whose two ends we might call "Principle" and "History." Despite employing historical illustrations, Aristotle situated his analyses fairly close to the continuum's Principle end: regardless of their proximity or distance in space and time, one regime differed from another to the extent that their rationales, premises, or organizing principles differed. Historical encyclopedias, in contrast, frequently place themselves at the continuum's other end, treating regimes as different to the extent that they operate in different times and places; historians speak of ancient Mesopotamian empires or the early modern European state (see, for example, Stearns 2001).

At both ends of the continuum, accounts of regimes become quite descriptive. At the Principle extreme appear attempts to capture the internal coherence of whole types such as fascism or state socialism. At the

History extreme, we find attempts to identify the particularities of Ming China or Tokugawa Japan. The extremes do not much interest us here, but location of competing regime classification regimes along the continuum matters, for explanatory strategies vary systematically along the continuum. Toward the Principle end concentrate inquiries into necessary and sufficient conditions for different types of regimes (Dogan and Higley 1998; Dogan and Pelassy 1984; Held 1996; Spruyt 2002). Toward the History end, we find searches for recurrent processes—notably including path-dependent processes—that regularly cause regime changes without producing identical outcomes (Collier and Collier 1991; Mahoney and Snyder 1999; Mahoney 2001, 2002).

Consider Marxist accounts. Beginning with Marx's own work on precapitalist economic formations (Marx 1964), Marxists have usually taken positions near the midpoint of the continuum, but on the History side: modes of production generate each other in well-defined historical sequences, with struggle that emerges from a given mode's internal contradictions driving the transition to the next mode (see, for example, Anderson 1974a, 1974b). But within each mode, the logic of productive relations shapes a political regime that implements the power of the mode's dominant class. Thus in the *Communist Manifesto* simplification bourgeois revolution destroys feudal regimes and replaces them with parliamentary regimes implementing bourgeois interests.

My great teacher Barrington Moore criticized the classic Marxist account but replaced it with another one located at almost precisely the same position on the Principle–History continuum (Moore 1966). A specialist in Russian politics and a close student of Russian history, Moore attributed more importance to class relations within agriculture than have most Marxists. While sharing with Marx the idea that parliamentary democracy resulted from bourgeois predominance, Moore argued that commercialization of agriculture, elimination of great landlords, and proletarianization of the peasantry (rather than the rise of industry itself) together opened the way toward bourgeois predominance. Yet for Moore, as for Marx, changing configurations of class generated regime transitions through struggle. Contention caused regimes.

Moore's analysis inspired a great deal of subsequent work on regime transitions (for example, Andrews and Chapman 1995; Collier 1999; Downing 1992; Rueschemeyer, Stephens, and Stephens 1992; Skocpol 1979; Stephens 1989). More than anything else, analysts in Moore's lineage have sought to explain how democratic regimes replace nondemocratic regimes. There they confront a host of theorists who operate closer to the Principle end of the continuum, looking for necessary and sufficient conditions of democratic regimes.

In a convenient if risky simplification, many students of contemporary democratization distinguish two main types of regime: authoritarian and democratic (for example, Przeworski et al. 2000). Their work ranges from close comparison of particular cases in a search for crucial differences to quantitative comparisons of many regimes in which authoritarianism and democracy become the low and high ends of the same variable: degree of democracy (APSA Task Force 2004; Anderson et al. 2001; Arat 1991; Bratton and van de Walle 1997; Burkhart and Lewis-Beck 1994; Collier and Levitsky 1997; Davenport 2004; Dawisha and Parrott 1997; Diamond 1999; 2002, Diamond et al. 2004; Engelstad and Østerud 2004; Fish 2005; Lijphart 1999; Linz and Stepan 1996; Morlino 2003; Vanhanen 1997; Yashar 1997).

A similar distribution of analyses appears in the comparative study of welfare states. Although often starting from the relatively historical account of British welfare policy formulated by T. H. Marshall (Marshall 1950; see also Barbalet 1988; Beland 2005; Turner 1997), recent efforts have concentrated on two largely unhistorical questions: What conditions promote the development of different degrees and kinds of social provisioning? What effects do different systems of social provisioning have on the actual social lives of citizens in different types of regimes?

Once again, the range runs from close comparison of particular cases in a search for crucial differences to quantitative comparisons of many regimes in which different levels or aspects of provisioning or social experience turn into variables to be explained by a variety of theoretically motivated predictors (Esping-Anderson 1990; Goodin et al. 1999; Hage, Hanneman, and Gargan 1989; Huber and Stephens 2001; Janoski 1998; Janoski and Hicks 1994; Ruggie 1996). These and similar studies provide intellectual resources—but not definitive answers—for the analysis of connections between regimes and political contention.

From Dahl to Finer

Rather than criticizing, codifying, or synthesizing these various approaches to typification of regimes and regime transitions, let me reconstruct just two exemplary analyses, one on the Principle side of our continuum, the other closer to History's end. For Principle, take Robert Dahl. For History, take S. E. Finer.

Robert Dahl's treatment of approximations to democracy has a distinctly Aristotelian air. As summarized in figure 1.1, Dahl's useful scheme distinguishes two dimensions of variation: inclusiveness, or the extent to which people under a given regime's jurisdiction have the right to participate at all, and liberalization, which is the extent to which participants in

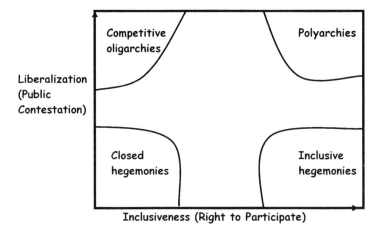

Figure 1.1. Robert Dahl's classification of regimes

the regime have rights to contest conditions of rule. Dahl adds to Aristotle the recognition of very inclusive regimes that allow little public contestation, which Dahl calls "inclusive hegemonies." He also leaves plenty of space between his four regimes where we might locate a great many other regimes—for example, the thinly ruled nomadic empires, urban federations, composite dynastic states, and city-empires that governed much of Europe five hundred years ago.

What Dahl calls "contestation" enters his classification as a bundle of rights at the liberal extreme:

- Freedom to form and join organizations
- Freedom of expression
- The right to vote
- Eligibility for public office
- Competition by political leaders for support
- Alternative sources of information
- Free and fair elections
- Institutions for making government policies depend on votes and other expressions of preference

Regimes vary enormously, as Dahl declares, "in the extent to which the eight institutional conditions are openly available, publicly employed, and fully guaranteed to at least some members of the political systems who wish to contest the conduct of the government" (Dahl 1975, 119; see also Dahl 1998; Lindblom 1977). His closed hegemonies accord such rights to no one, his competitive oligarchies extend them to a small elite, his inclusive hegemonies entertain no such rights, and his polyarchies open them to much of the population. Note that under the label "contestation" Dahl is speaking about institutionalized rights to opposition, not about the character or frequency of contention.

Noninstitutionalized public contention enters Dahl's story incognito. It appears as demands (of unspecified form) that regimes remove causes of extreme inequality, as disputes in which one segment of the population appears to threaten the survival of another, as the formation of revolutionary oppositions, and as foreign conquest. His scheme therefore challenges us to specify the interaction between regimes and the rights embedded within them, on one side, and contentious politics that sometimes adopt rightful means and sometimes defy them, on the other. The work at hand includes relating regimes and regime change to prevailing distributions of (1) actors, actions, and identities in contentious politics, (2) conditions for the emergence of such politics, and (3) their trajectories and outcomes.

Samuel Finer's *History of Government* provides another neo-Aristotelian handle for the classification of regimes. As its title implies, however, Finer's lengthy trilogy takes a significantly more historical position than Dahl's analysis. After stipulating that one can classify regimes along a territorial dimension (city, national, or empire), divide decisionmaking personnel into elites and masses, and distinguish decision implementation by bureaucracies and armed forces, Finer ultimately settles, like Aristotle, for a focus on the social character of a regime's ruling personnel. As illustrated in figure 1.2, Finer identifies four pure types: palace (monarch and following), nobility (privileged class), forum (segments or representatives of populace), and church (priesthood). The diagram's double-headed arrows portray paths of movement from one regime type to another and locations of mixed regime types.

Contention thrusts its way repeatedly into Finer's accounts of particular regimes. Speaking of Italian city-states, for example, Finer observes that thirteenth-century patriciates often closed their ranks to newcomers, but not without cost:

> They came under pressure from the less wealthy or newly wealthy elements demanding a due share in office; the so-called "democratic" movement. These elements, characteristically, used their guild organizations to channel their pressure, so that the struggle

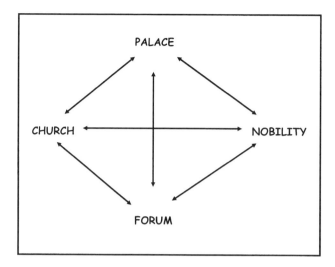

Figure 1.2. Samuel Finer's typology of regimes

looks like craft-guilds trying to break the political monopoly of the wealthier and more prestigious merchant-guilds. In Italy . . . these excluded elements formed themselves into sworn associations and called themselves the "People"—the *popolo*—and tried to assert their claims by revolt. But what happened in Italy is but the paradigm case of what was occurring in much of urbanized Europe as the thirteenth century began to close: resistance to the oligarchy, violence, even revolution. (Finer 1997, 2:954)

Pursuing other ends, however, Finer does not examine relationships—empirical or causal—among regime types, political transitions, and forms of contentious politics. This book concentrates, in contrast, on asking how and why political contention varies from one regime type to another, and how contention interacts with movement from regime to regime.

Our Problem Revisited

Following the premises laid out earlier, let us approach that pair of questions here in profound skepticism about the existence of neat correspondences between regime type A and action X, emergence process Y, or trajectory Z. On the contrary, we should search for rough empirical regularities in hope of accomplishing two distinct objectives: first, to specify what theoretically telling similarities and differences must be explained by any causal account of contention; second, to place firmly on the agenda how historically accumulated models, memories, understandings, and social relations—for example, residues of the Mongol empire's previous hegemony in a given region—affect the operation of contentious politics. The challenge is therefore to create two rough conceptual maps—one of regimes, the other of contentious politics—whose similarities and differences pose crucial questions of causation. We map regimes and repertoires separately, identify their correspondences, note their differences, and look for the causes that connect them: ways that regimes shape repertoires, ways that repertoires shape regimes.

Our basic map of regimes will remain very simple. In one dimension we place variations in governmental capacity—roughly speaking, the extent to which rulers' deliberate actions affect distributions of people, activities, and resources within the government's territory. Along the other dimension, we array regimes by their degree of democracy or nondemocracy, the extent to which persons subject to the government's authority have broad, equal rights to influence governmental affairs and to receive protection from arbitrary governmental action. That capacity-democracy space will allow us, for example, to compare the very different forms of politics that occur in high-capacity, democratic regimes and low-capacity, nondemocratic regimes. Chapter 2 will start the adventure of classifying regimes and their changes.

Forms of politics? The vignettes of Peru that started this chapter gave us glimpses of coups, civil wars, governmental thuggery, electoral competition, and more. Later sections of the book will take us on to a much wider variety of contentious politics. Those forms of politics will have in common that politically relevant actors are making consequential collective claims on other politically relevant actors. Generally speaking, they are struggling for power and advantage.

As links between regimes and contention, we will discover several partly independent clusters of causes, especially structures for political opportunity and contentious repertoires. From the top down, governmental policies and relations among established political actors constitute a political-opportunity structure that limits the chances for ordinary people to make collective claims either on governments or on other actors.

From the bottom up, previously established performances and repertoires likewise limit the initiatives available to ordinary people. We will see how collective contention involves such performances as the street demonstration or the coup d'état, and how performances group into repertoires such as contemporary social movements' whole array of claim-making routines. But we will also see how the typical interactions of social movements, revolutions, and other forms of contention differ from each other because both the available repertoires and the prevailing structures for political opportunity favor different kinds and consequences of collective claim-making.

Let me say clearly what the book does not do, and what it only does halfway. It does *not* provide a comprehensive account of all change and variation in contentious politics. Instead, it concentrates on how regime change and variation affect contentious politics. Nor does the book offer a general description or explanation of regime change and variation, a topic I have dealt with extensively in other books. It singles out the kinds of change and variation in regimes that have the largest, most direct, and most visible impact on political contention. That means favoring shifts in alignments among major political actors and in forms of government over incremental transformations of economy, population, environment, and belief systems.

Although later chapters repeatedly call attention to the effects of contention on the form and operation of regimes, on balance they say much more about how regimes shape contention than vice versa. The book therefore says little about issues on which I have spilled a great deal of ink elsewhere—for example, the democratizing and de-democratizing effects stemming from different kinds of contention. The book's analyses center on how regime variation and change shape the ways in which people make consequential collective claims: their contentious politics.

The remainder of this book contains three main sections plus a conclusion. The next section (chapters 2–4) continues the relatively static and classificatory approach of this one, first by laying out some tools for the description and analysis of contentious politics, followed by reviewing intersections of regimes with various forms of contentious politics. Then a shift to dynamics occurs. Chapter 5 moves on to consider regime change, change in the forms of contentious politics, and interactions between them. Chapters 6–8 apply the insights of earlier chapters to three processes involving contentious politics: collective violence, revolutions, and social movements. The conclusion considers where we have arrived and where to go next.

CHAPTER TWO >>
How Regimes Work

THE VIGNETTES OF PERUVIAN POLITICS in chapter 1 introduced colorful political actors such as Alberto Fujimori, Vladimiro Montesinos, Abimael Guzmán, and Alejandro Toledo. They led us through a variety of struggles including Sendero Luminoso's sustained civil war and the expulsion of Fujimori from the Peruvian presidency. But they touched only lightly on the nature of the Peruvian regime, which was following a rocky path to democratization. Before knowing how to describe and place Peru's regime changes after 1990, we must adopt some new analytical tools.

We begin with a *government:* a coercion-wielding organization that enjoys priority over all other organizations in some connected set and over the populations attached to those organizations; in the Peru of 1989–2003, for example, we see a national organization including the presidency, the army, SIN, the judiciary, and the legislature. The organization never quite shatters despite intense internal divisions, and even in regions of civil war never quite loses the upper hand. A set of further definitions follows.

Governmental agents are members of organizations with the power to deploy their organizations' resources, to act on their organizations' behalf, and/or to speak for their organizations; they include both individuals and subdivisions of the government. In Peru we have already seen successive presidents, Vladimiro Montesinos, the armed forces, and legislators acting in the company of a great many other agents.

Major political actors, then, include all such organizations and agents plus other connected clusters of persons having recognized names and recurrent interchanges with the government; in Peru during the period in question we must add labor unions, political parties, organized indigenous groups, shantytown activists, media organizations, Túpac Amaru, Sendero Luminoso, plus a number of other actors not yet encountered.

A *regime* means repeated, strong interactions among major political actors including a government; for Peru, then, we single out the more salient patterns of interaction among all these actors: not only the army, the government, and political parties, but also labor unions, indigenous groups, shantytown activists, media organizations, progovernment and antigovernment militias, churches, associations, and organized segments of business. When interactions between a pair of actors recur in similar forms, we begin to speak of a *relation* between the actors. We then describe a regime in terms of prevailing relations among political actors, including the government.

We make a rough distinction among members, challengers, and outsiders: actors that have routine access to the government and each other, organized actors that are bidding for power but lack routine access, and outside actors (for example, the Chilean government, the Organization of American States, and the United States) that intervene in domestic politics without exercising routine membership. In later chapters, with respect to any particular regime, the term "power holders" singles out those members that currently exercise the greatest control over governmental agents.

Political resources divide broadly into coercion, capital, and commitment. The term "coercion" includes all concerted means of action that commonly cause loss or damage to the persons, possessions, or sustaining social relations of social actors. It features such means as weapons, armed forces, prisons, damaging information, and organized routines for imposing sanctions. Coercion's organization helps define the nature of regimes. With low accumulations of coercion, all regimes are insubstantial, while with high levels of coercive accumulation and concentration all regimes are formidable.

We have seen both the government of Peru and those of its opponents such as Sendero Luminoso deploying coercion extensively. In Peru, coercive means had accumulated widely, but the government had been unable to concentrate them in its own hands. When it comes to coercion, the combination of high accumulation with low concentration generally produces plenty of violent conflict, as multiple coercion-wielders compete with each other for power and plunder. Peru amply illustrates the case.

Capital refers to tangible, transferable resources that in combination with effort can produce increases in use value, plus enforceable claims on such resources. Regimes that command substantial capital—for example, from rulers' direct control of natural resources, itself often undergirded by coercion—to some extent substitute purchase of other resources and compliance for direct coercion of their subject populations. Vladimiro Montesinos used capital extensively in neutralizing possible opponents of the Peruvian regime. Vargas Llosa suspected that the García government had previously used its own capital to support Vargas Llosa's upstart opponent Alberto Fujimori.

Commitment means relations among social sites (persons, groups, structures, or positions) that promote their taking account of each other. Shared language, for instance, powerfully links social sites without any necessary deployment of coercion or capital. Commitment's local organization varies as dramatically as do structures of coercion and capital. Commitments can take the form of shared religion or ethnicity, trading ties, work-generated solidarities, communities of taste, and much more. To the extent that commitments of these sorts connect rulers and ruled, they substitute partially for coercion and capital. But commitment can also turn against a government, as in the indigenous highland communities where Peru's Sendero Luminoso and Túpac Amaru guerrillas recruited extensive followings.

Contention in general includes any individual's or group's making of consequential claims on another individual or group. "Consequential" means the claims would, if realized, affect their object's interests. You and your spouse may contend over spending money, visiting relatives, cleaning out closets, or any number of other issues. Contention becomes *political*, however, when the claims are public and collective, at least one of the parties is already a political actor, and a government is at least a party to the claims in the sense that successful pressing of the claims will involve government agents as monitors, regulators, guarantors, or implementers.

Although contention among political actors and contention between spouses resemble each other in some regards, I single out political contention. Political contention matters because it always has implications for a regime's future and engages the coercive power of governments. In Peru, we witness intervention of police, the army, and government-backed death squads.

Public politics within a regime consists of claim-making interactions among agents, polity members, challengers, and outside political actors as well. Most public politics does not involve contention in the strong sense of the word used here. It includes elections, voter registration, legislative activity, patenting, tax collection, military conscription, group application for pensions, and many other transactions to which governments are parties. Most public political transactions within most regimes—even the turbulent Peru of 1989–2003—pass without open contention.

Contentious politics occurs, then, when connected clusters of persons make consequential claims on other clusters of persons or on major political actors, just so long as at least one government is a claimant, an object of claims, or a third party to the claims. In the case of Peru, we must include not only the civil wars and the gigantic struggles that brought regime changes, but also a wide range of meetings, strikes, demonstrations, and armed attacks my brief account has omitted.

In light of the foregoing analytic tools, box 2.1 summarizes the book's organizing arguments. The box's thirteen items identify a clear set of problems and a distinctive approach to resolving them. Following the leads in this introduction, the approach begins with changes and variations among different types of regime. It moves on to map changes and variations in contentious politics, relying heavily on the analysis of contentious repertoires. Next comes the identification of systematic variations in repertoires across different sorts of regime. That static effort leads to an analysis of dynamics: how regimes and repertoires change in connection with each other. The book's later sections apply the lessons of the earlier ones to three main categories of contentious politics: collective violence, revolutions, and social movements. Those three discussions are intended to show that the earlier analyses provide fresh, useful, consistent explanations for highly diverse forms of struggle.

Types of Regimes

How should we connect regimes with contentious politics? We can take our lead from Aristotle, creating a simple taxonomy of regimes on the way to reasoning about variations, trajectories, and transformations of contentious politics. Let us distinguish two dimensions of variation:

Governmental capacity (degree to which governmental actions affect distributions of populations, activities, and resources within the government's jurisdiction, relative to some standard of quality and efficiency): low (0) to high (1).

Democracy (extent to which persons subject to the government's authority have broad, equal rights to influence governmental affairs and to receive protection from arbitrary governmental action): low (0) to high (1).

In human history, no pure zeros or ones on either dimension have ever lasted long in populated areas. At times a government has collapsed or

BOX 2.1 This Book's Organizing Arguments

1. The location of a regime within the capacity-democracy space strongly affects its rulers' approach to generating and controlling contentious politics.
2. The previous trajectory of a regime within the same space, however, supplies much of the concrete means by which rulers and citizens engage in contentious politics.
3. In particular, changes in the multiplicity of independent centers of power within the regime, openness of the regime to new actors, instability of current political alignments, availability of influential allies or supporters, and the extent to which the regime represses or facilitates collective claim-making (which together comprise political opportunity structure, or POS) strongly affect the levels and loci of claim-making within the regime.
4. Rulers and citizens bargain out a set of understandings concerning possible and effective means of making collective claims within the regime.
5. The "bargaining" often involves vigorous, violent struggle, especially in nondemocratic regimes.
6. From the top down, those understandings identify sets of prescribed, tolerated, and forbidden claim-making performances, with likely governmental responses to each of them.
7. From the bottom up, the performances clump into repertoires that describe the forms of claim-making available to any particular set of political actors, including the government, and the likely consequences of making such claims.
8. Both internal mutations within contentious politics and external alterations of regimes and ruler–citizen relations create the repertoires that prevail in any particular time and place.
9. Contention itself reshapes regimes both incrementally and in bursts of struggle.
10. Not all contentious performances, repertoires, and episodes are causally coherent in the sense that systematic regularities across time and place govern their existence, change, and variation.
11. Some contentious performances, repertoires, and episodes, however, have *symbolic* coherence in the sense that naming them is a consequential political act, classifying a new instance as like its predecessors has political impact, and their existence provides models for claim-making even if they are not causally coherent.
12. Any analysis of regimes and repertoires must both distinguish causal from symbolic coherence and examine their interplay with care.
13. These lessons apply to collective violence, revolutions, and social movements.

failed to form, leaving a regime near or at zero on capacity. But no government has ever come close to complete control over the populations, activities, and resources within its territory, despite the efforts of absolutist and totalitarian rulers. Far more regimes have hovered near the bottom than the top of the continuum from nondemocratic to democratic regimes: plenty of governments have imposed or tolerated narrow, unequal rights, supported arbitrary policies or agents, and refused to consult subject populations. None, however, has ever come close to complete breadth, equality, consultation, and protection.

Capacity and Democracy

Capacity and democracy interact. In general, substantial increases in governmental capacity propel a broadening of rights when the essential resources for the government's operation come from the population within the government's jurisdiction. Struggles over those resources lead to provisional bargains that establish mutual rights and obligations between governmental agents and resource providers. Conversely, rentier and satellite states whose crucial support comes from outside—think of oil-exporting monarchies—often survive with narrow, unequal rights.

Governmental capacity strongly affects the chances for democratic processes. That statement could be read as a tautology, if capacity simply meant coordination among all political actors. Michael Mann makes the important distinction between despotic and infrastructural power: "We must distinguish between the two principal meanings of a strong regime: power over civil society, that is, *despotism;* and the power to coordinate civil society, that is, *infrastructural* strength" (Mann 1986, 477). In Mann's terms, governmental capacity centers on top-down despotic power: the extent to which the actions of governmental agents affect the distributions and deployments of people, activities, and resources within the government's territory. Infrastructural power, in the same terms, refers to consequences of the regime as a whole, certainly including governmental agents, but also including members, challengers, and citizens at large.

In principle, one could imagine broad political participation, relative equality of individuals or other social units, binding collective consultation, and protection in the absence of an enforcing government. Anarchists and utopians have often taken the relative democracy of some crafts, shops, and local communities as warrants for the feasibility of stateless democracy on a large scale. The historical record, however, suggests another conclusion: where governments collapse, other predators spring up. In the absence of effective governmental power, people who control substantial concentrations of capital, coercion, or commitment generally use them to forward their own ends, thus creating new forms of oppression and inequality. If ample governmental capacity does not define democracy, it looks like a nearly necessary condition for democracy on a large scale.

We cannot, however, draw from such an observation the comforting inverse conclusion: the expansion of governmental capacity reliably fosters democracy. In fact, expanding governmental capacity promotes top-down tyranny more often than it causes democracy to flower. In the abstract calculation that sums over all governmental experiences, the relationship between governmental capacity and democracy is no doubt asymmetrically curvilinear: more frequent democracy from medium to medium-high governmental capacity, but beyond that threshold substantial cramping of democratic possibilities as governmental agents come to control a very wide range of activities and resources (Tilly 2005d).

Citizenship, in this view, only forms above some threshold of capacity and democracy. Citizenship means mutual rights and obligations directly binding governmental agents to whole categories of persons defined by their relationship to the government in question. We can therefore only begin to speak of citizenship where governmental capacity is relatively extensive, rights extend to some significant share of a government's subject population, some equality of access to government exists among political participants, consultation of political participants makes a difference to governmental performance, and political participants enjoy some protection from arbitrary action. Although citizenship of a sort bound elite members of Greek city-states to their governments and elite members of many medieval European cities to their municipalities, on the whole citizenship at a national scale only became a strong, continuous presence during the nineteenth century.

Democracy builds on citizenship, but does not exhaust it. Indeed, most Western states created some forms of citizenship after 1800, but over most of that period the citizenship in question was too narrow, too unequal, too nonconsultative, and/or too unprotective to qualify their regimes as democratic. The regimes we loosely call "totalitarian," for example, typically combined high governmental capacity with relatively broad and equal citizenship, but afforded neither binding consultation nor extensive protection from arbitrary action by agents. Some monarchies maintained narrow, unequal citizenship while consulting the happy few who enjoyed citizenship and protecting them from arbitrary action by governmental agents; those regimes thereby qualified as oligarchies.

As we search for democratic regimes, we can take relatively high governmental capacity for granted; it is a necessary condition for strong consultation and protection. We will recognize a high-capacity regime as democratic when it installs not only citizenship in general, but broad citizenship, relatively equal citizenship, strong consultation of citizens, and significant protection of citizens from arbitrary action by governmental agents.

Both consultation and protection require further stipulations. Although many rulers have claimed to embody their people's will, only governments that have created concrete preference-communicating institutions have also installed binding, effective consultation. In the West, representative assemblies, contested elections, referendums, petitions, courts, and public meetings of the empowered figure most prominently among such institutions; whether polls, discussions in mass media, or special-interest networks qualify in fact or in principle as democratic preference-communicating institutions remain highly controversial.

On the side of protection, democracies typically guarantee zones of toleration for speech, belief, assembly, association, and public identity, despite generally imposing some cultural standards for participation in the polity. A regime that prescribes certain forms of speech, belief, assembly, association, and public identity while banning all other forms may maintain broad, equal citizenship and a degree of consultation, but it slides away from democracy toward populist authoritarianism as it qualifies protection. In high-capacity, democratic regimes, previous historical experience has laid down a set of models, understandings, and practices concerning such matters as how to conduct a contested election. This political culture of democracy limits options for newcomers both because it offers templates for the construction of new regimes and because it affects the likelihood that existing power-holders—democratic or not—will recognize a new regime as democratic.

Regime Space

We can simplify the work of analyzing regimes and contention, then, by thinking of a two-dimensional space: capacity democracy. Degree of democracy or nondemocracy provides the horizontal dimension of regime space. The vertical dimension represents governmental capacity, conceived as the extent to which governmental agents control resources, activities, and people anywhere within the government's jurisdiction.

Figure 2.1 represents the regime space with which the rest of this book works. Its lower-left corner (very low governmental capacity, no democracy) contains fragmented tyranny. In that portion of the space rival claimants to governmental power always arise and compete. Its upper-left portion includes a zone of authoritarianism, where high-capacity governments make few concessions to rights, consultation, or protection. The

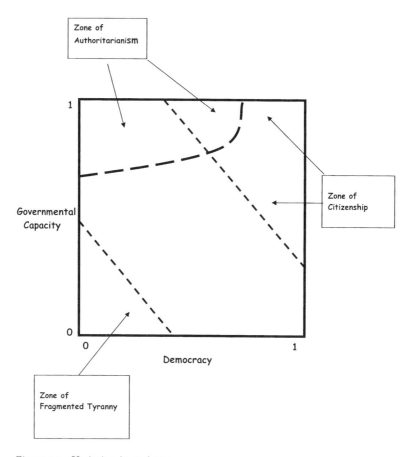

Figure 2.1. Variation in regimes

figure's upper-right corner (high-capacity, extensive democracy) contains full citizenship.

We can use the space in a static or a dynamic way. Statically, it allows us to place different regimes—for example, comparing Peru of 1980 (an incipient democracy with a medium- to high-capacity government) to Costa Rica (a fairly extensive democracy with medium-capacity government) in the same year. Dynamically, it allows us to sketch trajectories, for example the movement of Peru from the petty tyrannies of the nineteenth century to the higher-capacity, semi-democracy of the twenty-first.

Although both the static and dynamic versions of the regime space reappear later in the book, we will most often work with the simplified illustration of figure 2.2. It reduces the space to four crude types of regime: low-capacity, nondemocratic; high-capacity, nondemocratic; high-capacity,

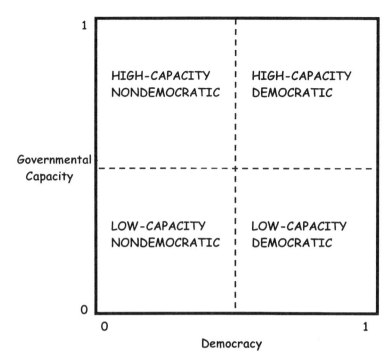

Figure 2.2. Crude regime types

democratic; and low-capacity, democratic. Examples of each type include the following:

High-capacity, nondemocratic: China, Iran.

Low-capacity, nondemocratic: Somalia, Congo (Kinshasa).

High-capacity, democratic: Germany, Japan.

Low-capacity, democratic: Belgium, Jamaica.

Throughout human history the distribution of regimes has occurred unevenly across the types. By far, most regimes have fallen into the low-capacity, nondemocratic sector. Many of the biggest and most powerful, however, have dwelt in the high-capacity, nondemocratic sector. High-capacity, democratic regimes have been rare and mostly recent. Low-capacity, democratic regimes have remained few and far between.

Over the long run of human history, then, the vast majority of regimes have been nondemocratic; democratic regimes are rare, contingent, recent creations. Partial democracies have, it is true, formed intermittently at a local scale—for example, in villages ruled by councils incorporating most heads of household. At the scale of a city-state, a warlord's domain, or a regional federation, forms of government have run from dynastic hegemony to oligarchy, with narrow, unequal citizenship or none at all, little or no binding-consultation, and uncertain protection from arbitrary governmental action.

Before the nineteenth century, furthermore, large states and empires generally managed by means of indirect rule: systems in which the central power received tribute, cooperation, and guarantees of compliance on the part of subject populations from regional power-holders who enjoyed great autonomy within their own domains. Seen from the bottom, such systems often imposed tyranny on ordinary people. Seen from the top, however, they lacked capacity; the intermediaries supplied resources to rulers, but they also set stringent limits to rulers' ability to govern or transform the world within their presumed jurisdictions.

Not until the nineteenth century was there widespread adoption of direct rule, creation of structures extending governmental communication and control continuously from central institutions to individual localities or even to households, and back again. Even then, direct rule ranged from the unitary hierarchies of centralized monarchy to the segmentation of federalism. On a large scale, direct rule made substantial citizenship, and therefore democracy, possible. Possible, but not likely—much less inevitable. Instruments of direct rule have sustained many oligarchies, some autocracies, a number of party- and army-controlled states, and a few fascist tyrannies. Even in the era of direct rule most regimes have remained far from democratic.

Of course, we could array regimes along other dimensions than capacity and democracy—size, dominant classes, relations to markets, multiplicity of internal governments, and directness of central control immediately come to mind. Let us retain our grip on the problem, however, by following the leads drawn from Aristotle, Dahl, and Finer and concentrating on two sorts of regime variation: from nondemocratic to democratic regimes, and from low-capacity to high-capacity governments. We should concentrate on these two aspects of regime variation for several reasons:

- They have attracted more theoretical and empirical attention from students of popular politics than have such aspects as uniformity of governmental administration or multiplicity of governmental units.

- Within recent centuries they have made very large differences to the character, trajectories, and dynamics of contentious politics.

- Even over the longer run, the position of a regime with respect to capacity and democracy has (as any good Aristotelian would expect) profound effects on the quality of its contentious politics.

We of the twenty-first century easily fall into thinking of regimes as exercising control over contiguous, bounded territories. Historically, however, regime boundaries have typically blurred, jurisdictions have overlapped, and governments have also exercised nonterritorial forms of jurisdiction. Most of the world only mapped into mutually exclusive territorial jurisdictions identified with autonomous national governments during the twentieth century. Even today, citizens of one country commonly enjoy special rights when they travel in another country's territory.

In fact, over the entire history of regimes two rather different principles of attachment to government have regularly competed: (1) control over a territory, its people, its resources, and its activities; (2) control over certain organizations and their members, regardless of their geographic location. If the second principle seems strange, just think of a fief, an international church, a global trading network, or a national army on foreign soil. In recent years transnational jurisdictions and organizations (for example, the European Community, the United Nations, Royal Dutch Shell, the World Bank, and Helsinki Watch) have become so influential that analysts have started to talk about transnational power structures and global civil society (see, for example, Anheier, Glasius, and Kaldor 2005; Fischer 2003; Horn and Kenney 2004; Kriesi 2003; O'Neill 2004; Tarrow 2005).

For convenience's sake, I usually speak here of regimes as if they attached to mutually exclusive territories, only qualifying when nonterritorial and extraterritorial jurisdiction become serious issues. Nevertheless, we will see that how continuously and territorially a government exercises surveillance and control makes a large difference to the everyday operation of regimes and to the interplay of regimes with contentious politics. In the case of Peru's recent past, we already noticed a large difference between the government's relatively secure control of the lowlands and its constant challenges in the high mountains.

With a clear, if simplified, understanding of regimes, we can begin to ask this book's main question: how do change and variation in regimes interact with change and variation in the character of contentious politics? To get a grip on that question, we must approach contention itself more closely. Analysis of contentious repertoires will bring us within viewing distance.

CHAPTER THREE >>
Repertoires of Contention

SUPPOSE THAT, HAVING CELEBRATED well into the previous night, you wake up stylishly late on New Year's Day 2005. No one is delivering newspapers on the holiday, and you don't feel like bundling up to brave January's cold. (Since it's summer down south and since newspaper deliveries occur mainly in urban regions, your story clearly unfolds somewhere in the thickly settled temperate zones of the Northern Hemisphere, which is in fact where I am weaving this plot.) As your tea or coffee brews, you use your web-surfing skills to connect with two sources for the day's news: the Reuters and BBC online dispatches. Amid the usual reports of celebrities, business coups, natural disasters, and predictions for the coming year, you find plenty of political news. Tuned to the definitions of chapter 1—this is a fantasy, after all!—you scan Reuters and BBC for episodes of contentious politics. Box 3.1 shows what you find.

You read about a wide variety of contention, much of it viciously violent. Through these online reports from the Middle East, South America, Africa, and South Asia you are witness to thousands of people making different kinds of claims on governments, on major political actors, and on clusters of ordinary people. The claims range from lethal direct attacks to public statements and mass demonstrations. None of the reports is self-explanatory; you must already know a good deal of context, for example, to understand that the Iraqi people Reuters calls "insurgents"

BOX 3.1 Contentious Politics on the Reuters and BBC Newswires, January 1, 2005

Iraq ushered in the new year on Saturday the same way it ended the last one—with a string of assassinations and bombings by insurgents bent on wrecking a landmark January 30 election. Three militant insurgent groups in Iraq have warned Iraqis not to vote in the January 30 election.

Gunmen hoisted Mahmoud Abbas on their shoulders as thousands of Palestinians gave the presidential election frontrunner a hero's welcome Saturday in a Gaza refugee camp shattered by fighting with Israel.

Saudi Arabia says one of the kingdom's most wanted militants was among five suicide bombers killed in twin attacks on government targets in the past week.

A Colombian rebel leader being held in custody in the United States on drug trafficking and other charges will appear in court next week, a Justice Department official said on Saturday. Ricardo Palmera, also known as Simon Trinidad, was extradited from Colombia to the United States after the Revolutionary Armed Forces of Colombia, or FARC, failed to comply with a government ultimatum to free 63 hostages including three Americans. Left-wing rebels killed at least 17 peasants in northeast Colombia on New Year's Eve in reprisal for cooperating with far-right militaries, police, and local authorities said Saturday.

An armed group led by a radical former soldier stormed a police station in a poor southern town [in Peru] and took 10 officers hostage on Saturday to demand the resignation of Peruvian President Alejandro Toledo. Some of the group, joined by townspeople, later peacefully took over the town hall, RPP radio reported from the scene.

The Catholic conservative movement Opus Dei has lost a legal battle to force a Chilean newspaper for homosexuals to change its name from Opus Gay.... A gay rights group, the Movement for Homosexual Integration and Liberation, called the ruling an "unprecedented victory" against powerful groups in Chilean society.

Lords Resistance Army rebels in northern Uganda have delayed signing a cease-fire to end the bloody 18-year conflict, the government says. President Yoweri Museveni [of Uganda] has vowed to step up military action against rebels in northern Uganda, after a seven-week truce expired without agreement.

Tsunami survivors in India's Andaman Islands have accused the authorities of underplaying the extent of devastation and failing to hand out aid. Frustration boiled over in the town of Campbell Bay when a crowd demanding food and water assaulted an official.

Thousands of people have rallied in the Nepalese capital, Kathmandu, demanding peace talks between the government and Maoist rebels.

Police in Pakistan's mountainous northern district of Chitral say two employees of an aid agency have been killed by masked gunmen.

armounting armed resistance to the American-led occupation of their country, attacking both Americans and fellow Iraqis who collaborate with the Americans, and trying to block an American-backed election that is likely to legitimate a governing coalition excluding them from power.

Similarly, you begin to think more systematically about those "masked gunmen" in Pakistan once you recall that the Pakistani president, Pervez Musharraf, came to power in a military coup, still heads the armed forces despite an overdue promise to step down from his military post, faces strident Islamist opposition within his own government, has survived several assassination attempts, is engaged in a military standoff with India over Kashmir, and has not succeeded in flushing out al-Qaeda chief Osama bin Laden, who is said to be hiding somewhere along Pakistan's mountainous frontier with Afghanistan. Chances are that the masked gunmen are connected with one or another of these opposition factions.

Again, to interpret the Uganda report (see box 3.1) you must take into account the nearly twenty years during which Joseph Kony's Lord's Resistance Army, originally a conventional guerrilla force, has claimed religious inspiration, has abducted thousands of Ugandan children for military and sexual services, has received intermittent aid and asylum from nearby Sudan, and has managed to avoid capture. At the same time, it will clarify what is happening to recognize that Sudan's government, under great international pressure, is negotiating a settlement with southern rebels but enduring (and, according to many reports, supporting) civil war in its northwest Darfur region. All these episodes of contentious politics connect closely with their political contexts—that is, with the regimes in which they occur.

Notice that participants in these tumultuous events are making three somewhat different sorts of claims. We can call them "identity," "standing," and "program" claims. Identity claims assert the presence of a substantial collective actor; further stories on the Peruvian hostage-taking make clear that the attackers represented a nationalist group demanding recognition of its stand against Alejandro Toledo's alleged sellout of Peruvian interests to foreign powers. Standing claims say that we *Xs* not only exist, but occupy a certain position within the regime; Chile's organized gays have already achieved some recognition of their existence, but they are also asserting their weight as major political actors protected by law. *Program* claims call for their objects to take an action, adopt a policy, or otherwise commit themselves to a change; among other things, Iraqi assassins call for the authorities to suspend national elections.

The three sorts of claims build in rough order: without a recognized identity, it is hard to demand political standing; without standing, it is hard to voice support for a program. Hard, but not impossible. Now and then, a new political actor moves onto the political stage by coordinated support for a program in the name of a previously unknown group. That happens repeatedly, for example, when factions employing violence against a government regroup in response to repression.

The high proportion of violent events in New Year's Day reporting could, however, mislead you. Visibly violent events are much more often the lead story than are nonviolent events, even when the claims resemble each other.[1] That is true for two reasons. First, disruptions of routine, especially violent disruptions of routine, receive much more attention in general from media than does conformity to routine; just think of a North American metropolitan newspaper's "rape and murder" page. Second, collective violence often occurs when governmental power is at stake: civil wars rage, revolutions displace governments, governmental forces strike back at dissidents, dissidents mount attacks at governmental agents, or all at once. Threats to governmental power generate more news than does its maintenance. In all the countries on the roster, especially the less authoritarian ones, the great bulk of collective claim-making actually goes on without violence, and passes unreported by international media such as Reuters and the BBC.

With that important qualification, note some important regime-contention parallels for future reference. The Peruvian episode in which an armed band led by an ex-soldier seized a police station should remind you of the Peruvian government's vulnerability to military bids for power, both from guerrilla movements and from the official armed forces. A retired army major, Antauro Humala, organized the hostage-taking deep in the Andes. Humala had also led the attempted coup when Vladimiro Montesinos returned from Venezuela in 2000, shortly before Alberto Fujimori fled to Japan. A month before the hostage-taking, the army had forced Humala into retirement (Economist 2005, 38). But the incident embarrassed the government sufficiently that the Peruvian interior minister soon resigned.

As compared, say, to Argentina or Mexico (both of which have had long histories of military intervention in or control of national politics but now keep their armies out of civilian politics), Peru clearly has not yet managed to insulate military forces from civilian government. Note the contrast with neighboring Chile, until recently just as roiled by autonomous military power. There, the standoff between Opus Dei and Opus Gay shows us a nonmilitary contentious politics greatly resembling that of other Western democracies; a court ruling defends a stigmatized but mobilized minority against a powerful religious group, and has some prospect of sticking.

---

1. For selective reporting of contentious episodes, see Almeida and Lichbach 2003; Earl, Martin, McCarthy, and Soule 2004; Hocke 2002; Hug and Wisler 1998; Koopmans 2004; McCarthy, McPhail, and Smith 1996; Mueller 1997; Oliver and Maney 2000; Oliver and Myers 1999; Rucht 2004.

More generally, we observe three patterns of correspondence. First, we have regimes in which rival armed groups are openly competing for power, however unevenly: Iraq certainly, but also Colombia, Uganda, Nepal, and (at least in some regions) Pakistan. Second, in some regimes the military serve under civilian rule but figure prominently in the squelching of domestic opposition and dissent; in the New Year's Day headlines, Saudi Arabia provides the prime example. (On other days, reports from China and Iran would put them in the same category.) Finally, whatever part the national armies play in foreign wars and border control, we have a set of regimes in which the armed forces remain largely insulated from domestic contentious politics: India except for its conflict-filled northeast frontier and Kashmir, Chile since the end of the Pinochet regime (1998), perhaps even the Peru that is now emerging.

To be sure, the three-way split leaves out the volatile situation involving Palestine and Israel, which lurches from month to month in and out of the first category, where rival armed groups openly compete for power, however unevenly. Nevertheless, the three categories correspond broadly to three of our four broad types of regime: low-capacity nondemocratic, high-capacity, nondemocratic, and (relatively) high-capacity democratic. If the headlines had brought us contentious episodes from a relatively low-capacity democratic regime such as Switzerland, we would witness a marvelous multiplicity of local and sectional claims (Frey and Stutzer 2002; Giugni 1995; Giugni and Passy 1997; Kriesi 1980, 1981; Kriesi et al. 1981; Trechsel 2000; Wimmer 2002). Each type of regime features a characteristically different pattern of political contention.

Regime, therefore form of contentious politics! If only it were that simple. Although systematic differences in the forms of contentious politics by regime do exist, each specific form lives embedded in the history of its regime. The differences between our reports from Iraq, Colombia, Uganda, Nepal, and Pakistan—all more or less low-capacity nondemocratic regimes—should tell us as much. This book's problem is to describe and explain change and variation in the forms of contentious politics, then to relate the change and variation systematically to the variable operation of political regimes. Resolving the problem requires careful specification of how contention articulates with its social setting. We are looking for regularities falling somewhere between the particular histories of individual regimes and the general history of all regimes.

Performances and Repertoires

We can capture some of the recurrent, historically embedded character of contentious politics by means of two related theatrical metaphors: performances and repertoires.[2] Once we look closely at collective claim-making, we can see that particular instances improvise on shared scripts. Presenting a petition, taking a hostage, or mounting a demonstration constitutes a *performance* linking at least two actors, a claimant and an object of claims. Innovation occurs incessantly on the small scale, but effective claims depend on a recognizable relation to their setting, to relations between the parties, and to previous uses of the claim-making form.

Performances clump into *repertoires* of claim-making routines that apply to the same claimant-object pairs: bosses and workers, peasants and landlords, rival nationalist factions, and many more. The theatrical metaphor calls attention to the clustered, learned, yet improvisational character of people's interactions as they make and receive each other's claims. Claim-making usually more resembles jazz and commedia dell'arte than the ritual reading of scripture. Like a jazz trio or an improvisatory theater group, people who participate in contentious politics normally can play several pieces, but not an infinity (Sawyer 2001).

Repertoires vary from place to place, time to time, and pair to pair. But on the whole, when people make collective claims they innovate within limits set by the repertoire already established for their place, time, and pair. Thus social-movement activists in today's European cities adopt some mixture of public meetings, press statements, demonstrations, and petitions, but stay away from suicide-bombing, hostage-taking, and self-immolation. Their repertoire draws on a long history of previous struggles (Tilly 2004a).

To appreciate how much repertoires vary historically, let us take three giant strides across French history from the seventeenth century to World War II. After the partial respite that followed the closing of the Wars of Religion in 1598, France resumed various forms of civil war in 1616 that continued into the 1620s. In the 1630s, under Richelieu's guidance, the country also returned to heavy involvement in international conflict. That meant a renewal of military recruitment in France as well as the wholesale

---

2. For descriptions and surveys of contentious performances and repertoires (by no means all of them using these terms), see Archer 1990; Barber 2002; Beckwith 2000; Beissinger 1998; Borland 2004; Bourguinat 2002; Chabot 2000; Chabot and Duyvendak 2002; Ekiert and Kubik 1999; Ellingson 1995; Ennis 1987; Esherick and Wasserstrom 1990; Farrell 2000; Fillieule 1997; Granjon 2002; Greiff 1997; Hanagan 1999; Heerma van Voss 2001; Jarman 1997; Lafargue 1996; Lofland and Fink 1982; McPhee 1988; Mueller 1999; Oberschall 1994; Pigenet and Tartakowsky 2003; Plow, Wall, and Doherty 2004; Robert 1996; Salvatore 2001; Scalmer 2002a, 2002b; Schwedler 2005; Sowell 1998; Steinberg 1999; Stinchcombe 2000; Szabó 1996; Tarrow 1998; Tartakowsky 1997; Thornton 2002; Traugott 1995; Wood 2004.

engagement of mercenaries from elsewhere. On May 16, 1640 the regional military commander for Sens wrote to the local royal prosecutor:

> [A]yant apris que les habittans de Villeneufve-le-Roy, Chaulmon, Rouseneau, et Esgriselles le Bocage et autres lieux des environs de Paris s'estans assemblez en armes le iiie de ce mois, sont allez charger la recrue du regiment de Razilly qui passoit aud. Chaumont et a Rouchon suivant sa routte pour aller joindre son corps ont tué et blessé plusieurs soldats de lad. recrue et sont cause qu'il s'en est dissipez grand nombre et mesme ont enleve des chevaux et du bagage des officiers dud. regiment, ce qui ceux de Villeneufve-le-Roy ont fourny des armes aux autres pour commettre cet attentat, Et voulant que ceux qui en sont autheurs et coupables en soyent chastiez exemplairement comme le merite un crime de si grande consequence. (Archives Historiques de l'Armée, Vincennes, AA A1 59)

> Having learned that residents of Villeneuve-le-Roy [now Villeneuve-sur-Yonne], Chaumont, Rousson, Egriselles-le-Bocage and other places near Paris [sic], having assembled with arms the third of this month, attacked the Razilly regiment's contingent of recruits which was passing through said Chaumont and Rouchon on its way to join its unit, killed and wounded many soldiers of said contingent, caused many of them to run away, and even took horses and baggage of the officers, and people of Villeneuve-le-Roy gave weapons for the attack to the others. Wishing that those who were guilty of being the originators of the attack be given exemplary punishment, as such a great crime deserves.

The letter goes on, inevitably, to request prosecution of the attackers. It merits an extensive gloss for the military history of the Thirty Years War, the brutal methods of military recruitment then in vogue, the depradations of soldiers who lived on the land, and the legal relationship between military and civil authorities. But what happened was banal enough in that wartime year: People from several adjacent villages and a river town (Villeneuve) took up arms and attacked a military contingent as it passed through their territory. In those days, soldiers shared reputations with rats and vultures.

Almost 150 years later, on July 13, 1789 Parisian bookseller Siméon-Prosper Hardy noted in his journal:

> Toward five o'clock [p.m.] I see a detachment of the bourgeois militia of the district of the Mathurins passing beneath my windows on the rue Saint-Jacques, already in formation, proceeding in good order and very deliberately, three men per row, to the Hôtel de Ville. That militia looked good and had an upright air. . . . In addition, we see a sub-

stantial detachment of other people armed with swords and wearing a green cockade at the wine merchant's by the corner of the rue des Noyers and the rue Saint-Jacques; they stopped to drink for a while, holding out a first-story window a sort of white flag made of a stick and a towel, as if to encourage passersby to join the action. . . .

A little after seven o'clock, another detachment of bourgeois militia, this one including about 120 people, came down the rue Saint-Jacques three by three on their way to the Hôtel de Ville, taking care to say that it was the Third Estate going to the Hôtel de Ville, in order not to frighten anyone. People were surprised that what one might have thought a day of public mourning was instead a celebration, given the cheers and indecent laughter that we heard everywhere, and all the vulgarities people acted out in the streets as if it were Mardi Gras. (Bibliothèque Nationale, Paris, Fonds Français 6687)

This text, too, deserves a thorough analysis. On July 11, King Louis XVI had dismissed popular chief minister Jacques Necker. (Hence Hardy's reference to a "day of mourning.") Fearing popular rebellion, the king had ringed Paris with troops. In response, within two days local assemblies formed throughout Paris, and many of them created their own militias. Some of the militias patrolled their own neighborhoods, some went searching for arms, and some marched to the Hôtel de Ville (Paris's long-standing site for civic assemblies) for a meeting with deputies from the Estates General, where a municipal electoral assembly continued all night. Their green cockades sported the color of the Duke of Orleans, a reputed reformer whom the king had exiled for his alignment with the political opposition in 1787. Crowds calling for Necker's return had carried Orleans's bust through the streets on July 12.

The next day, as we now know but Hardy did not yet know, culminated in an attack on the nearby Bastille. Hardy had watched part of the prologue to a great revolutionary drama. Now he watched mobilized militias simultaneously making program, identity, and standing claims: political reform including reinstatement of Necker, recognition as militias from different Parisian districts, and acceptance as valid interlocutors with deputies, city officials and, indirectly, royal power.

Another century and a half passed. In June 1940 German forces occupied Paris and soon established tight control. On October 30 they arrested the famous physicist and Popular Front activist Paul Langevin. After several small collective manifestations of disapproval, students organized a major action on Armistice Day, November 11. According to interviews with participants conducted by Raymond Josse:

On the Champs-Elysées some menacing gatherings formed that morning. Starting at 8:30, people of all ages, some individually and some in groups, started to parade before either the statue of Clémenceau at the foot of the Champs-Elysées or the tomb of the Unknown Soldier, by the Arc de Triomphe. Only one incident occurred, toward 11:45, when a hundred or so young men and women started to move down the avenue in groups of about ten; some of them wore big tricolor cockades in their buttonholes. The police blocked their march and tried to get rid of the cockades. One demonstrator protested vehemently and was immediately arrested by an inspector; he was a professor of natural sciences at the lycée Lakanal, René Baudoin. (Josse 1962, 18.)

Later in the day, student groups from all over Paris converged on the Champs-Elysées and the Arc de Triomphe, occasionally shouting "Vive la France," "Vive de Gaulle," and "France for the French." Altogether, three thousand people or more reached the area, but not without several run-ins with both fascist youth groups and the Parisian police.

In general, the French police merely contained the crowds, separated them from the fascists, and kept them moving. But around 6:00 P.M. German troops occupied the Rond Point of the Champs-Elysées and the corner of the avenue George V. From those bases German soldiers began to clear the streets by zigzagging military vehicles through them, striking members of the crowd with rifle butts, then machine-gunning in the side streets. Within an hour the German forces had cleared the neighborhood. The day's encounters among students, fascist youth, police, and troops constituted one of the early Resistance's great protests against German occupation and French collaboration.

With three small incidents drawn from three hundred years, one can infer anything and nothing. We could contextualize and compare the events in a dozen ways: as evidence concerning changes in military organization and politics, as interrogations concerning the connections between war and domestic conflict, as reflections of alterations in patriotism, and much more. They also raise questions about change and variation in popular repertoires. Every historian of popular politics knows events of this kind—movements of struggle and contestation. Those who deal with substantial blocks of space and time recognize, at least by implication, the dramatic variation among places and times in the forms taken by struggle and contestation.

In Villeneuve's conflict of May 1640, for example, we see a characteristic seventeenth-century interaction, a community's collective attack on unwelcome representatives of royal power; if we could peer farther into the place and time, we would find an accumulating local history of struggles over military billeting, pillaging, brawling, forced recruitment, taxation, and harassment of young women. We would discover local power-holders caught between their parochial patronage and the allure of alliances with agents of the monarchy. We would witness a rural world being penetrated by a demanding state.

As for the Paris of July 1789, historians have made it easy to recognize the crucial importance of that series of local assemblies, creations of militias, and dispatches of delegations to the city hall; it initiated one of the major forms of popular participation in what was soon to be a deep revolution. In the same city under German occupation, we observe a risky and loosely coordinated version of a routine French people had been using frequently for almost a century: a sort of demonstration.

The social underpinnings of the three events obviously differed enormously: clearly constituted village communities in 1640, Parisian neighborhoods with their assemblies and militias (not to mention the Estates General) in 1789, political associations, student groups, police, and military forces in 1940. The personnel differ, their organizations differ, their actions differ, the political consequences differ. In each case, the action articulates with a distinctive social and political context. But in each case, we also witness complementary program, identity, and standing claims.

In each of the three episodes, French people made collective claims by drawing on available repertoires of contention. During the seventeenth century ordinary people interacted with authorities (such as the Razilly regiment) by means of a cramped array of performances: humble petitions, armed opposition, intervention in public ceremonies, and vengeful attacks of the sort the army's archives describe for 1640 (Tilly 1986). Some of the same performances remained available early on during the Revolution, but by then the citizens' assembly and the sort of militia march that Hardy observed had joined the repertoire. As of 1940, despite the occupying Germans' repression, Parisians knew very well how to stage a demonstration, signaling their solidarity both to the authorities and to each other.

Exactly how people draw on contentious repertoires remains variable and controversial. Think first about a repertoire's flexibility. All performances that characterize the interaction among a specified set of collective actors constitute that set's repertoire of contention. Repertoires vary from nonexistent to weak to strong to rigid. Each position on the continuum identifies a different relationship between the familiarity of a previous performance and the likelihood that it will again appear in a similar situation, ranging from no relationship to perfect repetition.

Figure 3.1 describes four positions on this continuum. In the case of *no repertoire,* the previous familiarity of a performance does not affect the

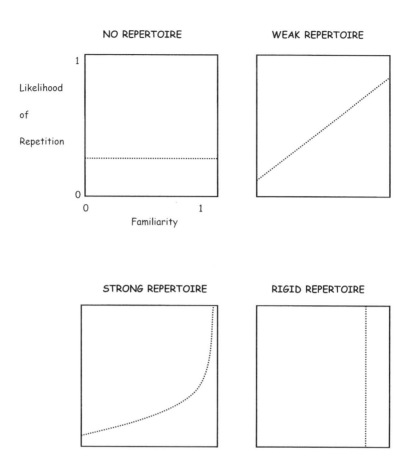

Figure 3.1. Types of repertoire

subsequent likelihood of its appearance. If past familiarity increases the likelihood of subsequent performance in a more or less linear manner, we are probably seeing the effects of learning, but not of strong preference; let us call that situation a "weak repertoire." If familiar performances receive strong preference but some unfamiliar performances also occur in the form of innovations, we are dealing with a flexible repertoire, which we can also call "strong." If nothing but very familiar performances ever appear despite changing circumstances, the repertoire is called "rigid."

For believers in the irrationality of crowds, popular contention lacks a repertoire; performances spring from either the moment's madness or primal urges having little or nothing to do with learning in previous contention. Strict theorists of rational action, oddly enough, place themselves in a similar position, implying that actors have perfect information and choose the most efficient means possible, which in principle also means no repertoire. If they recognize information costs, bounded rationality, and the effects of previous learning (as many institutional economists are inclined to do), rationalists may also concede a weak repertoire, but not a strong one. Strong or rigid repertoires imply great embedding of contention in previously existing history, culture, and social relations.

In the times and places that have been the subjects of my study, strong repertoires prevailed. Ritual political performances do take place, and take on an air of sedulous rigidity (Kertzer 1988; Muir 1997). But when people intervene in such rituals to make collective claims, they bend them back toward the strong repertoire. Periods of rapid political change and clashes of previously insulated political traditions appear to weaken contentious repertoires, as the ordinary preference for familiar claim-making routines dissolves in spurts of innovation. Most of the time, however, the forms of this year's claim-making in a given place greatly resemble the forms of last year's.

Why Repertoires?

Why should that be? Why should contentious politics behave like loosely scripted theater? First we must rule out two tempting bad answers: dumb habit and technological determinism. Repetition of similar claim-making routines from one year to the next might seem to result from force of habit, which blinds people to other possibilities. No one who has looked closely at contentious politics, however, is likely to find that explanation credible. On the contrary, participants impress us with their unceasing small-scale innovation. Remember those Parisians of November 1940, who certainly knew about demonstrations from the fractious street politics of the prewar years, but had not once before mounted a demonstration by walking in groups of ten or so with tricolor boutonnières.

Note the paradox of contentious claim-making: genuinely unfamiliar performances almost always misfire, but perfect repetition from one performance to the next breeds boredom and indifference on the parts of claimants and their objects alike. Effective contention does not resemble a marching band's precision drills, but the clash of championship football teams. Habit does not explain the pattern of incessant innovation. Innovation within the script matters.

As for technological determinism, every time claimants adopt a new technology someone comes along to argue that the technology itself caused them to make claims, or at least transformed claim-making. Technology analyst Howard Rheingold argues that mobile electronic communication makes possible the formation of "smart mobs"—that is, groups of people who act together without even knowing one another. As an example, Rheingold describes "netwar," which allows military attackers to remain dispersed until the moment of action. He identifies netwar as first cousin to the Seattle mobilization against the World Trade Organization (1999), the Manila mobilization against Philippine president Joseph Estrada (2001), and worldwide support for the Zapatista movement of Chiapas, Mexico (1994–2003):

> The Chechen rebels in Russia, soccer hooligans in Britain, and the FARC guerrillas in Colombia also have used netwar strategy and swarming tactics. The U.S. military is in the forefront of smart mob technology development. The Land Warrior experiment is scheduled to field-test wearable computers with GPS [Global Positioning Systems] and wireless communications by 2003. The Joint Expeditionary Digital Information (JEDI) program links troops on the ground directly to satellite communications. (Rheingold 2003, 162)

In such a view, technology drives political and military innovation. Unquestionably faster, more effective, more mobile electronic communication figures in all these innovations, and more. Technological zeal may actually be guiding American military policy. In all the nonmilitary instances of contentious politics Rheingold cites, however, closer examinations demonstrate the subordination of technical innovations to local political processes (Hellman 2000; Smith 2002, 2004; Tilly 2004, chap. 5; Tishkov 2004). Yes, activists adopt new technologies when those technologies serve their purposes. But purposes override techniques.

What does account for the clustering of claim-making performances in repertoires? The major causes sort into three main categories: (1) connections between claim-making and everyday social organization, (2) cumulative creation of a signaling system by contention itself, and (3) operation of the regime as such. Repertoires draw on the identities, social ties, and organizational forms that constitute everyday social life. From those identities, social ties, and organizational forms emerge both the collective claims that people make and the means they have for making them. In the course of contending or watching others contend, people learn the interactions that can make a political difference as well as the locally shared meanings of those interactions.

Palestinian gunmen's hoisting of Mahmoud Abbas on their shoulders signals military support for a hero in that local idiom (see box 3.1), just as

Nepalese rallying for peace in the streets of Kathmandu adopts a widely recognized performance, viewable on television throughout much of the semi-democratic world, but taking on local meanings in relation to a troubled monarchy. The regime itself sorts performances into prescribed, tolerated, and forbidden, dispensing threats and penalties to claimants who move onto forbidden ground. The changing interaction of these three elements—everyday social organization, cumulative experience with contention, and regime intervention—produces incremental alterations in contentious performances. At any given moment, however, that interaction promotes clustering of claim-making in a limited number of recognizable performances, a repertoire.

How and Why Repertoires Vary

It will take the rest of this book to spell out the logic of contentious repertoires in full. Let us settle here for a preliminary statement of hypotheses. My most general arguments concerning repertoires run like this: in routinely operating regimes with relatively stable governments, strong, flexible repertoires prevail. Daily social life, existing social relations, shared memories, and the logistics of social settings—whether, for example, women gather daily in a town's central market—shape the forms of contention. In that sense, they are simultaneously deeply cultural and deeply structural; they certainly rest on shared understandings and their representations in symbols and practices (that is, on culture), but they also respond to the organization of their social settings.

Within those limits, contenders experiment constantly with new forms in the search for tactical advantage, but do so in small ways, at the edge of well-established actions. Few innovations endure beyond a single cluster of events; they endure chiefly when associated with a substantial new advantage for one or more actors. Over the long run, nevertheless, innovations accumulate into substantial changes of repertoire; the history of contention therefore significantly affects its current operation.

At this point, we must revive the contested notion of political opportunity structures (POS).[3] Any regime, according to POS analyses, creates a specific environment of political opportunities and threats to which

---

3. Goldstone and Tilly 2001; Goodwin and Jasper 2004; Meyer 2004; Tarrow 1998, chap. 5. The contest concerns two issues: (1) whether it is possible to identify opportunities and threats reliably and independently of the contention they are supposed to explain, and (2) to what extent the causes of contention lie in the perceptions and creativity of individual actors rather than in the environments they inhabit.

makers of claims necessarily respond. Changes in that environment, so the argument goes, produce changes in contention. We can usefully include in POS (a) the multiplicity of independent centers of power within the regime, (b) the openness of the regime to new actors, (c) the instability of current political alignments, (d) the availability of influential allies or supporters, (e) the extent to which the regime represses or facilitates collective claim-making, and (f) decisive changes in a to e. (It would be easy to add other features of regimes that affect, in principle, the opportunities and threats impinging on their participants; the six simply include those having the most obvious effects.)

From the perspective of a whole regime, the instability of alignments and the availability of allies amount to the same thing. Stable alignments generally mean that many political actors have no potential allies in power. By such a definition, however, POS varies somewhat from one actor to another; at the same moment, one actor has many available allies, another few. For all actors, in any case, threats and opportunities shift with fragmentation or concentration of power, changes in the regime's openness, instability of political alignments, and the availability of allies.

Rapidly shifting threats and opportunities, I suggest, generally move power-holders toward rigid repertoires and challengers toward more flexible repertoires. Power-holders cling to proven performances, including repression of challengers; meanwhile, challengers seek new means to outwit authorities and competitors. (Complication: as the POS argument implies, rivalry among power-holders often leads some of them to form alliances with challengers, which limits the power-holders' movement toward rigidity as well as the challengers' move toward flexibility.) Since some repertoires link challengers to power-holders, rapidly shifting threats and opportunities thus introduce more uncertainties into the relations between claimants and objects of their claims. Programs, identities, and political standing all shift more rapidly.

In times of rapidly changing political opportunity, therefore, we find both recurrent innovation and frequent misapprehension among parties to contention, especially in the case of popular challenges to power-holders. A spiral of contention ensues as each new round of claim-making begins to threaten the interests of (or provide new opportunities for) previously inactive political actors. The extreme arrives in a revolutionary situation: a deep split in control of coercive means during which every actor's interest is at risk, prompting many to mobilize for action.

Such cycles usually end with the rapid demobilization of most actors, especially those who have challenged and lost. At that point, repertoires crystallize as the pace of innovation in performances slows. Some innovations that appeared during the cycle remain part of the repertoire, while some old performances or features of performances disappear. Association with the gain or loss of political advantage by one actor or another strongly affects innovations' survival and disappearance, although changes in the conditions of everyday existence and in actors' internal organization as a consequence of the struggle also affect the viability of different performances.

Incremental changes in repertoires are less dramatic but more decisive in the long run. There are three principal reasons for their occurrence:

1. The same sort of innovative response to rapidly changing POS occurs on a smaller scale in lesser crises and confrontations, whence innovations accumulate in a similar manner.
2. Incremental changes in the dispersion of power, the openness of political institutions, the instability of political arrangements, the availability of allies or supporters, and regime repressiveness—that is, in POS—likewise occur.
3. Potential actors' organization, shared understandings, and interests change incrementally as well.

In combination, these three effects identify intertwined strands of change in contentious repertoires, attributable to the internal history of struggle, transformations of regimes, alterations of social structure and culture outside the government, and their interaction.

Observing Contention

Peru's Fujimori/Montesinos debacle, our New Year's Day news stories, and long-term shifts in the character of French repertoires pose a serious problem for us. How can we possibly discipline descriptions of contentious politics? How can we avoid the two tempting but destructive extremes: sum up all sorts of contention into something abstract like "turbulence," "conflict," or "disorder," thereby losing all sense of connections with the political context; or describe each episode in all its particularity, thereby making comparison among places, times, and regimes impossible. We must find a middle ground.

Most serious students of contentious politics search for that middle ground by adopting one version or another of the same strategy. They identify some variety of contentious episode, collect multiple instances of that sort of episode, place the instances in their settings, and compare them. The instances range from rare, complex phenomena to frequent, more elementary phenomena. At the rare, complex end of the range we find revolutions, social movements, and wars (Cioffi-Revilla 1990;

Goodwin 2001; Kriesi et al. 1995; Parsa 2000). At the frequent, elementary end we find attempts to break contentious politics into discrete particles, such as single actions, interactions, or claims (Franzosi 1998; Shapiro and Markoff 1998; Sugimoto 1981). In between lie multiple efforts to define "events" having sufficient coherence for systematic comparison and for aggregation into larger summaries by place, time, issue, or participants (for surveys, see Olzak 1989; Rucht and Koopmans 1999; Rucht, Koopmans, and Neidhardt 1998; Tilly 2002a).

Over a long career in the study of contentious politics, my own work has spanned the entire range from individual interactions to whole revolutions (for examples at each end of the range, compare Tilly 1997a with Tilly 1993). That work has convinced me that no single unit of observation has priority; it depends on the question, the argument, the sources, and the historical context. Where governments or labor organizations have bureaucratized the collection of reports on strikes, for example, analysts can (with due allowance for reporting biases) compare industries, regions, or periods that differ significantly in their levels of strike activity on the way to pitting contradictory explanations of industrial conflict against one another (Biggs 2002; Church and Outram 1998; Cohn 1993; Franzosi 1995; Haimson and Sapelli 1992; Sandoval 1993). But if you have devised a promising general theory of what causes revolutions, you have little choice but to compare multiple examples of revolutions, near-revolutions, and nonrevolutions to see if the theory actually accounts for the differences among them.

On exactly this point, however, I must sound a warning that will echo throughout the rest of this book. The naming of a phenomenon provides no warrant that the phenomenon exists, much less that it is causally coherent. Many observers of violent contentious politics speak of street violence as "rioting." Riot, however, is an authority's name for public behavior of which the authority disapproves. Under King George I (1714–27), English law codified that perception in the Riot Act. The act provided that if twelve or more persons assembled with what a competent authority judged as the intent to commit an illegal act and refused to disperse within an hour of being warned, they qualified as felons. The Riot Act remained part of English law until 1973. Did riots exist? Do they still exist?

We have three choices: (1) declare that English authorities saw a distinct, coherent phenomenon and took steps to suppress it; (2) decide that the term "riot" actually refers to a legal encounter in which authorities manage to apply the Riot Act or its equivalent to some gathering; and (3) conclude that riots as such have no coherent existence and search for separate sets of regularities in street gatherings, authorities' responses to street gatherings, and interactions between the two. This book opts emphatically for the third approach, remaining suspicious of such catchwords as riot, disorder, and disturbance. Yet I also lay out a number of concepts—for example, regimes, performances, and repertoires—with the claim that the phenomena they name exist, are observable, and exhibit enough causal regularities for us to consider them coherent and worth analyzing systematically.

In this spirit, the book's later analyses often reject or recast a widely used concept on the ground that, at least as ordinarily used, it does not identify a distinct, causally coherent phenomenon. Chapter 6, for instance, where I analyze collective violence, challenges the existence of a distinct, uniform variety of action called "terrorism" and a distinct, uniform class of political actors called "terrorists." It goes on, however, to concede that a *strategy* we can reasonably call "terror" exists, has some common properties, and shows up in the performances of a wide range of actors across a considerable variety of circumstances.

Causal and Symbolic Coherence

A delicate problem arises at exactly this juncture. Even when they point to causally heterogeneous phenomena, everyday categories such as riot, disorder, disturbance, and terror have two kinds of significance for the analysis of regimes. First, the very labeling of a performance as one thing or another regularly has consequences for the participants. During the years of the Riot Act, authorities who called a worrisome assembly a "riot" assumed the right to use force against the assembled crowd. These days to identify a group as terrorist threatens that group's very survival.

Second, whether or not authorities do the labeling, once a certain sequence of performances acquires a name and notoriety, it can serve as a model for subsequent performances. Even if not all members of the category involve the same causes and effects, once observers, participants, or authorities have labeled a sequence as a "revolution" or a "strike," later contenders can draw on the model to say "We're making a revolution" or "We're striking." Thus when analyzing categories of political performances we must distinguish carefully among three different sorts of statements:

1. Performances of this kind are causally coherent; they result from similar causes, involve similar internal cause-and-effect sequences, and produce similar effects. As analysts, we can therefore hope to identify systematic regularities in their precipitating conditions, changes, variations, and consequences.

2. When participants, observers, or authorities identify a performance as an *X*, that label authorizes and/or promotes specific reactions to the performance that would not otherwise occur.
3. Once a performance acquires visible effectiveness, it becomes available as a model for later performances.

Given the importance of the second and third types of statements, we must distinguish between two kinds of coherence: causal and symbolic. *Causal* coherence refers to the systematic cause-and-effect properties of a phenomenon. *Symbolic* coherence singles out the extent to which participants or observers of a phenomenon attribute to it unity and significance. I have already claimed that both regimes and repertoires qualify as causally coherent phenomena. I have written this book, indeed, to identify the systematic causal properties of regimes and repertoires. But I have just denied that riots, as such, constitute causally coherent phenomena. In terms of the distinction between types of coherence, however, riots qualify as symbolically coherent phenomena, at least in the context of eighteenth-century Britain. I will make similar claims concerning revolutions, social movements, and many other forms of contentious politics—symbolically, but not causally, coherent.

The distinction clarifies the explanatory task at hand. It also has some interesting implications that are not obvious at first glance. It is possible in principle that participants and observers of contentious politics understand what is going on so well that they give symbolically coherent names to phenomena that are also causally coherent. When analyses of contentious politics feed back to participants, they sometimes insert causally coherent explanatory terms (for example, "regimes" and "repertoires") in the participants' vocabularies.

Within a given symbolic world, furthermore, agreement on the meanings of certain performances, repertoires, and types of episodes sometimes generates empirical regularities that cry out for explanation. In the world of contemporary North American social movements, for example, participants spend enough energy emulating, interpreting, and labeling each other's actions that their interaction follows recurrent, recognizable patterns. To explain the patterns, however, we must step out of the symbolic frames within which participants operate.

More generally, both labeling of contentious phenomena and emulation of existing models have general properties that are themselves causally coherent. Repertoires of contention provide a case in point. The rest of this chapter identifies ways in which they are causally coherent. Part of their coherence, it shows, results precisely from the fact that they involve consequential naming of performances and permit emulation of previously existing models. We must maintain the distinction between causal and symbolic coherence, but then look closely at their connections.

Contentious Events

The questions that motivate this book concern the interplay between regimes and repertoires. For that purpose, comparisons of revolutions or of strikes might help, but most likely we will need a more general characterization of claim-making and regime change. My own more general surveys of whole regimes have centered on collective making and receiving of claims, especially those linking distinct political actors with each other rather than, say, the members of a constituted group having their own leaders. They single out, furthermore, *discontinuous, public,* and *collective* claim-making: occasions on which people break with daily routines to concert their energies in publicly visible demands, complaints, attacks, or expressions of support before returning to their private lives.

Such an angle of vision obscures some important aspects of contentious politics: backroom deals, patron–client relations, organizing efforts that precede claim-making, official responses to claims, and interpretations by third parties. In my previous work, I often tried to reduce those blind spots by shifting to other vantage points, for example by studying official correspondence concerning a given episode I first found reported in a yearbook such as the *Annual Register* or an online wire service such as Reuters. Still, the collection of public, collective, discontinuous episodes of claim-making constitutes my principal evidence for what must be explained. For comparison over space, time, group, and issue, it has the advantage of coming close to what other analysts have in mind when they speak of social movements, popular protest, disorder, conflict, or collective action.

These points will come across more clearly with an extended example from my research: a study that examines changing forms of claim-making in Great Britain from the 1750s to the 1830s (for details, see Tilly 1995a). My research group painstakingly assembled a body of relevant evidence. It consists of machine-readable descriptions of just over eight thousand "contentious gatherings" (CGs) that occurred in southeastern England (Kent, Middlesex, Surrey, and Sussex) during thirteen selected years from 1758 to 1820, or anywhere in Great Britain (England, Scotland, and Wales) from 1828 to 1834.

A CG is an occasion on which ten or more people gathered in a publicly accessible place and visibly made claims that, if realized, would affect the interests of at least one person outside their number. In principle, CGs include almost all events that authorities, observers, or historians of the time would have called "riots," "outrages," or "disturbances" as well as even more that would fall under such headings as "public meeting," "procession," and "demonstration".

By no means do these sorts of CGs exhaust contentious politics, even in Great Britain between 1758 and 1834. For one thing, the threshold of ten persons gathered in a single place eliminates both smaller contentious gatherings and individual actions coordinated among spatially scattered actors. For another, our observations capture the time of coordinated public claim-making but neither the preparation nor the follow-up that also belong to contentious politics. Without those two restrictions, the study would have collapsed of its own weight. But we must recognize the parallel with a surveillance camera: it may do a fine job of registering who enters and leaves a bank, but it does not follow them off the scene. Exactly as intended, the CG procedure selects for public, collective making of claims, then relies on other evidence to trace relations between such events and their contexts.

The standardized descriptions of CGs came from periodicals: the *Annual Register, Gentleman's Magazine, London Chronicle, Morning Chronicle, Times, Hansard's Parliamentary Debates, Mirror of Parliament,* and *Votes and Proceedings of Parliament*. We read these periodicals exhaustively for the years in question plus January to June of 1835. Although we frequently consulted both published historical work and archival sources such as the papers of the Home Office in interpreting our evidence, the machine-readable descriptions transcribed material from the periodicals alone. We sought not to find every event about which information was available or even a representative sample of such events, but a complete enumeration of those described in standard periodicals whose principles of selection we could examine, and sometimes even test.

Unlike investigations singling out events in advance for their importance (whatever the standard of importance), this sort of inquiry leads almost inevitably to a sense of *déjà vu,* to a realization that the events in any particular time and place fall into a limited number of categories repeating themselves with only minor variations. Yet different settings and periods produce different arrays of events: collective seizures of grain, invasions of enclosed fields, and attacks on gamekeepers in one place and time; sacking of houses, satirical processions, and sending of delegations in another; demonstrations, strikes, and mass meetings in yet another.

Prevailing forms of action likewise vary by the social class of the actors (burghers dealing with nobles act differently than do peasants dealing with burghers), the contentious issues at hand (disciplining a fellow worker differs from seeking royal favors), and the immediate occasion for gathering (festival, election, meeting of legislative assembly, and the like). The arrays of actions obviously bear a coherent relationship to the social organization and routine politics of their settings. They therefore vary significantly from one setting to another. The word "repertoire" points to that variation.

Changing Repertoires

In the case of Great Britain between the 1750s and 1830s, we can distinguish sharply between the repertoires prevailing at the beginning and the end of that period. Forms of contention that occurred frequently in the southeast during the eighteenth century's middle decades included:

- Mutinies of pressed military men
- Breaking windows of householders who failed to illuminate
- Collective seizures of food, often coupled with sacking the premises of the merchant
- Verbal and physical attacks on malefactors seen in the street or displayed in the pillory
- Taking sides at public executions
- Workers' marches to public authorities in trade disputes
- Ridicule and/or destruction of symbols, effigies, and/or property of public figures or moral offenders
- Pulling down and/or sacking of dangerous or offensive houses
- Donkeying, or otherwise humiliating, workers who violated collective agreements
- Breaking up of theaters at unsatisfactory performances
- Liberation of prisoners
- Fights between hunters and gamekeepers
- Battles between smugglers and royal officers

Outside of the southeast, the comparable list includes not only all of these but also destruction of tollgates, invasions of enclosed land, and disruptions of public ceremonies and festivals (Archer 1990; Bohstedt 1983; Brewer 1976; Brewer and Styles 1980; Charlesworth 1983; Farrell 2000; Hanagan 1999; Harrison 1988; Hayter 1978; Stevenson 1979).

On the whole, these constitute parochial, particular, and bifurcated forms of action: *parochial* in concentrating on local targets, and basing themselves on local groupings rather than local segments of regional and national groupings; *particular* in having highly differentiated forms of action for different groups, situations, and localities; and *bifurcated* in dividing between direct action with respect to nearby objects of claims and action mediated by dignitaries and powerful people with respect to distant objects of claims.

The "eighteenth-century" repertoire reflected a politics in which many corporate groups and communities had established local rights; policing was relatively ineffectual in the absence of local consensus; authorities commonly used exemplary punishment and ordinary people sometimes followed their example; most people condoned direct action against moraloffenders; rights of assembly faced stringent limits; all power-holders and contenders employed elaborate, symbol-drenched stagecraft; ridicule and shunning served as powerful punishments; and the distinction between private and public life remained quite blurred. Yet during the eighteenth century the capitalization of the economy and the expansion of the state were threatening many of the rights and local memberships that underlay such a politics. For that very reason, they generated widespread contention.

Remember the essential qualifications: "eighteenth century" is only a rough approximation of a more complex timetable; some actions combined more than one of these forms; no single category of actors carried on all these actions; each form of action linked at least two actors, at a minimum one of them taking the other as a target and the other often riposting with a different action; and innovation and improvisation occurred incessantly within the broad limits set by each of these forms. In London itself, furthermore, the distinction between local and national blurred, since king, Parliament, financial magnates of the city, and national power-holders such as the East India Company lay close at hand; some relatively ordinary people (London's tailors and Spitalfields' weavers, for example) intermittently laid claims directly on those who ruled the land. But even they adopted forms of action in the eighteenth-century mode.

The point is simple: the number of standard forms was strikingly limited. It excluded a number of other actions—armed insurrection, the formation of popular political parties, ritual execution, mass meetings, and so on—that could, in principle, likewise have taken place. Indeed, in the 1760s and 1770s some new forms of contention did gain ground amid the eighteenth century's standard routines. In retrospect, we discover seeds of the demonstration, the mass meeting, and the social movement.

By the 1830s, Great Britain's "eighteenth century" forms of action had almost entirely disappeared. A set of mainly nonviolent ways of associating and making collective claims had displaced them. Most of these new forms still exist today. They include turnouts and strikes, demonstrations, electoral rallies, public meetings, petition marches, planned insurrections, occupations, blockades, invasions of official assemblies, organized social movements, and electoral campaigns. Some of them occurred, of course, during the eighteenth century. But they only became the predominant forms of popular contention during the nineteenth.

The emergence of the social movement as we know it today epitomizes the new repertoire (Tilly 2004a, chap. 2). As it developed in the West after 1750, the social movement emerged from an innovative, consequential synthesis of three elements:

1. A sustained, organized public effort making collective claims on target authorities; let us call it a *campaign*.
2. Employment of combinations from among the following forms of political action: marches, rallies, processions, demonstrations, occupations, picket lines, blockades, public meetings, delegations, statements to and in public media, petition drives, letter-writing, pamphleteering, lobbying, and creation of specialized associations, coalitions, or fronts; call the variable ensemble of performances the *social-movement repertoire*.
3. Participants' concerted public representations of worthiness, unity, numbers, and commitment (WUNC) on the part of themselves and/or their constituencies; call them *WUNC displays*.

Unlike a one-time petition, declaration, or mass meeting, a campaign extends beyond any single event—although social movements often include petitions, declarations, and mass meetings. Campaigns center on claims—claims for the adoption of abolition of public programs, claims for recognition of the claimants' existence, and/or claims for ratification of their standing as specific kinds of political actors such as indigenous peoples or constituted parties. A campaign always links at least three parties: a group of self-designated claimants, some object(s) of claims, and a public of some kind. The claims may target governmental officials, but the "authorities" in question can also include owners of property, religious functionaries, and others whose actions (or failures to act) significantly affect the welfare of many people. Not the solo actions of claimants, object(s), or public, but interactions among the three, constitute a social movement.

The social-movement repertoire overlaps with the repertoires of other political phenomena such as trade-union activity and electoral campaigns. During the twentieth century, special-purpose associations and crosscutting coalitions in particular began to do an enormous variety of political work across the world, well outside of social movements. But the integration of most or all of these performances into sustained campaigns marks off social movements from other varieties of politics.

The term "WUNC" sounds odd, but it represents something quite familiar. WUNC displays can take the form of statements, slogans, or labels that imply worthiness, unity, numbers, and commitment: Citizens United for Justice, Signers of the Pledge, Supporters of the Constitution, and the like. Yet collective self-representations often act them out in idioms that local audiences will recognize, for example:

Worthiness: sober demeanor; neat clothing; presence of clergy, dignitaries, and mothers with children.

Unity: matching badges, headbands, banners, or costumes; marching in ranks; singing and chanting.

Numbers: headcounts, signatures on petitions, messages from constituents, filling streets.

Commitment: braving bad weather; visible participation by the old and handicapped; resistance to repression; ostentatious sacrifice, subscription, and/or benefaction.

Particular idioms vary enormously from one setting to another, but the general communication of WUNC connects those idioms.

Taken singly, each of these elements drew on and adapted previously existing political practices, for example sporting of electoral colors, humble petitions to kings, or marches of militias, artisans' guilds, and religious organizations. But the combination of campaign, repertoire, and WUNC displays acquired a generality and staying power none of its predecessors had ever achieved. Together, furthermore, they made a powerful assertion of popular sovereignty: we, the people, have the right to voice on our own initiative; worthy, united, numerous, and committed, we have the capacity to change things.

In contrast to the parochial, particular, and bifurcated character of eighteenth-century repertoires, then, these forms of action constitute a relatively *cosmopolitan, modular,* and *autonomous* set. They qualify as cosmopolitan because they facilitate making claims on scales far larger than the locality: whole cities, regions, countries, even international mobilizations such as the British-led antislavery movement of the 1820s and thereafter. "Modular" means that the performances in the repertoires transferred easily from place to place, issue to issue, group to group. The term "autonomous" calls attention to the greatly diminished roles of patrons and intermediary authorities in making claims; the people involved spoke directly to the objects of their claims, including national authorities.

We should resist the temptation to label one of the two repertoires as more efficient, more political, or more revolutionary than the other. Nor does it help to call one repertoire "traditional" and the other "modern," any more than one can say that contemporary English is superior to that of Shakespeare, as if one were clearly more efficient or sophisticated than the other. We must recognize that repertoires of contention are sets of tools for the people involved. Backward/forward, prepolitical/political, and similar distinctions do not classify the tools but the particular circumstances for using them. The tools serve more than one end. Their relative efficacy depends on the match among tools, tasks, and users. A new repertoire emerged in nineteenth-century Britain because new users took up new tasks and found the available tools inadequate to their problems and abilities. In the course of actual struggles, people making claims and counterclaims fashioned new means of claim-making.

Neither the new tasks nor the new forms of action were intrinsically revolutionary. After all, the English had managed two revolutions in the seventeenth century with repertoires similar to those that prevailed in the eighteenth, but never managed to make one in the nineteenth or the twentieth century with their new repertoires. A larger share of actions in the older repertoire (such as Rough Music and the pulling down of poorhouses) involved direct action against adversaries, while a much greater proportion of the actions in the newer repertoire (such as the public meeting and the mass petition) took for granted the continued existence of the national structure of power. Furthermore, large segments of the population (for example, agricultural laborers and women who worked at home) lost their major means of making collective claims as the new repertoire replaced the old. In all these regards, the old repertoire was arguably more revolutionary than the new. Both reflected and interacted with the organization of power within their own historical contexts. The difference between them lay in the relations of repertoires and actors to their political settings.

Warning: like most useful dichotomies, the reduction of many repertoires to just two simplifies radically for the sake of clarity. No actual group employed all the means of action within either of the repertoires; no pair of actors shifted abruptly from one repertoire to the other; no sharp break in repertoires occurred in 1800 or at any other date. We are examining a history of continuous innovation and modulation. Yet surges of change in repertoires did occur, alterations in the contentious repertoires of one pair of actors induced alterations in adjacent pairs, broad conflicts produced more extensive repertoire changes than narrow ones, and some innovations caught on much more rapidly and durably than others. For these reasons, the exaggerated division of continuously changing multiple repertoires into eighteenth- and nineteenth-century sets serves as a useful guide to a complex history.

Why the Change?

Why did the shift of British repertoires occur? The most general explanation goes back to our three factors: connections between claim-making and everyday social organization changed, contention itself produced cumulative changes in the signaling system, and political opportunities or threats offered by the regime changed. More concretely, six sets of changes occurred:

First, the concentration of capital and the related proletarianization of the British workforce altered the interests of workers and employers, and of several third parties to their relationship—parish officers, royal functionaries, and others. Increasingly employers broke through the constraints of local crafts and made decisions based on the logic of national and international markets. For their part, workers increasingly found they could not exert effective pressure on employers without expanding their scale of organization and redefining solidarity in terms that cut across individual crafts. These changes, in turn, pushed contention toward a larger scale and a national arena.

Second, urbanization, migration, and rapid population growth transformed the organizational bases of local contention, adding weight to those actors who could create, adapt, or infiltrate flexible, efficient associations and assemblies. Associations and assemblies provided the means of connecting and maneuvering substantial numbers of people rapidly.

Third, the rising intensity of British military efforts, at least through 1815, impelled an expansion of taxes, national debt, and service bureaucracies, which increased not only the state's size but also its weight within the economy. In the process, Parliament—critical to every decision concerning governmental revenue, expenditure, and personnel—occupied ever more space in political decisions. These changes, too, promoted a shift toward contention that was large in scale and national in scope. In addition, they enhanced the strategic advantage and maneuverability of formally constituted associations, especially those with national constituencies, as bases for contention. They made parliamentary elections more critical to national issues, encouraged contested elections, drew nonvoters more intensely into electoral campaigns, and encouraged the formation of "para-parliamentary" politics in such guises as national social movements, national petition drives, and calls for a mass platform. All such activities in turn expanded the utilization of local assemblies such as vestries in national struggles over power and policy. These processes sharpened the conflict between two different conceptions and organizations of national politics: one vesting fundamental power in a compact between regime and parliament, the other treating both of them as instruments of a sovereign people.

Fourth, short-run shifts in the mobilization and strategic advantage of different parties to conflicts of interest strongly affected the ebb and flow of contention. The shifts often resulted from circumstances external to the conflicts themselves, as when the end of the Napoleonic Wars brought many former soldiers back into the civilian labor force but simultaneously reduced the demand for industrial labor.

Fifth, struggles laid down their own history, both because participants in a given struggle generally will remember what had happened before and plan their actions accordingly, and because the outcome of any particular struggle alters the positions of the participants, including third parties. Concessions the government made to a specific type of action by a certain actor, for example, made it easier for other actors to press claims by means of that same type of action. The success of one petition drive opened the way to new petition drives, as one association's pressing of its claims set a precedent for another association to press its own claims. Contention, however, also generated repression, which in turn shaped the possibilities for future contention.

A deep change in British policing, for example, occurred between 1750 and the 1830s; that change involved agents of the state in anticipatory control of potentially unruly crowds. In the course of that internal history of struggle, collective-action innovators and entrepreneurs such as John Wilkes, Lord George Gordon, Orator Hunt, Daniel O'Connell, John Doherty, and Feargus O'Connor sometimes had major impacts on prevailing forms of action. They helped create the social movement, with its devices of meeting, marching, petitioning, displaying, and attacking, as a standard means of pursuing shared ends.

Sixth, the particular history of Great Britain set off British contention from struggles in other Western countries. British capitalism and the British state both followed distinctive trajectories over the years from the 1750s to the 1830s, and those paths of change strongly affected the ways that ordinary British people acted together on their interests. On the side of capitalism, British landlords and entrepreneurs invested early and heavily in large-scale marketing and relatively concentrated means of production. They thus promoted proletarianization of workers in both agriculture and manufacturing. Their reorganizations of production likewise stimulated rapid shifts from agriculture to manufacturing and services as well as from rural to urban population, which in its turn favored a substitution of relatively long distance, definitive migration for the swarming short-distance movement that had characterized the previous centuries.

On the side of the state, war drove a great expansion of the Britishstate apparatus. Yet, as compared with other European powers, the British state continued to do much of its work through co-opted members of the ruling classes (notably as the parsons and landlords who served as justices of the peace) and operated increasingly within limits set by a mighty Parliament. Inside Parliament, furthermore, the Commons gained greater and greater weight.

These political arrangements had emerged from earlier struggles, including multiple rebellions and two revolutions (Tilly 2004b, chap. 5). In 1750, the Glorious Revolution lay only six decades back, the contested settlement of Germany-based Hanoverians on the British throne was only thirty-six years old, and major rebellions against royal power had shaken Scotland or Ireland several times in the memory of living men and women. In the course of those struggles, Britain's people had gained unusually extensive rights to assembly, association, petition, privacy, and criticism of authorities. During the ninety years following 1750, however, two monumental changes altered the everyday uses of those rights, and established new ones: (1) the formation of a new class system, more strongly marked by industrial capitalism, and (2) bargaining out of mass citizenship on a national scale. In both regards, British experience preceded that of most European neighbors.

The foundations of repertoire transformation in Great Britain between the 1750s and the 1830s take us back to this book's main problem: the interplay of changes in regimes and repertoires. Although alterations of economic organization and population distribution figure importantly in the story I have just told, their effects on repertoires filter through regime changes—including the creation, destruction, and reshaping of major political actors. In the story, we witness shifts in relationships among major political actors including government deeply influencing the character of popular contention, but we also see contention itself having profound effects on the regime. Without mass mobilizations of the 1820s and 1830s in the social-movement mode, for example, Britain would not have expanded the franchise, granted voting rights to Catholics and Protestant Dissenters, or abolished slavery in its colonies.

We have no reason to expect, however, that a single model of relationships among political transformation, social-structural transformation, and struggle will account for the character of contention in all times and places; on the contrary, we should expect the laws of contention to vary significantly among agrarian empires, urban representative democracies, and clan-organized nomadic systems. Nor do we have any warrant to postulate general tendencies toward more modern, differentiated, or effective performances and repertoires; only within particular historical eras characterized by directional changes in states and nonstate social structures should we discover directionality in contention.

In all eras, on the other hand, we should find a significant weight of history: the previous trajectory of contention should visibly constrain present possibilities for collective claim-making. Some causal mechanisms, furthermore, should recur in a wide variety of situations, such as the ways that the creation of networks and solidarities in routine social life selectively facilitates the contention of some, but only some, populations that share interests and opportunities. Although such recurrent mechanisms account for profound regularities in contention across history, with them alone we will never be able to account for the issues, actors, situations, and forms of interaction that characterize a given region and era. Like geologists accounting for particular land masses and their transformations, we have no choice but to examine the relevant history.

Our opening New Year's Day 2005 scenario, then, makes no more than a quick, tentative pass through the relevant history. We could try to place the contentious episodes on that day's newswires in their repertoires, perhaps by locating them somewhere between the poles parochial-particular-bifurcated and cosmopolitan-modular-autonomous. We could guess at the changes in everyday social processes, regimes, and contentious experiences that lay behind those episodes. For a serious effort at explanation, however, we must assemble much more extensive and systematic evidence about their contexts. Tracing causal connections between regimes and repertoires requires a serious historical and comparative effort.

CHAPTER FOUR >>
Repertoires, Meet Regimes

AS PERVERSE AS IT MAY SEEM, I have always enjoyed reading the *Annual Register*. It gives me pleasure for the same reason that I enjoy reading the *Economist:* like the market-mongering magazine, the venerable yearbook of world political affairs states its arguments so vividly and elegantly that it is a gratifying challenge to work out how and why I disagree with them. Both publications also overflow with news about contentious politics near and far. Edmund Burke himself founded the *Annual Register* as a chronicle of British and world politics in 1758. Burke started the yearly publication more than thirty years before his famous dissenting essays on the French Revolution.

By no means did the Irish-born Burke always agree with British authorities. During the 1760s and 1770s, for example, he plumped for American rights so long as American leaders kept their demands principled and decorous. In keeping with Burke's political positions over the previous three decades, nevertheless, his essays on the French Revolution began by criticizing British supporters of the revolution, who praised a form of contention that Burke considered improper and dangerous. Ordinary people, he insisted, should not take the law into their own hands. Burke cast a long shadow over the yearbook's subsequent editors.

By a rhetorically convenient coincidence, the collapse of state socialist regimes in 1989 arrived exactly two centuries after the French Revolution began. Commenting on the tumults of 1989, the *Annual Register*'s editorial for that year shook a finger in self-conscious emulation (and citation) of Burke. The editorial warned that excesses of revolution and democracy could lead to new tyrannies. "Two hundred years later," the editorialist declared, "Burke's perceptive judgment has lessons for us and for the euphoric reformers of the communist bloc."

> There, Mr Gorbachev's policy of *glasnost* (openness) was the catalyst of one of the swiftest and furthest-reaching changes in the political scene the modern world has ever experienced, concentrated in the last three months of 1989. Only a few years ago, the expected response to anti-government demonstrations in Eastern Europe would have been Soviet intervention, military repression and reaffirmation of centralized communist supremacy, a smothering of the fire that would have continued to smoulder until struck into irresistible heat.
>
> The contrast with the sequence of events in China in the past year was no accident. The cheering demonstrators in Beijing's Tienanmen Square, superficially very much like those in Wenceslas Square in Prague, neither had coherent and definite objectives nor were they the brave youthful front of a nation-wide mass emotion. They proclaimed general aspirations rather than demanding particular means of realizing them, save a boneless plea for "democracy." It was a courageous adventure which will have its reward one day; but, without a mass will behind it, it succumbed to the military power of the state. (*Annual Register* 1989, 3)

Thus, according to the *Annual Register*, the Chinese regime avoided the popular excesses that, as Burke had warned two centuries earlier and Aristotle had feared two millennia earlier, would bring first demagoguery and then new tyranny. When the Chinese people as a whole were ready, the yearbook's editor implied, they would earn and acquire democratic institutions.

Now *there's* an argument worth disagreeing with! As later chapters make the point in detail, I think that democratization always occurs in part as a result of contention and always generates extensive contention; a peaceful maturing into orderly democracy is a crippling myth. This chapter will do its work, however, if it simply maps out systematic connections between regimes and repertoires, for example by showing how the characteristic claim-making performances of a China-like regime differ from those of a Soviet-style regime. Systematic differences will clarify what we have to explain and provide a first grasp of possible explanations.

A Panorama of Repertoires and Regimes

Let us continue to work with the *Annual Register,* which has the great advantage of surveying all the world's national regimes. Just remember, however, its limitations. Like the New Year's Day 2005 dispatches at the beginning of chapter 3, the *Annual Register*'s descriptions of contentious politics across the world in 1989 understandably gave disproportionate attention to very large and/or violent episodes such as China's confrontation at Tienanmen Square, Beijing, or the assault on the Berlin Wall.

Nevertheless, with due allowance for that perspective, the year's reports covered a wide variety of regimes and their contentious performances. Consider this selection from the yearbook for a relatively democratic high-capacity regime:

> On 16 January the national holiday in memory of Martin Luther King was marred by race rioting in Miami following the shooting of two blacks by a policeman. The riot was quelled after two days but at least one person died, 11 were wounded and almost 400 arrested. There was violence in Georgia too when black and white marchers were attacked by members of the Ku Klux Klan for entering an all-white county. A larger demonstration followed on 24 January under the protection of the state militia . . . . On 23 August a white gang killed a black youth in an attack on four black youths in Bensonhurst, a largely Italian neighbourhood in Brooklyn. Subsequent black protest demonstrations in the area met with abuse from white onlookers. Further demonstrations and confrontations took place when New York blacks marched in memory of Huey P. Newton, one of the founders in the 1960s of the Black Panthers, who was found shot dead in Oakland, California, in what appeared to be a drug-related killing on 22 August. (*Annual Register* 1989, 53–54)

By the standards set forth in chapter 3, the *Annual Register*'s descriptions of contentious interactions lack essential detail. "Riot" and "violence" stigmatize those interactions but fail to say how they occurred. Even this terse account, however, indicates that in the American regime specialized police rather than the national military or government-backed death squads regularly confront, contain, or even protect protesters; that ethnic and racial divisions have political edges; and that street demonstrations or marches recur as ways of making identity, program, and standing claims. These features bring out resemblances between U.S. contention and that of other Western-style democracies such as Canada, Great Britain, France, Germany, and Australia.

For a very different picture, look up the *Annual Register* entry for Peru in the same year, remembering the Peruvian regime's precarious location at the edge of democracy and in a zone of uncertain governmental capacity:

> Violence escalated steeply, 690 deaths being recorded in the first three months of the year. On 28 April the Peruvian army successfully ambushed a column of the Tupac Amaru Revolutionary Movement (MRTA) near the village of Molinos (in Junin department), killing 62. But the hard-line Maoist Sendero Luminoso (SL) remained active. Following the assassination of a deputy of the ruling Aprista Party on 6 May, the Prime Minister, Armando Villanueva del Campo, resigned and was immediately replaced by the 88-year-old First Vice-President, Luis Alberto Sanchez. . . .
>
> On 10 May the SL declared an "armed strike" in the central Andean departments of Junin, Pasco and Huancano, whereafter both the violence and criticism of President Alan García spread rapidly. The death on 25 May of a British tourist at Olleros (Ancash department) was thought to represent a deliberate extension of violence. An "armed strike" in Lima in July was successful in keeping the buses off the streets and closed many shops in the shanty towns but had little effect on industry. Later in the year SL tactics focused on the disruption of the municipal elections on 12 November. A daring demonstration in the heart of Lima on 1 November became a lengthy gun-battle in which several passers-by were casualties, and led President García to place the capital under martial law. In the countryside, where more than 50 mayors had been killed and many candidates had in consequence withdrawn, it proved impossible to hold elections in some sparsely-populated areas. (*Annual Register* 1989, 73)

By now, of course, we already know something about the partial democratization of the Peruvian regime over the previous decade, not to mention the contested election that would bring Alberto Fujimori and Vladimiro Montesinos to power the following year. We observe a formally democratic regime seriously threatened by armed challengers, and responding with military power.

For another regime about which we already know something, we can turn to Uganda. There we learn that President Yoweri Museveni (who had seized power militarily in 1986) shook up his military administration in 1989. In fact, Museveni fired his own brother as army commander and replaced him with a reputedly incorruptible young colonel. But even that decisive move did not give the Museveni government secure control over all of Uganda's territory.

As of 1989, from all we know, Uganda clearly belonged in the low-capacity, nondemocratic quadrant of the regime space defined by figure 2.2. The year's report commented:

> The security situation improved, despite continued rebel activity in the northern Gulu district, and in the east around the town of Soroti. More than 50 "Holy Spirit" rebels died in clashes with government forces in northern Uganda early in April and some 370 in May; a number of Ugandan soldiers and civilians were also killed. The rebellion, formerly led by the warrior priestess Alice Lakwena, was now led by Joseph Kony, another mystic, and had degenerated into revenge killings motivated by clan rivalries. In July the army admitted responsibility for the deaths in eastern Uganda of 47 youths who suffocated in a railway wagon where, with some 200 other suspected rebels, they had been locked overnight. Amnesty International (AI) accused the army of human rights violations, but conceded that the gross violations perpetrated by previous regimes had ended. (*Annual Register* 1989, 252)

Once again the news of Uganda's contentious politics reveals an nondemocratic regime low—indeed, threatened—in capacity that regularly uses military force against its violence-wielding challengers.

The range of regimes will become clearer if we take up reports from three countries that have yet to make their entrance: Morocco, Jamaica, and India. Morocco has more than a thousand years of history as a Muslim power, including a period when it ran its own small empire. The territory endured French and Spanish occupations during the twentieth century, but became an independent monarchy in 1956. As of 1989, Hassan II, son of the dynasty's founding king, was running a relatively high-capacity, nondemocratic regime. The government had long been engaged in war with rival claimants (the Polisario Front) to the former Spanish Sahara, now known in Morocco as its province of Western Sahara. During the year, the regime accepted a UN-promoted truce with the Polisario.

Soon after, the regime's own contained version of contentious politics accelerated:

> In March there were calls for a general amnesty for political prisoners by the Moroccan Association for Human Rights, which was associated with the Union Socialiste des Forces Populaires. In June a general amnesty was granted to over 200 political prisoners by King Hassan, including members of the "March 23 Group" and the banned Marxist-Leninist Ilal-Amam movement. Several political prisoners held in Casablanca prison went on hunger strike in June

in protest against poor conditions and in September their case was taken up by Amnesty International. Legal proceedings were taken in September against Mohamed Idrissi Kaitouni, editor of the Istiqlal party's newspaper, *L'Opinion,* for publishing a statement by human rights groups in Morocco. (*Annual Register* 1989, 239–40)

Here we get news of fairly effective repression backed by an active military under royal and civilian control. External pressure, especially from Europe and the United Nations, was mitigating the harshness of royal rule, but by no means moving the regime rapidly toward democracy. Under Hassan's son Mohammed VI, who became king in July 1999, some room opened up for trade unionists, students, and religious activists to write, agitate, and demonstrate.

But not much room. After the September 11, 2001 attacks on New York and Washington, and (especially) after suicide bombings in Casablanca on May 16, 2003 killed thirty-three people, Mohammed's government cut back civil rights markedly in a drive against Islamic militants. According to the international monitoring organization Human Rights Watch (HRW), the antimilitant drive largely undid the progress made since Mohammed VI's accession. In HRW's cautious summary:

> Important elements of the progress made during the last fifteen years are now endangered by the way that authorities have rounded up and imprisoned thousands of Moroccans accused of links to terrorism. The credible reports of torture and mistreatment of these suspects, and the clear denial of their civil rights during the judicial process, suggest that the broader freedoms Moroccans have enjoyed during the last decade and a half can be reversed. (Human Rights Watch 2004a, 1)

At that point, the regime as a whole remained in the high-capacity, nondemocratic quadrant.

Jamaica belongs in the opposite quadrant of our regime space from Morocco, with governmental capacity low enough to threaten its relatively democratic institutions. Jamaica went from British colony to independent country in 1962, but remained within the British Commonwealth. The regime's fragility remained visible in 1989. During the campaign for the general election of February 9, activists of the People's National Party (PNP) and the Jamaica Labour Party (JLP) frequently attacked each other, with a toll of thirteen deaths and 108 injuries (*Annual Register* 1989, 83). As for the election, the PNP won forty-five seats to the JLP's fifteen. Years later, Jamaica-born Harvard sociologist Orlando Patterson explained the Jamaican organizational background:

A politician's political survival depends entirely on his or her ability to win repeatedly at the local level. One sure method of ensuring repeated victory is to create what is called a garrison constituency: a pocket of housing erected with public funds, with carefully screened residents who will constitute the unbeatable core of the politician's voters.

These began with Edward Seaga, now the leader of the Jamaica Labor Party, when he was in office during the 1960s and 80s. The leading politicians of the other main party soon followed his lead. There are now about 15 hard-core garrison constituencies, and political fights between them during elections have spilled over into broader, ongoing turf wars. The resulting gangs, initially formed for political purposes, now also serve the drug trade. During the 80s, many of these gangs migrated to America, where they became known as posses and soon forged a reputation for violence.

These gangs have increasingly worked to generate unrest as a political tactic. This may have been a cause of the recent violence, which was as much a police riot as a counterattack by political thugs against police. The violence took place in garrison constituencies loyal to the opposition party, and many commentators here see it as an attempt by the opposition to pressure the government to call an early election. (Patterson 2001, 1)

Even at times other than electoral campaigns, however, Kingston's armed gangs frequently shoot each other up, contributing to Jamaica's unenviable position as possessor of one of the world's highest murder rates.

Nor did Jamaican criminals simply attack each other. Jamaica's businesses suffer widespread protection rackets and property crimes. A 2002 UN survey of four hundred Jamaican firms found that two-thirds of all firms reported being victims of at least one property crime during 2001. Smaller firms suffered more from extortion, fraud, robbery, burglary, and arson than large ones (World Bank 2004, 89–90). At the same time, Jamaican police have acquired a worldwide reputation for brutality, which includes not only rough treatment of criminals but also attacks on gays (Amnesty International 2001c; Human Rights Watch 2004c). Jamaica serves as an important transit point for Colombian cocaine on its way to the United Kingdom and the United States, which helps explain the intensity of turf wars, the heavy armament of politically aligned gangs, and police brutality as well (Grimal 2000, 175). The power of drug-based gangs threatens to diminish hard-won and long-established Jamaican democracy (Sheller 2000).

India's Turbulent Democracy

A final vignette from 1989 takes us to the world's largest and most complicated democracy—India. During the year the country underwent a lively national election campaign that removed Rajiv Gandhi (who had become prime minister in 1984 after a Sikh activist had assassinated his mother, prime minister Indira Gandhi) and his Congress Party from power:

> [A] pre-election outburst of Hindu-Muslim strife in the populous Hindi-speaking belt of north-central India provided additional assurance that communalism would be an important electoral factor. The latest violence, in which over 100 people died, arose from attempts by Hindu extremists to "liberate" the Ram Janmabhoomi holy site in eastern Uttar Pradesh from the dominance of the Babri Masjid mosque built there in the 16th century. . . . Held on 22–26 November, the elections were for 525 of the Lok Sabha's 545 seats. . . . Serious campaign violence claimed some 128 lives (three times as many as in 1984), making the election the bloodiest since independence. (*Annual Register* 1989, 303–4)

Contemporary India remains fascinating because at the regional (that is, "state") and national levels its politics qualify as more or less democratic, with relatively broad, equal, and protected consultation for its vast numbers of citizens. Indian electoral campaigns proceed with colors, symbols, tableaux, and rituals more reminiscent of Paris in 1789 than of any Western country in 2005 (Brass 2003; Hansen 1999; Kakar 1996; Varshney 2002). But they proceed as genuinely contested campaigns. The national and state governments also exercise substantial control over people, activities, and resources within their territories. In that sense, India also qualifies as a fairly high-capacity regime.

Yet the Indian regime exists with sharp, politicized divisions by caste, class, region and, especially, religion. It maintains military forces in divided Kashmir, faces armed autonomist insurgencies in its mountainous northeastern regions, and experiences levels of domestic collective violence far surpassing those of other large democracies. In 1992, for example, the Babri Masjid dispute peaked in a Hindu militant attack on the Ayodhya, Uttar Pradesh mosque that reduced it to ruins. The attack precipitated nationwide struggles eventually killing more than two thousand people (Bose and Jalal 1998, 228; Madan 1997, 56–58; Rajagopal 2001, chap. 4; Tambiah 1996, 251; van de Veer 1996). The campaigns behind that newsworthy event had actually begun much earlier. During the nineteenth century, a platform marking the supposed birthplace of Ram, epic hero of the Hindu classic *Ramayana*, stood adjacent to the mosque. It represented the historical assertion that during his sixteenth-century conquest the Mughal emperor had demolished an ancient Hindu temple and built a mosque in its place.

The platform supplied the occasions for repeated Hindu–Muslim confrontations and for the program of building a Hindu temple on the site (Brass 1994, 241). Colonial authorities scotched the program. Shortly after independence, fifty to sixty local Hindus occupied the site one night and there installed Hindu idols. In response to Muslim demands, however, the newly independent (and avowedly secular) Indian government seized and locked up the mosque. During the 1980s, militant Hindu groups centering on the nationalist organization Rashtriya Swayamsevak Sangh (RSS) started demanding destruction of the mosque and erection of a temple to Ram. Just before the 1989 elections, RSS-affiliated Bharatiya Janata Party (BJP) activists transported what they called "holy bricks" to Ayodhya and ceremoniously laid a foundation for their temple.

The following year, President Lal Advani of the BJP took his chariot caravan on a pilgrimage *(rath yatra)* across northern India, promising along the way to start building the Ram temple in Ayodhya. Advani started his pilgrimage in Somnath, fabled site of yet another great Hindu temple destroyed by Muslim marauders. "For the sake of the temple," he declared en route, "we will sacrifice not one but many governments" (Chaturvedi and Chaturvedi 1996, 181–82). Advani's followers had fashioned his Toyota van into a version of legendary hero Arjuna's chariot, an image familiar from Peter Brook's film *Mahabharata*.

As the BJP caravan passed through towns and villages, Advani's chariot attracted gifts of flower petals, coconut, burning incense, sandalwood paste, and prayer from local women. Authorities arrested Advani before he could begin the last lap of his journey to Ayodhya, but not before many of his followers had preceded him to the city. When some of them broke through police barricades near the offending mosque, police open fire, killing "scores" of BJP activists (Kakar 1996, 51).

Both sides represented their actions as virtuous violence—one side as defense of public order, the other as sacrifice for a holy cause. Hindu activists made a great pageant of cremating the victims' bodies on a nearby river bank, then returning martyrs' ashes to their homes in various parts of India. Soon the fatalities at Ayodhya became themes of widespread clashes among Hindus, Muslims, and the police. Those conflicts intersected with higher-caste students' public resistance to the national government's revival of an affirmative-action program on behalf of Other Backward Classes (Tambiah 1996, 249).

Hindu militants finally succeeded in destroying the Babri Masjid mosque on December 6, 1992. With authorization from the Uttar Pradesh regional (state) government, the BJP planned a demonstration there, issuing pink identity badges to journalists the day before. At dawn, loudspeakers began broadcasting chants in honor of the Lord Ram. As supporters stood in a large crowd, BJP volunteers infiltrated the grounds and climbed to the tops of the mosque's domes. A large crowd watched, many of them cheering, as activists began smashing the structure, then mixed cement to build a platform and wall on its rubble. Meanwhile, other volunteers blocked Ayodhya's perimeter to keep out government security forces, and still others attacked Muslim homes. At the site, nationalist leaders made fiery speeches and honored the mother of two brothers who had died during the events of 1990 while trying to attack the mosque. Although government forces secured the temple site late on the sixth, attacks on Muslims and their properties continued for another day, killing thirteen people. As news of the confrontation spread across India, another two thousand people died in clashes elsewhere.

In Pune, Hindu militants who had just returned from Ayodhya told Thomas Blom Hansen about the symbolic importance of the mosque's destruction:

> In Ayodhya the excitement was tremendous. Everybody felt this is the foundation of the Hindu nation. It happened because what was happening to Hindus had to be washed off. So many of our leaders had been insulted and so much wrong had been done to us. It had to stop somewhere. Whatever has been done [in Ayodhya] was to bring together the Hindus and show them how outsiders are violating them and their country. Once the Hindu power is established . . . the Muslims will be shown their place. (Hansen 1999, 118)

The dispute continued into the twenty-first century, with militant Hindu leaders frequently vowing to build (or, as they insisted, rebuild) their temple on the Babri Masjid site. In 2003, the Uttar Pradesh state court ordered the Archaeological Survey of India (ASI) to bring its scientific expertise to bear on the site. ASI excavations identified fifty pillar bases plus other artifacts in patterns characteristic of North Indian temples. Instead of settling the matter with the cool calm of science, however, the new discoveries incited sharp disagreements among archaeologists as they brought cries of triumph from Hindu activists. Lal Advani himself declared that the ASI report "gladdens crores [tens of millions] of devotees of Lord Rama" (Bagla 2003, 1305). A few weeks later, an Uttar Pradesh court dismissed criminal charges against Advani (then a plausible candidate for prime minister if the BJP had won the 2004 general election) that stemmed from his incitement of the 1992 attack on the Ayodhya mosque.

These dramatic events could not have unfolded anywhere else than in India. Yet they combined a campaign (not just to build a Hindu temple, but also to attract political support for the BJP), a series of social-movement performances (associations, meetings, processions, and more) along with sensational displays of worthiness, unity, numbers, and commitment. In those regards, the political work of India's Hindu organizers resembled that of nationalist social-movement leaders throughout the world, complete with the strident nationalist claim "We were here first."

Just as Mohandas Gandhi and his collaborators pioneered a distinctive Indian variety of social movement claim-making oriented to the British colonial system and taking the British government itself as one of its targets, the BJP integrated visibly Hindu references into its campaigns, performances, and WUNC (worthiness, unity, numbers, and commitment) displays as it sought power within a nominally secular Indian state. Indian campaigns could hardly have made the distinctive duality of social movements—simultaneously local and international in their forms, practices, and meanings—clearer.

Meanwhile, at India's edges loom violent encounters resembling those of Peru, Colombia, the Caucasus, and Uganda:

> In India's seven northeastern states, more than 40 mainly tribal-based insurgent groups sporadically attack security forces and engage in intertribal violence. The rebel groups have also been implicated in numerous killings, abductions, and rapes of civilians.... In a number of states, left-wing guerrillas called Naxalites control some rural areas and kill dozens of police, politicians, landlords, and villagers each year. Police also continued to battle the People's War Group, a guerrilla organization that aims to establish a Communist state in the tribal areas of Andhra Pradesh, Orissa, West Bengal, Jharkhand, Bihar, and Chhattisgarh. (Piano and Puddington 2004, 261)

If India's contentious repertoires resemble those of other high-capacity democracies, then, they do so only in general ways.

Regimes in Regime Space

Figure 4.1 approximately locates, with regard to capacity and democracy, the six regimes that have been this chapter's focus thus far. Their locations in the two dimensions reflect my judgment as to their place among all national regimes across the world in 1989. A fuller diagram would be harder to read, but would include more extreme cases. Although Uganda

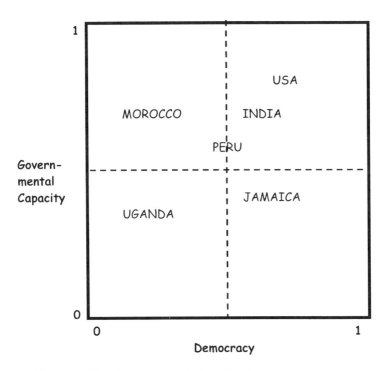

Figure 4.1. Rough placement of selected regimes in 1989

appears in the low-capacity, low-democracy quadrant of the space, for example, fragmented, chaotic Somalia anchors the lower-left corner. We can locate Iran and Norway as the next two corner-keepers in a clockwise rotation, with the lower-right corner—very high democracy, extremely low capacity—empty as usual. Uganda, Peru, India, and the United States then fall into something like a straight line, with increasing amounts of both capacity and democracy. But Morocco, as we have seen, stands off that line, with substantial governmental capacity and little democracy. Jamaica veers off the line in the other direction, with democracy threatened by weak governmental capacity.

The history of Peru has already shown us that regime locations fluctuate from year to year. Although I would hardly have believed it in 1989, my own reading of the U.S. trajectory is that between 1989 and 2005 the regime increased slightly in capacity but declined significantly in democracy. On one side, that is, investment in military forces and repressive means expanded the American state's control over people, activities, and resources within its territory. On the other, binding consultation declined as the national executive increasingly launched foreign military interventions without consulting the citizenry. Protection declined even more precipitously as the U.S. government used national security as a ground for abridging citizens' rights. Nevertheless, except in revolutions regimes do not make drastic shifts within the space from one year to the next. That is, indeed, how we distinguish revolutions from coups, rebellions, civil wars, and anarchy. Revolutions consist of rapid, drastic movements with regard to democracy and/or governmental capacity. (Chapter 6 examines how those rapid changes occur.)

As our vignettes of 1989 indicate, contentious repertoires vary systematically by location within regime space. Morocco's long war with the Polisario notwithstanding, struggles among autonomous military groups concentrate in the low-capacity, low-democracy quadrant. Figure 4.1 shows Peru as just exiting from the quadrant in 1989, as Túpac Amaru, Sendero Luminoso, and government-backed paramilitaries all start to withdraw from the public scene. The upper-left corner (high capacity, low democracy) includes regimes in which any public, collective claim-making occurs either within stringent limits imposed by the government or in niches that have somehow escaped governmental surveillance and control. The dispatches from Morocco make clear that the government leaves little room for public dissent.

In the upper-right corner (high capacity, extensive democracy) we could expect to find the familiar contentious politics of social movements: associations, meetings, statements, pamphlets, marches, rallies, petitions, lobbying, and (greatly increasing after 1989) electronic communication. On the whole, contention in that quadrant concentrates on nonviolent presentation of identity, standing, and program claims; violence occurs especially when one group (including police and other government agents) seeks to block another group's initially nonviolent making of claims. To be sure, the earlier vignettes from the United States and India display the limits of any such generalization: violence does attend some claim-making in the two countries. Nonetheless, as compared with contention in the nondemocratic half of the space, a large proportion of democratic claim-making goes off without brute force violence—without physical damage to persons or objects.

We should guard against an illusion easily brought on by the four categories of regimes. The four quadrants do not simply serve as pens in which different sorts of citizens carry on different sorts of claim-making. They also identify different relations between governmental agents and citizens. In high-capacity regimes, governmental agents participate more actively in all sorts of contention than do the governmental agents of low-capacity regimes. High-capacity agents participate by initiating claims, by receiving claims, by adjudicating claims, and by monitoring claims between nongovernmental parties. Among the regimes featured in this chapter, more contention goes on without some sort of governmental involvement in Uganda than in Morocco.

Almost by definition, democratic regimes leave more room for legitimate contention than do nondemocratic regimes. As we saw in chapter 1, Robert Dahl's "polyarchies" combine inclusive rights to political participation with extensive rights to public contestation. In the forms of social movements, industrial conflict, and ethnic, religious, or racial struggles, contestation within democratic regimes often feature groups of citizens pitted mainly against each other rather than against governmental agents. Nevertheless, in democracies governmental agents do not generally sit idle as contention proceeds. On the contrary, police forces, public officials, and legislators all keep their eyes on democratic contention, watching carefully to see whether it affects governmental interests and whether the means employed step beyond local rules of political decorum.

Such fragments of information begin to fit into a coherent pattern. Clearly, prevailing forms of public, collective claim-making—contentious repertoires—vary significantly from one location to another within regime space. We can arrive at that conclusion from either the bottom up or the top down. From the bottom up, we catalog different sorts of contentious performances and then notice where they occur most frequently within the space. We began chapter 3 with a bottom-up tour on New Year's Day 2005.

From the top down, in contrast, we proceed regime by regime, locating regimes within the space, then map what varieties of contention predominate in different kinds of regime. We have just finished an informal top-down tour. Now we should systematize such a view.

A Ruler's Eye View

Imagine yourself appointed ruler in one of these regimes—among all political figures, the one whose individual performance has the largest single impact on the way governmental agents behave. In India of 1989 you will be Rajiv Gandhi, at least until his December electoral defeat. In Uganda, you will undoubtedly step into the shoes of President Yoweri Museveni. In Peru, you will take the position of President Alan García, even if the following year you will have to decide whether President Fujimori or security advisor Montesinos deserves the nod. In Morocco, you will assume the royal robes of Hassan II. In Jamaica, you will have to choose between Jamaica Labor Party leader Edward Seaga and People's National Party Michael Manley; although Manley's PNP made him prime minister in February, he replaced Seaga in a post that has repeatedly bounced between the parties. In the United States, President Ronald Reagan will start the year for you, but will soon yield the baton to George H. W. Bush.

In the case of President Bush, you may begin to wonder how much of a ruler he is as his nominee for secretary of defense, John Tower, fails to receive confirmation when Tower's former colleagues in the Senate bring up allegations of heavy drinking, sexual improprieties in office, and involvement in shady Pentagon procurement activities. If you are prescient, you may also notice that the senators accepted Bush's second nominee for secretary of defense, Richard Cheney, whom the *Annual Register* describes as "the conservative Republican Whip in the House of Representatives," and the House then replaced Cheney with Newt Gingrich, described as "a hardline conservative who rejected the conciliatory approach" (*Annual Register* 1989, 48). You see two future candidates for ruler thus moving into positions of power.

From your vantage point as ruler, you see contentious repertoires in a somewhat different way: as forms of claim-making that can forward, impede, or threaten your own programs. Seeing how various performances affect (or would affect) your own interests, you can choose to anticipate performances before they occur or to respond after the fact. In either case, you deploy various combinations of available political resources: coercion, capital, and commitment. You can threaten or apply such coercive resources as prosecution and police force. You can pay off performers or their opponents. Similarly, you can draw on commitment either by activating the loyalty of performers to your regime (and, for that matter, to you personally) or by mobilizing their committed enemies.

Deploying those resources, you choose in effect among repression, facilitation, and a mixture of the two.[1] Your choices for dealing with different sorts of claim-making performance therefore look like this:

	Anticipatory	Responsive
Repression	Preventive actions and threats	Retaliation
Facilitation	Mobilization	Rewards

In a line of repression, you can take such anticipatory actions as spying on, incarcerating, or inhibiting the communications of likely participants in claim-making, closing off spaces where claim-making is likely to occur, and announcing penalties you will visit on anyone who organizes a certain

1. For surveys and syntheses concerning repression and facilitation, see Chalom and Léonard 2001; Davenport 2000; Davenport, Johnston, and Mueller 2005; Davis and Pereira 2003; Deflem 2002; Gerstenberger 1990; Goldstein 1983, 2000, 2001; Goldstone and Tilly 2001; González Callejo 2002b; Kotek and Rigoulot 2000; Lüdtke 1992; McCarthy, McPhail, and Crist 1999; Monjardet 1996; Oliverio 1998; della Porta and Reiter 1998.

kind of performance. But you can also send out your bailiffs, troops, or hit squads after someone has made claims in a way that meets your disfavor. (If you have limited means, furthermore, you can retaliate by means of exemplary punishment: ostentatiously hanging or torturing the few perpetrators on whom your agents can lay their hands.)

In the line of facilitation, you have a similar choice between anticipation and response: actively recruit participants for performances of which you approve before the performances occur, or reward those who turn out after the fact. All effective rulers carry on some combination of the four strategies. But regimes differ in relative emphasis. Authoritarian regimes, for example, invest heavily in anticipatory repression, not simply waiting until someone does something wrong to put them down. We have seen Human Rights Watch slapping Morocco's wrist for too much anticipatory repression. From the perspectives of democratic regimes, Morocco's preventive measures against Islamist activists threaten democracy twice: in general by abridging rights to assembly, association, and speech, and in particular by reducing protections of minorities against arbitrary actions of governmental agents.

Your combination of repression and facilitation divides claim-making performances into three categories. Some you *prescribe*, as when you demand public pledges of allegiance or collective financial contributions from your subjects. Some you *tolerate*, as when you accept humble petitions or let citizens assemble to deliberate. Some you *forbid*, as when you send your troops against any group that mauls your tax collectors or military recruiters. Various combinations of facilitation and repression (whether anticipatory or responsive) mark the boundaries among prescribed, tolerated, and forbidden. You may, for example, facilitate peaceful demonstrations, but set up serious penalties for any demonstrator who engages in a violent act. Again, you may threaten with prison anyone who refuses a prescribed performance such as reporting for military service or saluting the national flag.

Remember (from chapter 3) that political opportunity structure (POS) includes (a) the multiplicity of independent centers of power within the regime, (b) the openness of the regime to new actors, (c) the instability of current political alignments, (d) the availability of influential allies or supporters, (e) the extent to which the regime represses or facilitates collective claim-making, and (f) decisive changes in (a) to (e). As you lay out and enforce your preferences for prescribed, tolerated, and forbidden performances, you are actually helping form POS. You are especially shaping (b) and (e): the openness of the regime to new actors and the extent to which the regime represses or facilitates collective claim-making. If, for example, the only forms of claim-making that your regime tolerates are the ones that come easily to existing power-holders, and the ones you forbid belong especially to existing challengers, you are restricting POS for challengers actual and potential.

How do prescribed, tolerated, and forbidden performances vary within regime space? Both governmental capacity and democracy affect overlaps among prescribed, tolerated, forbidden, and contentious public political performances. How? First, democratic regimes absolutely prescribe relatively few such performances, but they tolerate quite a range; while military conscription, tax payments, and replies to censuses come close to being compulsory for affected parties in democracies, even registering to vote remains voluntary in most democratic regimes. High-capacity, nondemocratic regimes, in contrast, commonly prescribe a wide range of public political performances while tolerating few others. They also forbid a much wider variety of claim-making performances.

Second, democratic regimes draw contentious claim-making toward their prescribed and tolerated forms of expression because access to power and recognition regularly pass through effective uses of those forms; thus electoral campaigns and sessions of legislative assemblies become foci of claim-making, even on the part of contenders that currently exercise little or no power. High-capacity, nondemocratic regimes, in contrast, typically exclude contentious issues and actors from prescribed and tolerated forms of claim-making, with the consequence that dissidents make their claims either by covert use of tolerated performances such as public ceremonies or by deliberate adoption of forbidden performances such as armed attacks.

But governmental capacity matters as well. Low-capacity, nondemocratic regimes tolerate a relatively wide range of contentious claim-making for three reasons: (1) they lack the means to prescribe many performances, and therefore settle for tribute, ritual obeisance, and a few other services from subjects; (2) they also lack the means to police small-scale contentious claim-making throughout their nominal jurisdictions; (3) their efforts to impose cultural, political, and organizational uniformity throughout their jurisdictions remain weak and ineffectual, with the consequence that actions, emergence processes, and trajectories of contentious politics vary greatly from region to region and sector to sector.

On the democratic side, similar arguments apply. Low-capacity, democratic regimes have rarely formed in history, and even more rarely survived; most have taken no more than a local scale. When they have existed, however, they have typically prescribed few performances, tolerated a great many, and passed a great deal of their public life in contention among conflicting claims, factions, and forms of action. From long Mediterranean experience with city-states, Aristotle recognized the vulnerability of low-capacity, democratic regimes to be taken over by factions or by external conquest. They also appear to fragment easily into regimes organized around rival—or at least distinct—governments. Since many of today's emerging democracies build on relatively low-capacity governments, any leads we can find to the operation of low-capacity, democratic regimes should illuminate struggles going on in the contemporary world.

Repertoires within Their Regimes

We can do some rough reality checks by comparing my placements of regimes with those of a professional freedom-tracking agency. Since 1972, New York-based Freedom House has rated all the world's independent countries on political rights, civil liberties, and presence or absence of democratic elections. (For years one of my graduate school classmates, Raymond Gastil, collected and analyzed the data as well as refined the ratings.) A democracy, by Freedom House's fairly relaxed standards, maintains universal suffrage and competitive political parties; its last national elections is required to have been fair and free according to the House's expert evaluators. In 2003, using these rules, Freedom House proclaimed that 117 regimes (61 percent of the world total) were electoral democracies. For a selection of regimes including those we examined earlier, figure 4.2 shows the dividing line between democracies and nondemocracies by this criterion. With Russia, Colombia, and Albania all on the line's positive side, we can conclude that Freedom House uses the label "democracy" generously.

Freedom House also produces more refined ratings of political rights and civil liberties. In that dual scheme, countries run from 1 (high) to 7 (low) on each of the two. Box 4.1 lists the questions raters are supposed to ask about each regime. Although we might quibble over the neglect of such matters as arbitrary taxation, official corruption, and unequal liability to military service, Freedom House's questions cover the conventional range of democratic rights and liberties. The more emphatically raters can say "yes" to its array of questions, the more extensive the regime's political rights and civil liberties. In the Freedom House procedures, knowledgeable raters assign values from 0 to 4 for each required question, temper the scores with judgments about special circumstances, then combine them into overall assessments.

Broadly speaking, the Freedom House ratings for political rights address breadth, equality, and binding consultation, whereas civil liberties mainly concern protection. Neither deals with governmental capacity directly, although capacity figures indirectly in answers to such questions

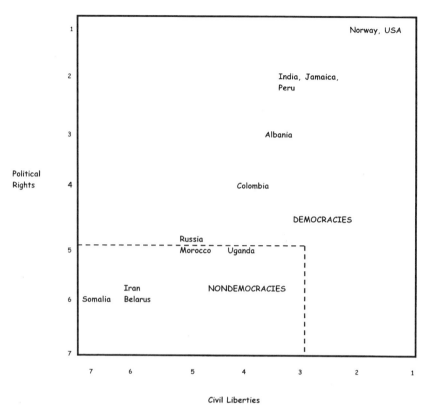

Figure 4.2. Freedom House ratings of selected countries on political rights and civil liberties, 2003
Source: Compiled from Piano and Puddington 2004.

as PR7 ("Are the people free from domination by the military, foreign powers, totalitarian parties, religious hierarchies, economic oligarchies, or any other powerful group?") and CL10 ("Are property rights secure? Do citizens have the right to establish private businesses? Is private business activity unduly influenced by government officials, the security forces, or organized crime?"). Remembering that higher scores are less democratic, then, think of the multiple Political Rights × Civil Liberties as a rough measure of democracy, mildly tinged by governmental capacity.

In addition to the dividing line between electoral democracy and nondemocracy, figure 4.2 arrays the same selection of countries on political rights (vertical axis) and civil liberties (horizontal axis). Regimes cluster along the diagonal, which means that regimes with high scores on political rights also tend to receive high scores on civil liberties, and vice versa.

BOX 4.1 Freedom House Checklist for Political Rights and Civil Liberties

POLITICAL RIGHTS

1. Is the head of state and/or head of government or other chief authority elected through free and fair elections?
2. Are the legislative representatives elected through free and fair elections?
3. Are there fair electoral laws, equal campaigning opportunities, fair polling, and honest tabulations of ballots?
4. Are the voters able to endow their freely elected representatives with real power?
5. Do the people have the right to organize in different political parties or other competitive political groupings of their choice, and is the system open to the rise and fall of these competing parties or groupings?
6. Is there a significant opposition vote, de facto opposition power, and a realistic possibility for the opposition to increase its support or gain power through elections?
7. Are the people free from domination by the military, foreign powers, totalitarian parties, religious hierarchies, economic oligarchies, or any other powerful group?
8. Do cultural, ethnic, religious, and other minority groups have reasonable self-determination, self-government, autonomy, or participation through informal consensus in the decision-making process?
9. (Discretionary) For traditional monarchies that have no parties or electoral process, does the system provide for consultation with the people, encourage discussion of policy, and allow the right to petition the ruler?
10. (Discretionary) Is the government or occupying power deliberately changing the ethnic composition of a country or territory so as to destroy a culture or tip the political balance in favor of another group?

CIVIL LIBERTIES

1. Is there freedom of assembly, demonstration, and open public discussion?
2. Is there freedom of political or quasi-political organization, including political parties, civic organizations, ad hoc issue groups, etc.?
3. Are there free trade unions and peasant organizations or equivalents, and is there effective collective bargaining? Are there free professional and other private organizations?
4. Is there an independent judiciary?
5. Does the rule of law prevail in civil and criminal matters? Is the population treated equally under the law? Are police under direct civilian control?

6. Is there protection from political terror, unjustified imprisonment, exile, or torture, whether by groups that support or oppose the system? Is there freedom from war and insurgencies?
7. Is there freedom from extreme government indifference and corruption?
8. Is there open and free private discussion?
9. Is there personal autonomy? Does the state control travel, choice of residence, or choice of employment? Is there freedom from indoctrination and excessive dependency on the state?
10. Are property rights secure? Do citizens have the right to establish private businesses? Is private business activity unduly influenced by government officials, the security forces, or organized crime?
11. Are there personal social freedoms, including gender equality, choice of marriage partners, and size of family?
12. Is there equality of opportunity, including freedom from exploitation by or dependency on landlords, employers, union leaders, bureaucrats, or other types of obstacles to a share of legitimate economic gains?

Source: Adapted from Karatnycky 2000: 584–585.

Although the distinction between Russia (with its contested, if distorted, elections) and Morocco (an authoritarian monarchy) is a close call, the countries qualifying as nondemocracies on electoral grounds also receive unfavorable ratings on political rights and civil rights.

The largest discrepancy between these ratings and my rough placements for 1989 in figure 4.1 concerns the relative positions of Uganda and Morocco. In 2003, the two regimes received equal Freedom House ratings on political rights (5, or fairly low), but on civil rights Uganda received a more favorable 4, to Morocco's 5. According to Freedom House, in fact, during the 1990s Ugandan civil rights improved slightly, while Moroccan civil rights decayed. In figure 4.1, by contrast, I rated Morocco as exercising much higher governmental capacity than Uganda, but standing roughly equal with Uganda with regard to democracy. Otherwise (remembering that the ratings neglect capacity), the orders of democracy in the two figures correspond to each other.

Repression, Facilitation, and Repertoires

What differences in contentious repertoires among these regimes do my earlier arguments imply? The differences by crude regime type run as follows:

Low-Capacity Nondemocratic: few prescribed performances; medium range of tolerated performances; much of contention via forbidden performances; low involvement of government agents in contention; high levels of violence in contentious interactions.

High-Capacity Nondemocratic: many prescribed performances; narrow range of tolerated performances; almost all contention by means of forbidden performances; high involvement of government agents in contention (often as principals); medium levels of violence in contentious interactions.

Low-Capacity Democratic: few prescribed performances; broad range of tolerated performances; extensive overlap of contention with both prescribed and tolerated performances; medium involvement of government agents in contention (often as principals); medium levels of violence in contentious interactions.

High-Capacity Democratic: few prescribed performances; medium range of tolerated performances; contention overlapping somewhat with prescribed and tolerated performances; high involvement of government agents in contention (often as third parties); low levels of violence in contentious interactions.

Ideally, evidence for or against these generalizations would take two parallel forms for each regime: (1) a collection of governmental actions that facilitate or repress different kinds of claim-making performances, thus dividing them into prescribed, tolerated, and forbidden; (2) a collection of claim-making performances by actors within the regime. Properly supplemented by continuous information on governmental action, catalogs of "contentious gatherings" collected according to the procedures described in chapter 3 supply evidence of just this sort. Alas, no one has yet prepared the essential catalogs for Uganda, Peru, Morocco, and the other regimes we have been comparing.

One More Round of Regimes and Repertoires

We can, however, get an inkling of what such catalogs would show by drawing on intermittent reports by Human Rights Watch (HRW) and Amnesty International (AI) plus the annual reports of Freedom House (FH). All three agencies concern themselves with violations of political and civil rights by governments and other holders of power. HRW and AI alternate between national surveys and reports on particular abuses, while FH issues an annual country-by-country survey to supplement its ratings for political rights, civil rights, and democracy. The three agencies' reports during the years 2000 through 2004 mostly ignore routine nonviolent making of claims, but they provide enough detail to tell the difference among regimes in their responses to contentious repertoires.

UGANDA We expect Uganda, a low-capacity, nondemocratic regime, to display few prescribed performances, a medium range of tolerated performances; much of its contention via forbidden performances; low involvement of government agents in contention; extensive use of coercive means (rather than capital or commitment) by government agents when they do intervene in contention; and high levels of violence in contentious interactions. Except that the monitoring agencies (concerned especially about governmental abuses) single out episodes involving government agents and therefore surely exaggerate the involvement of the government in all of contentious politics, the news from Uganda amply fulfills these expectations (Amnesty International 2004a; Human Rights Watch 2003a, 2003d; Piano and Puddington 2004, 590–94). It portrays a repressive regime that strikes at its opponents when it can, forbids democratic participation, but exercises only wavering control over much of its territory and population.

In 2002, for example, a Parliament dominated by President Yoweri Museveni's National Resistance Movement (NRM) passed a Suppression of Terrorism Bill that imposed dire penalties on violence or threats of violence for political, religious, or cultural ends, unlawful possession of arms, and publishing news "likely to promote terrorism." The same year its Political Organizations Law barred formation and registration of new parties as it forbade existing parties to hold rallies, take part in elections, or open offices outside of Kampala, the national capital. Uganda's Constitutional Court intervened against the law, but the NRM remained the only effective party-like force in Ugandan politics. (In 2005, the Ugandan Parliament compliantly revised the country's term limits so that President Museveni could run for a previously barred third term.)

Meanwhile, the government freely used charges of treason to imprison political dissidents and did not hesitate to break up opposition gatherings. "On January 12, 2002," reports HRW,

> police broke up a peaceful rally in Kampala organized by an opposition party, the Uganda People's Congress (UPC), by firing on demonstrators with live ammunition. They killed a young journalist, Jimmy Higenyi, and injured several other persons with gunfire. They briefly detained several UPC leaders and two journalists. Local elections held in February were the occasion for cases of manipulation and abuse by government forces. Plainclothes agents abducted a

campaign worker for Kampala's mayor, took him to the headquarters of Chieftaincy Military Intelligence (CMI, a government security agency), and later to an unacknowledged detention center in Kampala. They accused him of cooperating with armed rebel groups and beat him severely. (Human Rights Watch 2003a, Uganda, 2)

But the government's actual capacity to repress legally forbidden performances fell off rapidly with distance from Kampala. In large northern and southern regions of Uganda, government military forces and their proxies were battling a variety of insurgents, frequently attacking local civilian populations presumed to support the insurgents. Their unsuccessful campaign against the Lords Resistance Army (LRA) in the north brought scorched-earth tactics and massive displacements of civilians from both the rebels and the Ugandan army. Although the Sudanese government at first suspended its support for the LRA in the immediate wake of the events of September 11, 2001, when the U.S. government identified the LRA as a terrorist organization, Sudan was soon again providing shelter and arms to the LRA, reportedly in retaliation against Ugandan support for separatist rebels in southern Sudan.

During the second half of 2002 alone, the LRA abducted nearly five thousand children in northern Uganda while killing 539 civilians and 122 Ugandan soldiers (Human Rights Watch 2003b, 5, 16). As the LRA advanced, local youths formed their own vigilante groups to hunt down LRA warriors (Amnesty International 2004a, 3). All this exemplifies the contentious politics of low-capacity, nondemocratic regimes across the world.

PERU Compare with Uganda, Peru's government exercises substantially higher capacity as its regime maintains at least some democratic freedoms. We might therefore expect its contentious politics to occupy an intermediate position: some prescribed performances; a medium range of tolerated performances; much contention by means of forbidden performances; higher involvement of government agents in contention (often as principals); and medium levels of violence in contentious interactions. Contrasted to bloody Uganda, Peru's contention during the early twenty-first century did look somewhat more like our idealized model of medium-capacity, semi-democratic regimes.

Nevertheless, human rights observers found plenty to concern them during those early years (Amnesty International 2000, 2001a; Human Rights Watch 2002a, 2004b; Piano and Puddington 2004, 444–48). In 2003, a Peruvian Truth and Reconciliation Commission reviewed the violence from 1980 to 2000, concluding that Sendero Luminoso had committed the major offenses of the period, but national military and security forces had done their share. (Former military chief Roberto Clemente

Noel replied by accusing commission members of being Marxists with connections to Sendero Luminoso; Anheier et al. 2005, 356).

Despite considerable resistance from the armed forces, the government actually began arresting veterans of Montesinos-sanctioned death squads that had engaged in abductions and killings of suspected rebels and dissenters during the 1990s, as well as media executives that accepted bribes for favorable coverage of Alberto Fujimori. It also began prosecution in absentia of Fujimori himself, and took steps to ask Japan for his extradition. During 2002 and 2003, Sendero Luminoso returned to the attack. A year later, high in the Andes, local people and leftist activists accelerated attacks on American gold-mining firms, which they accused of destroying the environment of indigenous people. Meanwhile, growing opposition to the new president Alejandro Toledo mostly took the form of election rallies, media criticism, and nonviolent demonstrations, sometimes violently suppressed.

MOROCCO As we saw earlier, the Moroccan regime clearly belongs in the high-capacity, nondemocratic quadrant of our regime space, despite the monarchy's occasional gestures toward popular political participation. In that quadrant we expect to find many prescribed performances; a narrow range of tolerated performances; almost all contention by means of forbidden performances; high involvement of government agents in contention (often as principals); and medium levels of violence in contentious interactions. With some interesting nuances resulting from the government's sensitivity to international pressure, the portrait fits Morocco better than Uganda or Peru (Human Rights Watch 2004a, Piano and Puddington 2004, 389–92).

After succeeding his father as king in 1999, Muhammad VI started a cautious move toward representative government—dismissing corrupt ministers, freeing political prisoners, allowing political exiles to return, and, in 2002, holding competitive elections to the national parliament. In 2003, the king proposed substantial increases in women's rights with respect to marriage and divorce. Nevertheless, the government continued to insist on licensing all nongovernmental organizations and requiring permits for public gatherings.

As often happens in such circumstances, domestic human rights activists used the available openings to press for more change. On December 9, 2000, for example, the Moroccan Association of Human Rights organized a sit-in demonstration outside of the Parliament to commemorate the fifty-second anniversary of the Universal Declaration of Human Rights and to call for public inquiries into past human rights violations, including the unexplained disappearances of opposition leaders. Government security forces arrested forty-two of the demonstrators. On the tenth, follow-up demonstrations by members of a banned Islamist association, calling for the association's legalization, occurred in Rabat, Casablanca, Marrakesh, Fes, Tetouan, Agadir, Oujda, and El-Jadida. In those encounters, security forces beat some of the demonstraters and arrested hundreds more (Amnesty International 2001b). Muhammad VI's liberalization had strict limits.

In any case, suicide-bombings in May 2003 soon reversed the government's direction. According to HRW:

> The police carried out massive arrests and home searches without judicial warrants, mostly in poor neighborhoods that are suspected Islamist strongholds. At least 2,000 were detained in the months following the attacks, according to human rights organizations. Many reported that they were then transported to a detention center in Temara, outside Rabat, that is operated by the General Directorate for the Surveillance of the Territory [DGST or DST] . . . the main domestic intelligence agency. While Moroccan authorities deny the existence of a DGST-run detention center, the testimonies we collected affirm earlier accounts of suspected Islamists who said they were interrogated by the DST at such a center. (Human Rights Watch 2004a, 2)

Government agents rounded up suspected Islamists and quickly tried many of them under procedures that domestic and international human rights organizations judged unfair. The government delayed municipal elections from June to September, and put increasing pressure on the (legal) Islamist Justice and Development Party. The party responded by contesting only a few seats in Casablanca, Fes, and Rabat. Meanwhile, the government used newly passed laws against terrorism to muzzle and press and convict journalists for "insulting the king" (Slyomovics 2005). Despite some royal gestures toward democratic participation, the regime remains in the zone of high capacity and low democracy.

JAMAICA As of 2003, Freedom House rated diminutive Jamaica (2.6 million people) as a flawed democracy: 2 on political rights, 3 on civil liberties. Its relatively weak government allowed plenty of scope for violent gangs that drew revenue from the cocaine trade but also often provided strong-arm support for local politicians when needed. That weakness combined with the sluggishness and corruption of courts to promote the police's taking of law into its own hands. In addition to its spectacular homicide rates, Jamaica registers one of the world's highest frequencies of police-killing (Piano and Puddington 2004, 288). An Amnesty International report declared in 2001:

The loss of life at the hands of the Jamaican Constabulary Force (JCD) borders on a human rights emergency. The rate of lethal police shootings in Jamaica is one of the highest per capita in the world. More than 1,400 people have been shot dead by police over the past 10 years in Jamaica; in a country whose population is only 2.6 million. (Amnesty International 2001c, 2)

Gangs and police both often attacked gays, who were also recurrent targets of vituperation by reggae singers (Amnesty International 2004b). In response, five Jamaican human rights organizations launched a 2004 campaign against victimization of gays:

> For this courageous act they were accused by a representative of the Jamaica Police Federation of joining Human Rights Watch "to spread lies and deliberately malign and slander the police force and the government." In its letter of November 25 published in the *Jamaica Observer,* the Federation was not content to defame these advocates and Human Rights Watch. It demanded that the government "slap on sedition charges where necessary to both foreign and local agents of provocation." (Human Rights Watch 2004c, 1)

Despite violent struggle, however, Jamaica's political parties continue to mobilize their followers, to respect election results, and to succeed each other in power. Widespread election violence, rampant gangs, corrupt courts, and abusive police combine to make Jamaica a very troubled democracy.

INDIA With a little over a billion people—four times the U.S. population—India stands as by far the world's largest democracy. Judging its governmental capacity is made even more difficult because of the country's federal structure; the unevenness of governmental writ by region, class, and caste; the presence of large patron–client structures within parties and regions; and the persistence of armed rebellion on the country's northwestern and northeastern frontiers. Nonetheless, on balance it seems right to locate the Indian regime as a whole well into our high-capacity, democratic quadrant. There we expect to find few prescribed performances; a medium range of tolerated performances; contention overlapping somewhat with prescribed and tolerated performances; high involvement of government agents in contention (often as third parties); and low levels of violence in contentious interactions. As compared with Uganda, Peru, and Morocco, India fulfills our expectations, except for higher levels of violent contention than most other regimes in its category (Amnesty International 2003a; Human Rights Watch 2002b, 2003a; Piano and Puddington 2004, 258–62).

Indian violence occurred in three rather different settings: clashes between government security forces and separatist guerrillas in Kashmir and multiple sites along the northeastern border, confrontations of religious groups contending for political power in the country's main political arenas, and clandestine attacks on national targets by Pakistani sympathizers or agents. In many states, higher-caste Hindus also employ violence to discipline outcast Dalits (the "Untouchables") who demand their rights. "Police, army, and paramilitary forces," reports Freedom House, "continue to be implicated in disappearances, extrajudicial killing, rape, torture, arbitrary detention, and destruction of homes, particularly in the context of insurgencies in Kashmir, Andhra Pradesh, Assam, and several other northeastern states" (Piano and Puddington 2004, 260).

The recent ascendancy of the Bharatiya Janata Party (BJP) and related Hindu nationalist parties has placed other religious groups—notably Muslims, Sikhs, and Christians—on the defensive and produced many a violent encounter. In February 2002, fifty-eight Hindu activists returning from a pilgrimage to that disputed site in Ayodhya died in a Godhra, Gujarat fire, after local Muslims attacked their train. With backing from police and politicians, organized Gujarati Hindus began chasing down Muslims through much of the state, eventually killing about one thousand people and leaving one hundred thousand homeless. Gujarat's Hindu nationalist government did little to apprehend the killers, and the BJP, with an openly anti-Muslim campaign, won a landslide victory in Gujarat's December 2002 elections. After September 11, furthermore, the national government itself began cracking down on Muslim activists who opposed the U.S. invasion of Afghanistan, firing on demonstrators and banning the Students Islamic Movement of India.

Despite all this, India provides a remarkable model of peaceful political mobilization within the limits of the standard social-movement repertoire: associations, public meetings, press statements, demonstrations, petitions, and lobbying. Tracing back to the period of anti-British independence movements, Indian activists have mainly hewed to their own domesticated forms of the Parliament-oriented claim-making they deployed so effectively in pressing for Indian rights. During the first half of 2003, for example, the following Indian events attracted international attention:

- January 2–7: Fifteen thousand people participate in the First Asian Social Forum in Hyderabad.
- April 18: Twenty thousand people attend a rally in Srinagar, Kashmir, for a speech by Prime Minister Atal Bihari holding out the possibility of peace with Pakistan.

- June 29: India's first ever gay pride march takes place in Calcutta (Anheier et al. 2005, 351–55).

India retains its distinctiveness, but within the range of other relatively high-capacity, flawed democracies. In the face of dire predictions, the BJP's loss of governmental power in the 2004 national elections occurred without major new violence. A Prevention of Terrorism Act, first put in place by decree shortly after the attacks on September 11, passed parliament in 2002. It strengthened the state's police powers, but fell far short of silencing political contention across the country.

Lest North American readers congratulate themselves invidiously as they read these descriptions of imperfect democracy, let us remember that the United States, too, falls short of perfect breadth, equality, consultation, and protection. Amnesty International reports repeatedly score the United States for its widespread use of the death penalty and its resistance to international courts of justice. But after September 11, AI zeroed in on the treatment of prisoners and suspects in the War on Terror:

> A report by an independent US government watchdog agency, the Justice Department's Office of Inspector General, published in June 2003, found there were "significant problems" in the treatment of non-US nationals detained in the initial post September 11 sweeps in the USA. Hundreds of people were held, often for months, on minor visa violations in harsh conditions, and were deprived of rights including prompt access to attorneys. While the US government has undertaken to reform some of its procedures in response to that report, no such scrutiny has been permitted in the case of the hundreds of non-US nationals who continue to be held outside the USA in its ongoing "war on terror."
>
> The Department of Defence continues to hold hundreds of foreign nationals without charge or trial in the US Naval Base in Guantánamo Bay in Cuba. Many have been held there for more than a year in conditions the totality of which may amount to cruel, inhuman or degrading treatment. None was granted prisoner of war status or brought before a competent tribunal to determine this status as required by the Geneva Conventions. None has had access to any court or to legal counsel. Visits by family members have not been granted, thereby drawing relatives into the distress of this indefinite and unchallengeable detention regime. On 3 July 2003, it was announced that President Bush had named six detainees under the Military Order he signed in November 2001, making them eligible for trial by military commission. Any such trial would contravene international fair trial norms, and any executions carried out after such trials would violate

minimum international safeguards applying to capital cases. (Amnesty International 2003b, 1; see also Human Rights Watch 2003c).

In Morocco, India, and the United States alike, then, the government assumes the power to override its announced principles of civil liberty when it comes to what it defines as threats to its own survival. Our judgments of capacity and democracy always involve more or less rather than absolutes.

With that fundamental specification, vignettes of contention and its control in the regimes of this chapter indicate that locations of regimes with respect to capacity and democracy do, indeed, significantly affect the repertoires of contention that prevail in those regimes. They do so for two main reasons: (1) rulers in different sorts of regimes apply characteristically different combinations of coercion, capital, and commitment to the definitions of prescribed, tolerated, and forbidden forms of claim-making; and (2) a regime's cumulated experience with contention lays down a characteristically different structure of opportunity and threat for potential claimants. Repertoires meet regimes in collaboration and conflict.

CHAPTER FIVE >>
Trajectories of Change

SEGREGATED ALEXANDRA TOWNSHIP, just northeast of Johannesburg, South Africa, mobilized intermittent but sometimes fierce resistance to white rule from its founding in 1912 until the recent past. In 1986, as black mobilization accelerated through South Africa, Alexandra's people mounted their most sustained rebellion. It centered on the Six Day War, from January 15–20, when local authorities and external security forces alike ceded control of the township to young street fighters. Only in May did the army and police retake the local streets. During the interregnum, both sides sometimes engaged in public acts of vicious violence. National forces shot down unarmed citizens who had blundered into the line of fire. Street warriors, on their side, looped kerosene-filled auto tires around the necks and shoulders of suspected traitors or witches from the black community before setting them afire in plain view.

In Alexandra, early 1986 marked the most lethal interval in a long transition. As in the rest of South Africa, a dual shift was occurring: struggle was pushing a regime based on racial categories and white dominance toward some new form of political control with contours that remained uncertain. At the same time, the forms of struggle were changing rapidly. Alexandra and South Africa pose this chapter's more general problem: when regimes and repertoires alter simultaneously, how do those changes interact, and why? As we will soon see, the answer is far more complex and interesting than the simplest possibility—that regimes reshape themselves and thereby alter political opportunities, thus transforming repertoires. Changes in the forms, sites, and intensities of contentious claim-making produce shifts from one sort of regime to another. Trajectories of regimes and repertoires interact. This chapter closely tracks South Africa's mutual mutations of regimes and repertoires before treating interactions of regimes and repertoires much more generally.

Long before 1986, Alexandrans had occasionally joined protest marches; boycotted stores, buses, or schools; blocked bulldozers; and held mass meetings. In 1976, for instance, a brief series of attacks on government buildings, government-operated liquor stores, buses, and cars followed a similar rising in the huge black township on the opposite side of Johannesburg—Soweto (South West Township). During the following years, boycotts and other organized antigovernmental actions intensified. As in all contentious politics, Alexandra's contentious performances of 1986 drew on previously known performances. But a new repertoire was then emerging as the national and local regimes reached a point of crisis.

Speaking of Soweto, political ethnographer Adam Ashforth comments on the grim violence of that repertoire:

> In the political struggles of the late 1970s and 1980s, the heavy-handed response of the state's security forces solidified the sense of community among people living in Soweto. Although many of the older generation of residents were disturbed by the unruliness of the youth in their political struggles during those years—especially when comrades turned against suspected informers, imposed "stay-aways" and boycotts on hard-pressed workers and consumers, or spurred conflicts with the migrant workers from rural areas living in hostels—virtually no one in Soweto doubted the justice of their cause or the necessity of standing together against the hated and brutal "System." Even the "necklacing" of informers *(izimpimpi)* with petrol-filled tires, though appalling to most people, was understood as an unfortunate but necessary community defense against the secret agents of the evil system of apartheid. (Ashforth 2005, 102)

These local forms of resistance joined with national and international political changes to undermine what had once seemed an unshakably tyrannical regime.

Over the period from 1970 to 1995 as a whole, South Africa's elaborate system of apartheid collapsed as black Africans and their nonblack allies mobilized against exploitation, foreign governments and organizations organized more effective boycotts; demands for black labor increased and undermined existing systems of segregation; both domestic and overseas investment in the South African economy declined precipitously; prosperous whites fled the country; the ruling National Party itself split over competing programs of containment and accommodation; and some 30 percent of Afrikaner members left the party.

During the 1980s, the government alternated between attempts to co-opt South Africans of mixed-race ("Colored") and Asian background as well as compliant black leaders, on the one hand, and sustained repression, on the other. A complex series of strategic interactions connected competing black leaders; street-level black activists; representatives of other constituted racial-ethnic categories such as Afrikaners or Colored; the regime's military forces; and members of the government itself.

Coalitions made a critical difference. Leaders of the militant Black Consciousness movement (BC, founded by Steve Biko in 1969 in deliberate contrast to the nonracial African National Congress [ANC]), for example, started to form new coalitions during the 1980s (Marx 1991). BC played a central part in organizing the National Forum, a resistance front, and also aligned itself closely with militant black-based unions.

In competition and collaboration with the ANC, BC activists began organizing campaigns:

> Many BC activists, influenced by growing links with the ANC, concluded that a less ideological and more mass-based, locally organized resistance was now necessary. The state unintentionally encouraged this new strategy when in 1979, seeking to appease its opponents, it instituted reforms that provided breathing space for greater mass organization. Ironically, the emerging mass organizations benefited from reforms while publicly rejecting them to further bolster their popular appeal. For example, when P. W. Botha later proposed a new tricameral parliament intended to attract back the loyalty of coloureds and Asians by giving them limited representation, activists used the proposal as the impetus for a national unification of localized resistance under the United Democratic Front (UDF), founded in 1983. (Marx 1998, 202–3)

This organizing effort occurred amid widespread formation of local civic associations and significant expansion of worker militancy in general (Price 1991, 162–82).

History's Weight

The South African political actors who struggled with one another during the 1980s had emerged from two centuries of interaction between changing regimes and changing forms of contention. The Dutch who colonized the Cape of Good Hope along with adjacent territories during the seventeenth century and the other Europeans who joined them became Afrikaans-speaking Boers. Then British settlers began arriving in substantial numbers and competing with the Boers for control. British–Boer military struggles began in earnest during the 1790s and continued through the nineteenth century. They culminated in the South African war of 1899–1902, known as the Boer War to Britons, the Second War of Freedom to Afrikaners, and a time of troubles for black Africans. Britain's violent victory found a hundred thousand Boer women and children in concentration camps, more than a hundred thousand Africans likewise incarcerated, and Boer farms in smoking ruins.

Having already destroyed so much as to disperse and deplete the African labor forces of farms and mines, rulers of the new South African state eventually chose a combination of co-optation and transformation: first creating a partly autonomous Transvaal government, then integrating it into a new Union of South Africa, staffing its bureaucracies and coercive forces disproportionately with Boers, but deeply reorganizing controls over the non-European population. The latter process raised what South African and British elites referred to as the "Native Question," which actually consists in two closely twined conundrums: (1) how to integrate black Africans into the new state while keeping them compliant and subordinate, and (2) how to commit African labor to farms, to urban services and, above all, to man-devouring diamond and gold mines.

Both conundrums centered on effective means of exploitation, drawing black workers into work on white-dominated resources while excluding them from the full return of their effort. The first involved maneuvering among missionaries who considered themselves uniquely qualified to define and defend Native welfare, chiefs who claimed competing jurisdictions within predominantly African areas of settlement, and capitalists who already depended heavily on African labor. The second involved ensuring that each year pastoral and agricultural communities would continue to send several hundred thousand able-bodied workers, mostly male, for labor away from home, yet reabsorb them when employment slackened or they lost the strength necessary for the labor.

South African authorities sought to answer both questions with a series of efforts at category-building. The most general categorical cut divided Europeans from Natives, matching to those categories unequal and separate territories, protections, and rights of citizenship. At first, European settlers homogenized on both sides of the line, justifying a system of indirect rule in which co-opted African chiefs spoke for their own territorial segments of a presumably unitary Native population. White rulers justified the division as not only natural but also benign. In 1903 Lord Milner, high commissioner of South Africa, put it this way:

> The white man must rule because he is elevated by many, many steps above the black man . . . which it will take the latter centuries to climb and which it is quite possible that the vast bulk of the black population may never be able to climb at all. . . . One of the strongest arguments why the white man must rule is because that is the only possible means of gradually raising the black man, not to our level of civilisation—which it is doubtful whether he would ever attain—but up to a much higher level than that which he at present occupies. (Marks and Trapido 1987, 7)

The government adopted a harsh approach to enlightenment: it used taxation, deprivation of land, and outright compulsion to drive Natives into labor markets. Economic inequalities nevertheless paralleled legal inequalities: in the gold mines, law and standard practice strictly segregated white from black jobs; in mining, African cash wages were 8.6 percent of white wages in 1911, 7.0 percent in 1955, down to 4.8 percent in 1970 (Terreblanche 2002, 262; see also Moodie 1994).

Europeans also segregated themselves, but less rigorously, against Indians. South Africa's Indian-origin population descended chiefly from (especially Madrasi) indentured servants and (especially Gujarati) merchants who arrived between 1860 and World War I. Regional, caste, and religious divisions figured significantly within the Indian population—merchant elites, for example, tended to be Muslim or high-caste Hindu—but little affected the European/Indian division. On the European side an additional line between British and Afrikaners defined opponents in conflicts that several times approached civil war (Moodie 1975). A very unequal South African quadrilateral therefore distinguished British, Afrikaners, Indians, and Natives. Natives constituted the vast majority.

On the quadrilateral's Native side, however, South African authorities actually found not neat boxes but a kaleidoscope. Thousands of categories designated and divided different sets of the African population. Many of them fell into broadly similar linguistic groupings such as Xhosa, Zulu, and Sotho without their occupants' being much aware of the similarities. Some of those similarities harked back to kingdoms that had dominated different parts of the region before Dutch and British hegemony, but by the twentieth century few of them designated sharply bounded populations having long histories of geographic and social segregation.

At first British-oriented authorities sought to treat Africans as a homogeneous mass. But then Boer self-defense within the European population promoted a new view of South Africa as composed of multiple nations.

Those presumably distinct nations came to include major segments of the African population. In a remarkable series of direct interventions, the South African state set out to create racial categories that would serve as the basis of unequal rights and rewards.

From 1903 to 1981, state-appointed commissions repeatedly enlisted administrators, anthropologists, missionaries, professionals, and capitalists in the work of defining the major categories of South African Natives, assigning them collective characters and recommending policies based on those characterizations. They regrouped the thousands of available categories into a handful, attached them to territorial "reserves" currently little populated by Europeans, categorically differentiated their rights to work temporarily outside those reserves, and thus produced gradations of citizenship according to officially assigned ethnicity.

During the twentieth century, Boer intellectuals and administrators likewise codified official views of Afrikaner culture. They created not only a unitary, teleological history but also a standardized Afrikaans language to supplant a variety of Dutch-based dialects and creoles (Hofmeyr 1987). South Africa's so-called ethnos theory, modeled to some extent on Boer experience, preached that coherent social life depended on the maintenance of distinct cultural groups. Anthropologist W. M. Eiselen, who became permanent secretary for Native Affairs during the initiation of thoroughgoing apartheid in 1948, warned as early as 1929 of threats to the coherence of African cultures:

> [T]here is one factor, and that the most important factor, which I have not yet mentioned. That is the will of a people to stand on guard *(handhaaf)*, to remain immortal as a people. If such a will exists, then it can only operate through the medium of a unique ethnic language. From the history of the Boer we learn how a people can retain its identity despite insuperable difficulties and economic disadvantages. (Evans 1990, 26)

Ideologists of apartheid proposed an ingenious, pernicious solution: in addition to Afrikaner-English and black-white-Indian segregation, segregation within the African population. Although nineteenth century regimes had commonly applied the term "Colored" to all non-Europeans, officially designated "Colored people"—8 percent of the national population in 1936—now contained the overflow: nonwhite people who could not be forced into one of the standard categories (Goldin 1987).

Note one telling feature of South Africa's racial categories. Although few large states have ever adopted as explicitly and oppressively racist policies as South Africa, no consistent and durable set of beliefs drove the South African racial system. Racial distinctions enforced by the state shifted repeatedly over time. Although the African/European line stayed in more or less the same place, other divisions altered as a function of political expediency, practical feasibility, and struggle among the parties. Organizational convenience overrode and transformed prevailing beliefs.

Installation of apartheid from 1948 onward modified, and then reinforced, categorical differences previous administrations had created. It did so with greatly increased intensity: uprooting Africans and Colored people from long-established urban residences; herding Africans into small, fragmented, overpopulated homelands; even segregating European children into different schools according to the language spoken at home, English or Afrikaans.

The Tomlinson Commission of 1950–54, a prime architect of apartheid, enshrined ethnographers' distinctions among languages and cultures—Nguni, Sotho, Venda, and Shangaan-Tsonga—on the way to recommending separate lands and statuses for each of them. It also asserted that each of them divided into lineage-defined tribes, typically headed by a single chief. Thus for a series of South African peoples, including various categories of Europeans and Asians, the Tomlinson Report adopted a model of long-established nations that, as they matured, would acquire their own separate states (Ashforth 1990, 159). Indeed, the report recommended a kind of ethnic cleansing, exchanging white and black populations until they filled substantial homogeneous regions, with the black-occupied regions further segregated by assigned linguistic-cultural category (Ashforth 1990, 176). Over the next quarter-century, implementation of that policy displaced close to 4 million people (Marks and Trapido 1987, 22).

South African authorities undertook an immense political and geographic reorganization of the African population. The 1959 Promotion of Bantu Self-Government Act designated ten homelands to house separate "nations": Bophuthatswana for Tswana; Ciskei for Xhosa; Gazankulu for Shangaans and Tsonga; KaNgwane for Swazi; KwaNdebele for Southern Ndebele; KwaZulu for Zulu; Lebowa for Northern Sotho and Northern Ndebele; QwaQwa for Southern Sotho; Transkei for Xhosa; and Venda for Venda (Taylor 1990, 19). Of these, Transkei, Bophuthatswana, Venda, and Ciskei acquired nominal political independence as enclaves within South Africa between 1976 and 1979.

To be sure, white demand for black labor in cities, mines, and farms subverted all plans for total containment of South Africa's populations. The growth of manufacturing and services promoted such rapid expansion of the black urban population that by 1945 manufacturing had surpassed mining's contribution to South African gross domestic product (GDP) (Lodge 1996, 188). By 1960, fully 63 percent of the African population lived at least temporarily outside African reserves (Fredrickson 1981, 244).

Around that time, furthermore, what had been an urban labor shortage shifted to a labor surplus, so that African unemployment concentrated increasingly in cities and townships rather than rural reserves. South Africa's rulers had to manage the contradiction between treating Africans as conquest-formed Natives and recognizing them as capitalist-created workers. The contradiction led to costly efforts at segregating residence and sociability while drawing more and more Africans into the urban and industrial labor forces (Murray 1987, chap. 2, Terreblanche 2002, chap. 9).

Establishment of tribally defined segregation, moreover, responded not only to official conceptions of history but also to political convenience:

> The new system provided an expedient opportunity for the NAD [Native Affairs Department] to dilute the influence of chiefs it regarded as uncooperative. The popularly acknowledged Paramount Chief Sabata Dalindyebo, for example, saw his chiefdom arbitrarily split into two regions, Tembuland (later renamed Dalindyebo) and Emigrant Thembuland. In the latter region, Kaizer Mantanzima, a once obscure chief who early showed a genuine interest in the philosophy and practice and soon the material rewards of apartheid, was elevated to paramount chief. (Evans 1990: 44)

Urbanization, industrialization, and political expediency did not keep South African authorities from building racially defined categories deeply into the country's legal and economic structures. Even partial legalization of African unions in 1979 inscribed the government's own racial divisions into the law. Recipients of this organizational largesse faced an acute dilemma: accept state-endorsed categorization and retain meager claims to land and employment; or reject it and abandon all state-enforced rights whatsoever.

Separatist policies nonetheless had unanticipated consequences. First, they drove Africans, Indians, and Coloreds into a common front as apartheid governments increasingly deprived members of the latter two categories the distinctive rights they had previously enjoyed. Second, the apartheid regime's attempt to impose new chiefs and territorial units that would perform the work of indirect rule actually stimulated popular resistance to chiefly authority and beyond it to governmental control (Olivier 1991).

Separatist policies finally made government-defined African identities available as bases of political mobilization. "As the South African state in 1990 began to shift away from formal racial exclusion and segregation, toward 'non-racial' democracy," notes Anthony Marx, "racial identity and mobilization has lost some of its salience. In its place, political entrepreneurs have increasingly relied on 'tribal' or 'ethnic' identities as the basis of mobilization, as indicated by Zulu nationalism and 'coloured' fears of African domination under the ANC" (Marx 1995, 169).

Disaggregation occurred at two levels: the nonwhite front cracked, so that by 1996 Colored voters in the Cape were opting massively for the National Party, former architect of apartheid. But the categories African, Colored, and Indian also lost unifying force in favor of smaller-scale distinctions. The Zulu-based and formerly state-subsidized Inkatha movement of M. G. Buthelezi exemplifies the stakes even some Africans acquired in the categories earlier imposed by white South Africans to sustain their domination. We should therefore avoid any supposition that the political actors of twentieth-century South Africa had somehow formed prior to and independently of the successive regimes within which they lived and struggled (Jung 2000).

Regime Crisis and Change

In 1983, a shaken apartheid regime attempted to expand its support by establishing a thoroughly unequal tricameral legislature that incorporated representatives of the Asian and Colored populations into separate chambers. That measure, however, spurred mobilization among black Africans and among other nonblack challengers of the regime. At street level, informal groups of young activists called "comrades" alternately collaborated and fought with members of community organizations called "civics." The formation of a national United Democratic Front (UDF) from 575 disparate organizations—itself a great feat of coalition building—drew on connections established by the now-illegal BC and ANC, but went well beyond them. At its peak, the UDF claimed 2 million members (Johnson 2004, 187).

In 1985, a similar (and, in fact, overlapping) coalition of trade unions formed the Congress of South African Trade Unions (COSATU). Those well-brokered organizations coordinated widespread resistance to the regime. Threatened, the government declared successively more repressive states of emergency in July 1985 and June 1986. The later declaration "gave every police officer broad powers of arrest, detention, and interrogation, without a warrant; they empowered the police commissioner to ban any meeting; and they prohibited all coverage of unrest by television and radio reporters and severely curtailed newspaper coverage. The government had resorted to legalized tyranny" (Thompson 2000, 235).

The government detained thousands of suspects without trial. Despite the state of emergency, despite banning of many community organizations, and despite preventive detention of activists by the thousands, black mobilization actually accelerated during the later 1980s. Resistance combined with international pressure to shake up white control of public politics.

Under domestic and international pressure, even the once-solid Afrikaner bloc began to crack. In 1982 National Party members opposed to any compromise had already bolted the NP to form a smaller, more determined Conservative Party (CP). For five more years, NP governments (now harassed by right-wing pressure and the threat of autonomous Afrikaner military action) tried to subdue their opponents on both flanks by legal means and clandestine assaults. During 1988, the government intensified its attacks on the ANC and the government's liberal opposition, as the ANC's own sabotage campaign accelerated.

After the NP beat the CP badly in the white municipal elections of October 1988, however, president and NP head P. W. Botha announced dramatic concessions. They included reprieves of six ANC activists under death sentences and transfer of ANC leader Nelson Mandela from the hospital where he was being treated for tuberculosis to house arrest rather than back to the island prison where he had suffered for twenty-five years. On the international front, the militarily overstretched government finally took steps toward ending its occupation of neighboring Namibia, which South Africa had administered since Germany gave up the colony at the 1919 Treaty of Versailles.

Namibia (or South West Africa, as the South African government called it before the former colony's independence) lived under even more authoritarian control than South Africa, but underwent a parallel cycle of mobilization, resistance, and regime disintegration (Buende 1995). The United Nations General Assembly had declared South Africa's occupation of Namibia illegal in 1966, and the International Court of Justice had confirmed that ruling in 1971. South Africa had then defied international opinion. Its forces had held their grip on Namibia while sending troops into Angola to battle the exile armies of the South West African People's Organization and their Angolan rebel allies. In 1988, however, South Africa not only started moving Namibia toward independence but also began withdrawing its troops from the Angolan civil war as well.

The following year brought decisive steps toward settlement of South Africa's domestic standoff. In 1989, NP leader and premier F. W. de Klerk undertook negotiations with the previously banned ANC, including Mandela himself, freeing most of the ANC's imprisoned leaders. De Klerk's toleration of a thirty-five-thousand-person multiracial protest march cum celebration in Cape Town (September 1989) not only signaled a major shift of strategy but also encouraged multiple marches on behalf of reconciliation through the rest of South Africa. A welcome-home celebration for freed ANC prisoners at Soweto's Soccer City "became in effect the first ANC rally in 30 years" (*Annual Register* 1989, 295).

By 1990, de Klerk was governing in close consultation with the ANC. Released from house arrest, Mandela became a major participant in national politics. In 1991, COSATU activist Cyril Ramaphosa was elected to serve as the ANC's general secretary. Meanwhile, KwaZulu homeland chief Buthelezi's Inkatha Freedom Party, which had previously received clandestine support from the government and the National Party, found itself increasingly isolated. Inkatha stepped up attacks on its ANC rivals, but by the 1994 elections was only receiving about 6 percent of the national black vote, as compared with the 75 percent that went to the ANC. (Of the total vote, all racial categories together, the ANC received 63 percent, the NP 20 percent, and Inkatha 11 percent.) In a triumph that would have astonished almost any South African of any political category ten years earlier, ex-prisoner Nelson Mandela became president of South Africa.

Nevertheless, the ANC also had to negotiate between 1990 and its electoral triumph of 1994. The Soviet Union's partial disintegration in 1989 had two crucial effects in South Africa. First, since conservatives claimed to serve as a bulwark against South Africa's allies of an international communist conspiracy, it reduced the credibility of that claim. Second, it reduced external diplomatic and financial support for the ANC. Together, the two effects encouraged the United States to press both sides for a compromise solution far short of revolution. To assert its presence, the ANC declared 1991 its "year of mass action," calling its supporters to peaceful, disciplined strikes, boycotts, marches, and rallies (Jung and Shapiro 1995, 286). Step by step, the ANC presence undermined the NP plan of establishing some sort of power sharing.

Yet the ANC also worked to avoid complete polarization. It accepted "proportional representation for elections, job security for white civil servants, and an amnesty for security forces that admitted to crimes under the old regime" (Bratton and van de Walle 1997, 178). As Joe Slovo, a major leader in the ANC and the South African Communist Party, reflected in 1992:

> The *starting point* for developing a framework within which to approach some larger questions in the negotiating process is to answer the question: *why are we negotiating?* We are negotiating because toward the end of the 80s we concluded that, as a result of its escalating crisis, the apartheid power bloc was no longer able to continue ruling in the old way and was genuinely seeking some break with the past. At the same time, we were clearly *not dealing with a defeated enemy* and an early revolutionary seizure of power by the liberation movement could not be realistically posed. This

conjuncture of the balance of forces *(which continues to reflect current reality)* provided a classic scenario which placed the possibility of negotiations on the agenda. And we correctly initiated the whole process in which the ANC was accepted as the major negotiating adversary. (Saul 1994, 178)

Thus a semi-revolutionary situation yielded to a remarkable negotiated compromise.

KwaZulu Aflame

Take the case of Inkatha mobilization in Natal. As of the 1980s, the KwaZulu homeland headed by Chief Buthelezi consisted of twenty-nine major and forty-one minor tracts of land scattered through the hinterland of Durban. KwaZulu exported labor to urban and industrial areas throughout Natal, the larger region pivoting on coastal Durban and encompassing all of KwaZulu. It also sent substantial numbers of migrant workers to the Rand, around Johannesburg. Many of its emigrants (especially in the Rand) lived in hostels supplied by their employers, frequently within townships established for Africans under apartheid. As all-male groups in segregated quarters, they repeatedly clashed with township people, especially young males. Alexandra itself housed three huge hostels, whose residents often fought with local youths.

Throughout much of KwaZulu and its areas of emigration, warlords who controlled their own enforcers played the classic game of indirect rule. Within their own territories, they recruited and disciplined migrant workers; operated protection rackets; benefited from monopolies of such commodities as beer; and collected a variety of payments from local merchants. Chief Buthelezi's Inkatha Freedom Party long enjoyed their financial, political, and (when needed) military support:

> The various warlords tend to join Inkatha because in KwaZulu this relationship is based on a *quid pro quo*—as a reward for being left alone and allowed to follow their own devices they will undertake to deliver a certain number of men for Inkatha rallies and also provide "soldiers" for any fighting that needs to be done. Sometimes they bus vigilantes to other warlords who might need assistance or organise vigilante attacks on United Democratic Front/African National Congress . . . strongholds. (Minnaar 1992, 65)

Throughout the 1970s, an ANC-Inkatha alliance against apartheid seemed possible. By the early 1980s, however, Buthelezi and the ANC had become sworn enemies.

The 1983 formation of the UDF, the 1985 establishment of COSATU, and their joint efforts to coordinate opposition to the regime in Natal threatened Inkatha hegemony over workers in and around KwaZulu. Inkatha struck back. When COSATU-affiliated unions began organizing workers in the Pietermaritzburg region of Natal, for example, Inkatha created and installed a rival union, engineered the firing of UDF-affiliated workers, and began an aggressive campaign of forced recruitment in nearby townships. Struggles between the UDF and Inkatha accounted for about seven hundred deaths in the Pietermaritzburg region between 1985 and 1988 (Minnaar 1992, 7). Warlords and their followers od importantly as Inkatha enforcers.

During the mobilization that followed the recognition of African-based political parties in 1990, however, many warlords became even more active agents for Inkatha, not only continuing their usual activities but increasing their payment of tribute to Buthelezi's party, supplying personnel for public displays of Inkatha support, and organizing attacks on ANC activists. The ANC's rise to power, after all, threatened the warlords' whole way of life. Nelson Mandela described the lethal consequences:

> Natal became a killing ground. Heavily armed Inkatha supporters had in effect declared war on ANC strongholds across the Natal Midlands region and around Pietermaritzburg. Entire villages were set alight, dozens of people were killed, hundreds were wounded, and thousands became refugees. In March 1990 alone, 230 people lost their lives in this internecine violence. In Natal, Zulu was murdering Zulu, for Inkatha members and ANC partisans are Zulus. (Mandela 1994, 576)

Nationwide, over 5,500 people had died in South Africa's political conflicts between 1984 and 1989, but that number swelled to 13,500 or more, mostly Africans killed by other Africans, between 1990 and 1993 (Charney 1999, 184; see also Seidman 2000).

Meanwhile, Inkatha's opponents in the townships—especially students and unemployed ex-students—aligned themselves increasingly with the ANC. Civic associations formed widely to link young activists to older and more established members of their communities, as networks among civic associations formed connections from township to township. Thus webs of brokerage produced two formidable political forces in Natal.

As it does elsewhere, brokerage among disparate groups explains many alignments and realignments in South African politics between 1980 and 1995. Brokers connect previously unconnected sites, and thereby promote the creation of new collective actors and new relations with other actors, hence new identities. The enormous mobilization of

Africans that surged immediately after the beginning of 1990 relied less on drawing new people into contentious politics than on integrating those who had been involved in struggle at a small scale with much larger political actors.

Alexandra Again

Within this context of vast political changes, Alexandra's residents lived their own turbulent history. Historian Belinda Bozzoli has written a gripping, detailed, self-consciously theatrical narrative of the Six Day War's background and aftermath. Bozzoli advised defense attorneys in the 1987 Supreme Court trials of Moses Mayekiso and others; interviewed most of the defendants in that trial; had access to the 1987 trial records of Ashwell Zwane and others; interviewed Zwane and his attorneys; and attended the Alexandra hearings of South Africa's Truth and Reconciliation Commission. She constructed her narrative chiefly from those three large blocks of evidence, supplementing them with newspaper accounts, police records, and other observers' writings. Together, they supplied the materials for an epic ranging from individual turns to large set pieces involving the township as a whole.

Alexandra lived a profound drama, which Bozzoli conveys expertly. Established as a Native township in 1912, it housed around one hundred thousand people in the 1980s. It had become a place of misery and yet of spirit. Its residents got by mostly without electricity, rubbish removal, or a sewage system—cut off from nearby Johannesburg but bound to one another by kinship and relative equality. Like other black South Africans, Alexandra residents began mobilizing seriously with the UDF's campaigns of 1983 and thereafter. In boycotts and attacks on offenders, students and youths led the way, backed by organizations at least loosely affiliated with the ANC. Young men (connected by soccer, already used to gathering in the streets, and freer of household duties than their sisters) participated most actively.

Starting on New Year's Eve, the final day of 1985, the deaths of two local activists at the hands of security officers resulted in community mourning; public vigils; politicized funerals; attacks on shops, stores, and houses; burning of policemen, witches, and accused informers; and battles between marchers and police. On February 1, a security guard killed seventeen-year-old Michael Diradeng outside a Jazz Stores supermarket. Youth groups organized a mass funeral and vigil for the fifteenth, but police were on hand to break up the vigil with tear gas. "The next day," reported activist Mzwanele Mayekiso, who had only joined his brother Moss (Moses Mayekiso) in Alexandra the previous December, we tried to negotiate with the police to end the harassment. This was my first direct experience with the authorities in Alex. We negotiated that the funeral would go ahead. Moss was to be the master of ceremonies at the Alexandra Stadium. The funeral procession, which was initially blocked from moving to the cemetery, was then allowed to move. Even the most angry of the youth paid attention to us as we spoke, and followed our directions to conduct ourselves with dignity.

But then, as a crowd of 40,000 was returning from the cemetery to the Diradeng home for a traditional hand-washing ceremony, they came under tear gas attack by provocateur police. The youth responded with a barrage of stones, petrol bombs, and so forth. A dozen white- and Indian-owned shops on the outskirts were the subject of looting that night, as the anger bubbled to surface. In fear, the police left the township, and instead guarded the outskirts. Every weapon at the community's disposal was gathered. Trenches were dug to prevent police infiltration. A war had truly begun. (Mayekiso 1996, 60–61)

Local youths and police struggled for control of Alexandra's streets. With a vengeance that had already started to spread through other parts of South Africa, when the youths caught someone that improvised street courts pronounced a traitor, they commonly filled an automobile tire with kerosene or gasoline ("petrol" in Ashforth's and Bozzoli's accounts), hung the tire around the person's neck, and set her or him on fire. They called the practice "necklacing." That was the Six Day War, for which Bozzoli assembled revealing hour-by-hour chronologies. After the six days of open street warfare, night vigils, funeral services, and meetings in the streets, in churches, and in Alexandra's stadium brought much of the community into open resistance. They became displays of militant nationalism.

Bozzoli insists on the indigenous origins of Alexandra's shift to militancy, and portrays the ANC as seeking to catch up with and co-opt township militancy rather than to organize it. She sees the state's shift from township "welfare paternalism" to "racial modernism" during the 1960s and 1970s as having shaped a new militant generation in Alexandra and elsewhere. The "Comrade Generation," in her account, led the risings that became more frequent and lethal during the mid-1980s. Youth groups initiated the renaming of local zones, streets, and schools for nationally visible leaders and symbols. They likewise spearheaded the people's courts and attack squads that enforced boycotts, mounted anticrime campaigns, necklaced accused witches or informers, and threatened locals who remained on local councils.

Bozzoli's biographical sketches of the relatively young Albert Sebola, Ashwell Zwane, and Piet Mogano back up her generational account. However, her parallel biographies of the older activists—the Mayekiso brothers and Obed Bapela—underline the importance to the larger resistance movement of linkage by political leaders with longer experience and extensive outside connections. (Moses Mayekiso, for example, eventually acquired sufficient connections to become head of the South African National Civic Organization when it formed to coordinate and control the country's many local civics on behalf of ANC rule in 1992.) The elders also organized less violent, more "rationalist" varieties of local control in contrast to the "millenarian" dreams of the youth. Nevertheless, Bozzoli argues, the two generations converged in their support of African nationalism against the apartheid state's tyranny. By late April of 1986, the township council had resigned and the two groups of activists, in uneasy coalitions, provided whatever government existed in Alexandra.

But the central government counterattacked. After street battles, by mid-May the army and police had retaken control of Alexandra's perimeter and established a fearsome presence in township streets. Activism subsided or went underground. Arrests and trials for treason and sedition began in September 1986. Bozzoli titles the chapter in her book that relates the state's return "From Victory to Defeat." Her drama ends with the trials of activists and the reshaping of public memory they produced. Most remarkably, youth activists imprisoned for sedition largely disappeared from public life and memory, while the elders—all acquitted—came to represent Alexandra's nationalist resistance. The Truth and Reconciliation Commission, Bozzoli argues, cemented in place the myth of a unified, determined, deeply nationalist, but police-victimized community aligned closely with the ANC. The drama ends in myth.

The chronology in box 5.1 therefore deserves a close look. On the third day of the Six Day War, it shows us the weaving of a small number of contentious performances into a widespread rebellion. Different groups of youths stoned vehicles, buildings, or people; manufactured petrol bombs to launch at other vehicles or buildings; looted shops; hijacked buses; or staged brief confrontations with troops. At the same time, military forces patrolled in armored vehicles called "Casspirs," shooting and launching tear gas to disperse activist crowds. (The Casspir, the anagrammed acronym for the South African Police that commissioned it and the Council for Scientific and Industrial Research that developed it, deflected bullets, grenades, and even mines; it became a favorite armored crowd-control and antiguerrilla vehicle for South African forces during the 1980s.)

BOX 5.1   Events in Alexandra, South Africa, on February 16, 1986

11:00 a.m.	A house was attacked at 25 Fourteenth Avenue
12:00 noon	A Toyota Hiace was stoned on the corner of Tenth Road and Third Avenue
12:00 noon	A bus was stoned between Thirteenth and Fourteenth Avenues
12:00 noon	A Putco bus was stoned along Fifteenth Avenue
12:20 p.m.	Another Putco bus was stoned on Fifteenth Avenue
12:30 p.m.	Another Putco bus was stoned on the corner of Fifteenth Avenue and Selborne Road
12:30 p.m.	There was stoning on First St Marlborogh, the adjacent suburb
12:30 p.m.	A petrol bomb was thrown in Fifteenth Avenue
1:30 p.m.	A Volkswagen Combi was threatened on the corner of Sixth Avenue and Vasco da Gama Street
1:45 p.m.	There was stoning on Fourteenth Avenue
2:00 p.m.	A house was petrol bombed at 1018 Second Street Marlborough
2:00 p.m.	A motor vehicle was hijacked along Sixth Avenue
2:45 p.m.	A factory was petrol bombed at 1121 Second Avenue Marlborough
3 p.m.	There was stoning on the corner of Hofmeyr and Second Avenue
3:30 p.m.	A petrol bomb was thrown on the corner of Selborne and Third Avenue
3:40 p.m.	There was an "incident" on the corner of Ninth Avenue and Selborne Street
4:00 p.m.	An "unknown black male" died of bullet wounds on the corner of Twelfth Avenue and Roosevelt
4:00 p.m.	A motor vehicle was burnt at 1067 First Avenue Marlborough
4:15 p.m.	A Datsun was stoned on the corner of London Road and Thirteenth Avenue
4:30 p.m.	A motor vehicle was stoned on the corner of Thirteenth Avenue and Wynberg Road
4:35 p.m.	A Casspir was stoned at Fifteenth Avenue
4:35 p.m.	A "black female" was burned on Fifteenth Avenue
?	A firebomb was thrown on the corner of First Avenue and Hofmeyr Road
5:00 p.m.	A motor vehicle was stoned along Eleventh Avenue
5:20 p.m.	A motor vehicle was stoned along London Road
5:30 p.m.	Damage was done to the building of "Marlborough Panel Beaters"
6:30 p.m.	Youths were found making petrol bombs along First Avenue
7:25 p.m.	A policeman's house was petrol bombed at 16 Sixth Avenue
?	A building and cars were stoned at "Marlborough Panel Beaters," 21 First Street

7:30 p.m.	A motor vehicle was stoned in Phase 1
8:00 p.m.	A motor vehicle was stoned on Fourth Avenue
8:00 p.m.	Windows were broken and a petrol bomb thrown on the corner of Second Avenue and Second Street
8:00 p.m.	A petrol bomb was thrown on the corner of Selborne Street and Twelfth Avenue
8:30 p.m.	Erphraim Mambono took the corpse of an "unknown black male" who had been shot to the clinic
10:25 p.m.	A building was petrol bombed on the corner of Second Avenue and Sixth Street
10:25 p.m.	Police shot an "unknown black male" on the corner of Vasco da Gama Street and Fifteenth Avenue
11:30 p.m.	A motor vehicle was stoned near the Alexandra Flats, Phase 1 Several further shops and a bus were petrol-bombed during the night

Source: Adapted from Bozzoli 2004, 77

On Day Three:

Albert Sebola, a soccer player, and later an accused in one of the treason trials, arrived for his Sunday game at the stadium at midday, but it was disrupted by "unknown" young people. Later, when he returned to the stadium he found broken bottles on the field, from a nearby liquor store, "Square One Bottle Store," owned by the Town Council—which was being looted. There were many drunken people about. On his way back from the stadium to his clubhouse, he saw a bus, probably hijacked, being driven by a "young boy." Later a Casspir appeared, and fired a teargas canister at him and his soccer friends. He hid in the clubhouse the whole day and only ventured home at 7 P.M. He heard gunshots, was aware of heavy police presence and indeed feared for his life were he to venture out. (Bozzoli 2004, 76)

By the end of six violent days, Alexandra's own black police force had disintegrated in death, resignation, or flight, and national forces had retreated to the township's perimeter. Surrounded Alexandra lived under its own improvised authority for the next four months.

These brief accounts of South African contention in Alexandra, in KwaZulu, and in the country as a whole over the longer run of 1948–2000 make three facts abundantly clear. First, what we easily describe in retrospect as a single movement leading to the overthrow of apartheid and white supremacy actually consisted of successive contingent coalitions in which local activists were frequently moving in quite different directions from their would-be national leaders. Second, instead of a single set of claim-making performances directed uniformly against the white oppressor we see a wide variety of performances, including some that pitted blacks against other blacks. Third, prevailing repertoires shifted significantly from one phase of the struggle to another, largely as a consequence of changes in the regime's operation. Regime changes altered the political opportunity structure (POS), which reshaped repertoires.

In Alexandra and elsewhere, repertoire change between 1948 and 2000 fell into four rough phases:

1948–1970: imposition of brutal top-down controls over residence, association, and assembly, with a consequent strangling of nonwhite popular politics.

1970–1990: accelerating resistance to white rule by means of strikes, boycotts, and attacks on accused collaborators, based on networks of trade unions, civic organizations, and informal circles of young activists loosely affiliated with political parties (especially the banned African National Congress) and the United Democratic Front.

1990–1994: partial demobilization of local-level activists accompanied by competition for control of local organizations and spaces, revenge attacks on members of rival ethnic categories, and relatively nonviolent electoral mobilization.

1994– : further demobilization, more decisive shift to the nonviolent social movement politics of meetings, associations, demonstrations, and public statements.

By making black South Africa largely ungovernable, the second phase played a major part in producing a revolutionary transfer of power from a narrow white governing class to an unequal coalition of white liberals, African nationalists, an increasingly wealthy and educated black elite, and organized segments of the Asian and Colored populations. The third phase sorted out the locations of former activists and their enemies in a strikingly new regime, and the fourth consolidated into more routine and peaceful struggles in a political system dominated by a transformed ANC.

In the municipal elections of 2000, for example, a national turnout of about 48 percent gave the ANC control over 170 of the country's 237 municipalities; left thirty-six to Inkatha; awarded another eighteen to the recently formed Democratic Alliance; brought the likewise recent United Democratic Movement a single municipality; and established mixed governments in the final twelve (*Annual Register* 2000, 282–83). By that time a public politics centered on control over Parliament and the national executive had almost entirely displaced the politics of massive resistance. Collective acts of violent vengeance had not entirely disappeared, but they had shifted to attacks on accused criminals, witches, and, more rarely, corrupt local politicians (Ashforth 2005, chap. 4; Bozzoli 2004, epilogue). Most dramatically, young black people had largely abandoned local politics and their connections with the ANC (Lodge 2001, 8). Grassroots civic organizations, once central to local struggles, had lost much of their energy, power, membership, and connection with national political organizations (Zuern 2001, 2002).

South African Regimes and Repertoires

Figure 5.1 schematically summarizes the regime side of the story that has been unfolding in this chapter so far. The year 1948 marks the full implementation of apartheid in a regime that already qualified as fairly authoritarian. Apartheid, goes the argument, temporarily increased governmental

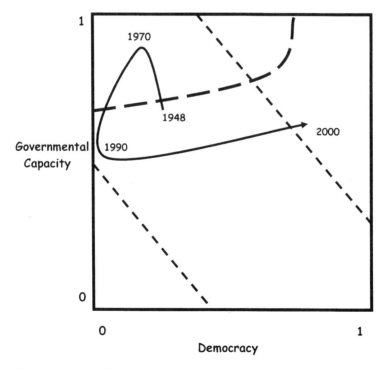

Figure 5.1. South African regimes, 1948–2000

capacity while further de-democratizing an already nondemocratic regime. Sometime around 1970, however, resistance and opposition began undermining governmental capacity, while the government's own increasingly repressive measures produced even more de-democratization. That trend continued to the end of the 1980s, when the momentous regime changes described earlier began. Then comes the riskiest part of the conjecture: the suggestion that transfers of power between 1990 and 2000 not only brought South Africa (just barely) into the zone of democratic citizenship, but also slightly increased governmental capacity.

Harking back to earlier arguments, what does this description of South Africa's regime trajectory imply for changes in contentious repertoires? We expect such a trajectory to create major shifts in political opportunity structure for all of South Africa's political actors, especially its challengers. Remember the elements of POS: (a) the multiplicity of independent centers of power within the regime; (b) the openness of the regime to new actors; (c) the instability of current political alignments; (d) the availability of influential allies or supporters; (e) the extent to which the regime represses or facilitates collective claim-mking; and (f) decisive changes in (a) to (e).

Figure 5.1 indicates that POS became less favorable to South African blacks between 1948 and 1970, but then reversed as independent centers of power, backed by foreign pressure, began to form, political alignments within the regime became more unstable, and influential allies and supporters became more available both domestically and internationally despite the government's own resistance to new actors and deployment of increasingly heavy-handed repression. Those changes facilitated black mobilization and resistance. By 1990, runs the analysis, all elements of POS were moving decisively toward greater opportunity for previously repressed political actors.

Contentious politics does not, however, operate like a hydraulic pump: increase the pressure or reduce the resistance and more water flows. South Africa brings out dramatically the influence of previously existing political institutions on forms and outcomes of contention. The boundaries about which South Africans mobilized and fought between 1948 and 2000 had emerged from the earlier operation of a racially oppressive regime, but continued to shift as the apartheid regime put new institutions into place.

Formation of a tricameral legislature in 1983, for example, did not split the nonwhite population as Premier Botha had planned, but it did provide a vehicle for dissident Asian and Colored allies of the excluded black population. Creation of homelands such as KwaZulu did not tame the African population, but it did establish a new arena for struggle between black resisters and collaborators. After 1994, the ANC's long history as emblem and means of black struggle against apartheid made it available as a formidable instrument of rule in the new regime. At each stage, political contenders drew on previously existing institutions, relations, and shared understandings to organize and make their claims.

Some further implications of earlier arguments are the following:

- The move of the South African regime even farther into the high-capacity, nondemocratic quadrant of regime space after 1948 produced greater emphasis on prescribed political performances, narrowed the range of tolerated performances, expanded the range of forbidden performances, and increased the share of all contention taking place by means of forbidden performances.

- After about 1970, the combination of further de-democratization and declining governmental capacity expanded the range of effectively tolerated performances—tolerated simply because the government was concentrating its repression elsewhere—while increasing the overlap between contention and tolerated performances.

- The dramatic democratization from 1990 or so, plus the slight increase in governmental capacity during the same period, narrowed the scope of prescribed performances, maintained the enlarged range of tolerated performances, shifted that range toward the familiar repertoires of social movements, increased the overlap between contention and both prescribed and tolerated performances, but decreased the frequency of contention by means of forbidden performances.

- In times of rapidly changing political opportunity such as 1980–94, we find both recurrent innovation and frequent misapprehension among parties to contention, especially in the case of popular challenges to power-holders.

- A spiral of contention ensues, as each new round of claim-making begins to threaten the interests of (or provide new opportunities for) political actors who had previously remained inactive. KwaZulu and Inkatha provide the clearest evidence of such a spiral.

- Such cycles usually end with rapid demobilization of most actors, especially those who have challenged and lost. At that point, repertoires crystallize as the pace of innovation in performances slows. Some innovations that appeared during the cycle remain in the repertoire, while some old performances or features of performances disappear. Even as civic organizations dwindled in energy and influence during the 1990s, their meetings, marches, and rallies continued to mark South African popular politics.

- Association with the gain or loss of political advantage by one actor or another strongly affects innovations' survival and disappearance, although changes in the conditions of everyday existence and in actors' internal organization as a consequence of the struggle also affect the viability of different performances.
- Since rapidly shifting threats and opportunities generally move power-holders toward rigid repertoires and challengers toward more flexible repertoires, the advantages of flexibility during 1948–90 shifted temporarily to black activists and their allies.
- The nationalization and eventual success of black resistance produced moves toward a cosmopolitan, modular, and autonomous repertoire for contentious claim-making in the social movement mode.
- Institutionalization of that repertoire marginalized those street-level activists who did not move into civic organizations as their major vehicles for claim-making, and limited the capacity of civics themselves to make effective claims beyond the local level.

Of course, my selective narratives fail to provide clinching evidence for these extensive arguments. The near disappearance of violent street politics instead of institutionalization of its major performances, furthermore, raises questions these principles do not answer. Severing the connections between the ANC and its belligerent street-level comrades seems to have combined with co-optation of some comrades into civic organizations and government offices in the demobilization of street-level activism. Nevertheless we can see an approximate fit between these theoretically expected patterns and the actual complicated experience of South African contention between 1948 and 2000. The major causal lines in the story are depicted in figure 5.2.

Here we see only the dominant causal links: governmental changes that alter relations between the government and major political actors (for example, organized Afrikaners); shifting relations within the regime that transform POS for challengers such as the ANC, UDF, and COSATU or local-level Comrades; mutations of contention that result from changes in POS; plus feedback from contention to governmental changes and relational shifts within the regime. We could obviously complicate the causal diagram by including external connections: increasing international pressure for reform, decreasing support for the Communist Party from a disintegrating Soviet Union, and so on. The main point would remain the same. Although the government played a

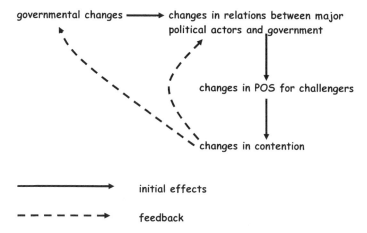

Figure 5.2. Major causal links in South African contention, 1948–2000

major part in initiating its own overturn, shifts within the regime over which the government exercised only partial control altered political opportunities for challengers. New forms of contention then transformed the regime.

Implications

If this account of interactions between regime change and contention in South Africa is accurate, what plausible alternatives does it rule out? How widely does its basic logic apply? Note that the account involves significant asymmetry between regime change and contention, with the initial impetus to alterations in repertoires coming from shifts within regimes. Such a causal story contradicts essentially bottom-up accounts in which structural changes and/or transformations of shared consciousness generate action that overthrows an oppressive regime. But it also disagrees with strictly top-down accounts in which a regime's change of location in the international system and/or alterations in ruling-class orientations determine the direction of regime change, producing popular protest or resistance, but not consequential political action on the part of popular activists.

Figure 5.2 surely does not exhaust the possible sequences of cause and effect. In other cases, for example, we would surely find changes in relations between major political actors and government preceding governmental changes as such; indeed, even in the South African case we might think of the split of hard-liners from the National Party (1982) and its effects on governmental policy as this sort of sequence. Changes in POS that stimulate increased contention, furthermore, do not always involve expanding opportunity for challengers; repression that directly threatens challengers' identities and survival regularly produces resistance rather than passive demobilization (Goldstone and Tilly 2001; Tilly 2005c). The figure simply identifies the largest causal connections.

How widely does the logic apply? The overall sequence of events in South Africa between 1948 and 2000 belongs to South Africa alone. Nowhere else—not even in adjacent Namibia—did a tight system of apartheid mutate into a fledgling democracy along the same trajectory. My scheme's claims to generality lie at two other levels. First, it offers a crude but serviceable model of how regime change *does* affect popular contention, from governmental change to regime realignment to alterations of POS to changes in contention. With appropriate adjustments, we can use it to map the interaction of changing regimes and repertoires in Uganda, Morocco, Peru, or the United States, as well as in South Africa.

Second, the scheme describes processes that commonly occur when a high-capacity, nondemocratic regime moves toward democracy. In a high-capacity regime, relatively little political contention occurs without involvement of governmental agents, but by that very token vigorous mobilization against the government produces changes in regime structure—either closing of ranks that reduces political opportunities for challengers or realignments that enhance those opportunities. In low-capacity, nondemocratic regimes, a great deal of contention occurs outside the reach of governmental agents, and consequently has less direct impact on the regime.

Think back to the trajectories of British regimes and repertoires between 1750 and 1840 described in chapter 3. Figure 5.3 reinterprets that earlier analysis in the light of this chapter's arguments. It shows a British state increasing greatly in capacity and de-democratizing as a consequence of military buildups and ever-expanding warfare between the 1750s (Seven Years War, 1756–63) and the end of the immense wars with France (intermittently 1792–1815), then democratizing significantly with a slight drop in capacity thereafter.[1]

Chapter 3's narrative followed the interplay of those regime changes with a massive shift in contentious repertoires from parochial, particular, and bifurcated forms of claim-making during the eighteenth century to cosmopolitan, modular, and autonomous forms during the nineteenth

---

1. For much more detailed analysis including spearate treatments of Great Britain and Ireland, see Tilly 2004c, chap. 5.

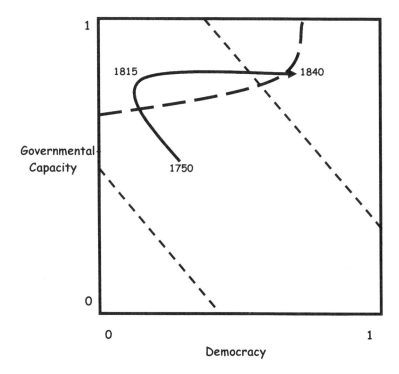

Figure 5.3. British regimes, 1750–1840

and thereafter. In the case of Great Britain, governmental changes unquestionably drove changes in relations between major political actors and government, those shifts certainly altered POS for challengers, alterations of POS surely stimulated changes in contentious repertoires, and contention itself clearly fed back to transformations of government and regime. To that small extent we can take comfort: South Africa's trajectories belong to a larger family of interactions between changes in regimes and repertoires.

No one has assembled the sort of systematic evidence for multiple regimes that is necessary for lining up case after case to determine whether the interplay of regime change and alteration in contentious repertoires does, indeed, generally conform to my simple model. In this book's second half, my strategy instead is to work out the model's implications for collective violence, revolutions, social movements, and democratization, then to see whether existing evidence on those contentious processes confirms this chapter's reasoning.

In the cases of collective violence, revolutions, social movements, and democratization, what should we expect to find? If my arguments thus far make sense, these closer looks at particular political processes should reveal at least the following:

- Distinctive differences in rulers' approaches to generating and controlling contentious politics (as represented by the distribution of prescribed, tolerated, and forbidden claim-making performances) depending on a regime's location in the capacity-democracy space.
- Distinctive differences in prevailing repertoires (for example, in the prevalence of parochial, particular, and bifurcated claim-making performances) depending on a regime's location in the capacity-democracy space.
- Transformation of prevailing repertoires (for example, increasing predominance of cosmopolitan, modular, and autonomous claim-making performances) by movement of regimes within the capacity-democracy space.
- Incremental transformation of prevailing repertoires (for example, mutual alterations in the tactics of demonstrators and police) through (a) the internal dynamics of struggle and (b) changes in the organization and relations of potential political actors.
- Innovations in claim-making performances accelerate during spirals of contention but slow during periods of little political change and of demobilization.
- During those accelerations, the performances of power-holders become more rigid while those of challengers become more flexible.
- Path-dependency: strong influence of a regime's previous trajectory within the same space on the concrete means by which rulers and citizens engage in contentious politics—for example, engagement of previously existing forms of religious, civic, and kinship organization in new varieties of struggle.
- Mediation of all those regularities by variations in political opportunity structure.

More particular changes and variations in collective violence, revolutions, social movements, and democratization follow from these general principles. We should, for example, find governments that increase in capacity exerting ever-greater control over violent specialists, with the interesting consequence that a rising proportion of all collective violence involves governmental agents as claimants, objects of claims, or intervening third parties. Again, we should discover that the campaigns, performances, and WUNC (worthiness, unity, numbers, and commitment) displays of social movements occupy a larger share of all contentious politics as democratic regimes emerge. Let us see how well these predictions hold up.

CHAPTER SIX >>
Collective Violence

WHAT IS COLLECTIVE VIOLENCE? Its many varieties have in common episodic social interaction that immediately inflicts physical damage on persons and/or objects ("damage" includes forcible seizure of persons or objects over restraint or resistance), involves at least two perpetrators of damage, and results at least in part from coordination among persons who perform the damaging acts. Collective violence, by such a definition, excludes purely individual action, nonmaterial damage, accidents, and long-term or indirect effects of such damaging processes as dumping toxic waste. But it includes a vast range of social interactions.[1]

Characteristic forms and intensities of collective violence differ dramatically from one type of regime to another. They also change significantly as regime change occurs. These variations mainly result from the fact that control of the means of collective violence varies greatly across different types of regimes, as do the alternatives to violent making of claims and counterclaims. This chapter shows how those two facts produce their effects.

First we need evidence of variation in collective violence. For quick surveys of collective violence throughout

1. For recent surveys of violence, individual and collective, see Barkan and Snowden 2001; Burton 1997; González Calleja 2002b; Heitmeyer and Hagan 2003; Jackman 2002; Krug et al. 2002; Kurtz 1999; Reiss and Roth 1993; Ruff 2001; Summers and Markusen 1999; Tilly 2003, 2005b; Wilson 2003.

the world, there is a wide range of sources from which to choose. Following the model of chapter 3, you could go to the Reuters and BBC newswires for violent incidents. Of the ten episodes in box 2.1, all but one—the judicial victory of Peruvian gay rights groups—mention violent claim-making. You could also refer to the U.S. State Department's congressionally mandated annual reports of human rights in country after country (for example, State 2005). Those country reports regularly describe violent acts by government agents and on the parts of other powerful nongovernmental figures—assassinations, massacres, kidnapping, attacks on property, and more.

Congress likewise requires the State Department to issue a parallel annual report on international terrorism throughout the world; that accounting focuses even more narrowly on collective violence than the human rights reports (for example, State 2004a). For less official but no less serious accounts, you could scan the frequent investigations of Amnesty International of the sort that provided information for country sketches in chapter 4, or the annual and special reports of Human Rights Watch (for example, Human Rights Watch 2005). Collective violence crops up in a wide variety of political reports.

More surprisingly, the annual survey of political rights and civil liberties by Freedom House that backed up the regime descriptions in chapter 3 also provides abundant vignettes of violence in country after country. In a chapter on India, for example, Freedom House's 2004 report looks back to February 2002:

> [A]t least 58 people were killed when a fire broke out on a train carrying members of a Hindu extremist group. A Muslim mob was initially blamed for the fire, and in the anti-Muslim riots that followed throughout Gujarat, more than 1,000 people were killed and roughly 100,000 were left homeless and dispossessed. The violence was orchestrated by Hindu nationalist groups, who organized transportation and provisions for the mobs and provided printed records of Muslim-owned property. Evidence that the BJP-headed state government was complicit in the carnage led to calls for Chief Minister Narendra Modi's dismissal, but the party leadership continued to support him. In state elections held in December in which Modi campaigned on an overtly nationalistic and anti-Muslim platform, the BJP won a landslide reelection victory. (Piano and Puddington 2004, 257)

This vignette takes us back to an earlier violent incident described in chapter 3. The "Hindu extremist group" struck by the train fire was returning from a pilgrimage to the site of the Ayodhya, Uttar Pradesh mosque (and legendary birthplace of the Hindu hero Ram) that Hindu activists had destroyed in 1992. Pilgrimage to the site had since become a mark of Hindu religious and political commitment.

As of late 2003, Freedom House was reporting the first convictions of Hindus for their attacks on Muslim villagers during Gujarat's 2002 rampage: "The right to practice one's religion freely is generally respected, but violence against religious minorities remains a problem and the government's prosecution of those involved in such attacks continues to be inadequate" (Piano and Puddington 2004, 259). Human Rights Watch agreed: "The Gujarat government's failure to bring to justice those responsible for massive communitarian riots in the state, in which thousands of Muslims were killed and left homeless, continues to be a source of tension throughout the entire country" (Human Rights Watch 2005, 280).

Compare India's situation with Peru's that same year. Remember how after decades of military rule, Peru had started its uneasy experiment with democratic civilian government in 1980: political struggle soon generated extensive collective violence against civilians by Túpac Amaru, Sendero Luminoso, government-backed paramilitaries, and the Peruvian army itself. Highland indigenous populations paid a higher price than anyone else. The 1990 election of Alberto Fujimori and his recruitment of Vladimiro Montesinos as his untitled but powerful security chief brought in a corrupt regime that finally collapsed in scandal as Fujimori and Montesinos fled the country late in 2000. A relatively clean 2001 election brought populist Alejandro Toledo to the presidency.

In 2003, according to Freedom House:

> The Truth and Reconciliation Commission presented its nine-volume report in August on the country's political violence that occurred in the 1980s and 1990s. The report, which accused both [Shining Path] and the military of atrocities, shocked many observers by more than doubling the estimated number of deaths during the protracted insurgency. These findings reflected the fact that nearly three-fourths of the victims of both the guerrillas and the military were Indian peasants living in rural areas, and that these rural poor have long suffered neglect at the hand of the central government. (Piano and Puddington 2004, 446)

Toledo's two-year-old government was trying to bring Peru a populist version of democracy with more protection and opportunity for the indigenous population, but it faced serious obstacles laid down by the legacies of corrupt and authoritarian previous regimes. The military, for example, continued to insist on trying charges against its personnel in separate military courts. Human Rights Watch summed up:

The inefficiency and inaccessibility of Peru's justice system, coupled with local government corruption and lack of transparency, have contributed to outbreaks of violence in rural areas, such as the lynching of a controversial mayor. Police use lethal force unjustifiably in dealing with public protests, sometimes with fatal consequences. Long-standing problems like torture and inhumane prison conditions continue to give cause for concern. Journalists in provincial towns and cities are vulnerable to physical attack and intimidation for criticizing local authorities. (Human Rights Watch 2005, 228)

When it came to collective violence, as of 2004 Peru did not yet give off the signals of a high-capacity, democratic regime.

In recent years, then, both India and Peru have experienced substantial, threatening collective violence. A simple comparison of violence in the two countries makes several of this chapter's most important points:

- Each regime has its own characteristic forms and mixtures of collective violence.
- The salience and coordination of collective violence vary from the deliberate use of destructive force against well-defined targets by specialists to scattered outcomes of predominantly nonviolent interaction.
- Far from expressing undifferentiated rage, tension, or despair, within each regime collective violence emerges from, and bears the stamp of, its broader patterns of contentious politics.
- A regime's prevailing claim-making repertoires (which we already know vary systematically from one sort of regime to another) significantly affect the forms, loci, participants, and prevalence of its collective violence.
- The character and intensity of collective violence within a regime depend especially on relations between violent specialists and the government, in a range running from largely independent of government supervision to closely controlled by government agents.
- Characteristic forms and intensities of collective violence therefore differ significantly according to a regime's location and trajectory within the capacity-democracy space.

In keeping with these points, this chapter first constructs a typology of collective violence that helps specify the sorts of variation we must explain. It then moves on to a broad analysis of how forms and intensities of collective violence vary across regimes. It closes by applying the analysis to civil war and terror, varieties of contention that combine several different types of collective violence.

Types of Collective Violence

Analysts of collective violence habitually choose among three descriptive strategies: lumping, everyday cataloging, and singling out. Some simply lump together all violent encounters—or at least all encounters above a certain scale—into general measures of total damage and death (Gurr 2000; Rummel 1994). If we were simply asking where and when the risk of death and destruction rises, that approach would serve us reasonably well. But it would not help us sort out interactions among regimes, repertoires, opportunity structures, and collective violence. It says too little about the what and why of the phenomena we are trying to explain.

A second group of researchers adopt categories that come to them from everyday discussions of the news. They seek to differentiate, describe, and explain the various sorts of events like those we encountered in chapter 3's surveys of repertoires in the United States, Peru, Uganda, Morocco, Jamaica, and India. An authoritative *Encyclopedia of Violence, Peace, and Conflict,* for example, includes articles on political assassinations; civil wars; clan and tribal conflict; interstate war; gang violence; genocide and democide; organized crime; police brutality; revolutions; sexual assault; terrorism; and a number of similarly identified collective and violent phenomena (Kurtz 1999). A World Health Organization report on violence and health (Krug et al. 2002) offers chapters on youth violence; child abuse; violence by intimate partners; abuse of the elderly; sexual violence; self-directed violence; and collective violence.

If the point were mainly to join public debate about the character and origins of these phenomena taken separately, it would make sense to address them as categorized in such widely recognizable terms. But the adoption of everyday terms assumes that names such as "civil war" and "gang violence" represent causally coherent phenomena, obscures relations among the phenomena, and makes it almost impossible to understand how one type of collective violence turns into another.

Third, and most frequently, analysts single out just one type of violent encounter for close attention. They ask when and why revolutions occur, under what conditions strikes become violent, what increases or decreases the frequency of gang wars, and so on. Each time a particular form of collective violence catches the public eye, some group of specialists appears to claim expertise on the subject. For example, the September 11, 2001 attacks on the World Trade Center and the Pentagon, coordinated by al-Qaeda, brought out a large number of previously obscure specialists in conspiratorial terror (Senechal de la Roche 2004; Lauderdale and Oliverio 2005). These specialized studies provide precious evidence for more general analyses of collective violence. But their typical assumption that they are dealing with distinctive, causally coherent phenomena keeps them from cumulating into more general analyses on their own.

None of the three conventional approaches, then, will solve the problem at hand. In order to discipline our inquiry into connections of collective violence to regimes and repertoires, we must specify the sort of variation we are trying to explain. To that end, I construct a two-dimensional map of interpersonal violence, including individual attacks of one person on another or on that person's property. This first dimension concerns the *salience of short-run damage*. We look at interactions among the parties, asking to what extent infliction and reception of damage dominate those interactions. At the low extreme, damage occurs only intermittently or secondarily in the course of transactions that remain predominantly nonviolent. At the high extreme, almost every transaction inflicts damage, as the infliction and reception of damage dominate the interaction. Routine bureaucratic encounters that occasionally lead to fisticuffs stand toward the low end of the range, attacks by genocidal militias toward the high end.

The second dimension represents *extent of coordination among violent actors*. The definition of collective violence with which this chapter began incorporated a minimum position on this dimension: it insisted on at least two perpetrators of damage and some coordination among perpetrators. Below that threshold, we call violence "individual." Nevertheless, collective coordination can run from no more than improvised signaling and/or common culture (low) to involvement of centralized organizations whose leaders follow shared scripts as they deliberately guide followers into violence-generating interactions with others (high). At the low end we find such events as barroom brawls, at the high end pitched battles between opposing armies.

This way of setting up analyses of collective violence emphasizes its connections with nonviolent political processes. Many violent incidents, for example, begin with nonviolent making of claims: initially orderly demonstrators scuffle with police sent to contain them, someone in a crowd that is stolidly blocking a tax collector throws a rock, or perhaps queuing petitioners turn on a late arrival who tries to jump the queue. How much coordination occurs among violent actors and how salient damage is to their interactions with others help pinpoint and explain the degree of destruction resulting from those interactions. Broadly speaking, destructiveness rises with both salience and coordination. Where the two both reach high levels, widespread destruction occurs. Gujarat's 2002 massacre of Muslim villagers combined high salience and coordination: organized Hindu hit squads went out prepared to kill and burn.

Figure 6.1 presents a typology of interpersonal violence produced by distinguishing salience and coordination as separate dimensions of variation. For the moment the diagram includes individual aggression (which does not qualify as collective violence) in order to specify its relation to other larger-scale forms of violence. The classification works as follows: we locate a clump of violent episodes in the salience-coordination space, for example in the upper-left corner, where high coordination among violent actors and relatively low salience of damage in all interactions among the parties coincide. Organized but passive resistance to an occupying force by means of foot-dragging, concealment, and occasional clandestine attacks illustrates the collective violence occurring in this corner. At the diagonally opposite corner of the collective space, barroom brawls regularly qualify as high in salience but low in coordination. So too does the

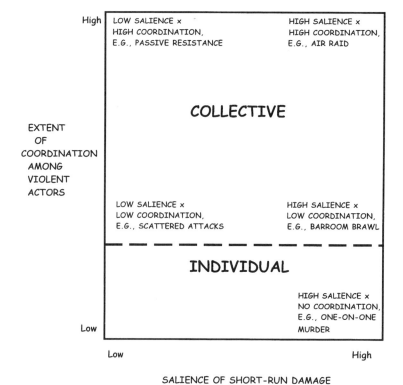

Figure 6.1. A typology of interpersonal violence

small-scale looting that often follows withdrawal of troops or police from an occupied territory.

We must keep the distinction between causal coherence and symbolic coherence clearly in mind. Here we are looking for causal coherence. Despite my earlier warnings about everyday labels, the following descriptions of the types may read as though we could simply drop conventional names for collective violence into the types: all civil wars into one type, all gang fights into another, and so on. Contrary to that impression, the whole point of turning to a more abstract typology is to bring out the change and variation in coordination and salience that occur within most conventionally named varieties of collective violence.

Interstate war, for example, qualifies as such not by the forms of violence in which the parties engage, but by the fact that two independent governments declare a mutual state of belligerency. In the course of their belligerency, the parties ordinarily carry on a wide variety of violent interactions, some of them high on coordination and salience, others at the opposite extreme. In what follows, nevertheless, concrete examples will make it easier to grasp differences among the abstractly defined types.

Let us be clear what the scheme does and does not represent. It does *not* summarize the conditions under which violent contention occurs rarely or frequently. We have no reason whatsoever to imagine that high-salience/low-coordination events form a smaller share of all collective violence than do high-salience/high-coordination events, or that low-salience/low-coordination events usually produce less violence than the rest. Scattered attacks can wreak havoc across an entire region, while high-salience/high-coordination collective violence sometimes involves no more than ritual wrecking of a fallen leader's statue.

The scheme comes closer to telling us where very high and very low levels of death and damage occur. On the average, collective violence in the upper-right corner (high salience/high coordination) does produce more deaths and physical damage per participant and episode than do other combinations of salience and coordination. Nevertheless, the less salient and less coordinated forms of collective violence sometimes cumulate into very high levels of damage simply because they occur with great frequency. While India's coordinated attacks such as the Gujarat massacres of 2002 far surpass smaller-scale Hindu–Muslim conflicts in sheer destructiveness when they do occur, a significant share of India's religious violence from one year to the next continues to take the form of less coordinated and less salient collective encounters (Brass 2003).

The salience-coordination scheme concentrates, in any case, on a different question: when collective violence does occur, what determines the form it takes? The scheme converts the question into another: when collective violence occurs, how and why does it vary from peripheral to salient, from fragmented to coordinated, or back in the other directions? In order to move on to overall levels of violence, we must consider interactions between these sorts of variations and the variable character of regimes.

Causes of Salience and Coordination

One part of the answer to the salience-coordination question comes from our earlier explorations of regimes and repertoires. We have good reasons for expecting the salience and coordination of collective violence to vary significantly from one sort of regime to another. Regimes affect salience directly by authorities' control over possession and use of violent means, including control of violent specialists such as soldiers, police, militias, and gangs. High-capacity regimes take command of the principal concentrated means of coercion within their territories, employ or license the bulk of violent specialists, and set obstacles in the way of anyone's accumulation of substantial autonomous coercive means or personnel. As an ironic consequence, when collective violence does occur in high-capacity regimes, government-controlled violent specialists much more often take part in it than is the case for low-capacity regimes.

Regimes affect salience more indirectly, but no less potently, by their influence over the formation, political standing, programs, and alliances of major claimants. But the organization of routine social life outside of contentious politics also weighs heavily on salience; in chapter 3, for example, I sketched how shifts in Great Britain's economy and demography between 1750 and 1840 promoted movement from a relatively violent repertoire to one that was relatively nonviolent.

Regimes also affect coordination among violent actors directly by their patterns of repression or facilitation of collective claim-making; their array of prescribed, tolerated, and forbidden claim-making performances; and the extent to which governments themselves control the prizes over which claimants struggle. Again, economy, demography, and routine social interaction strongly affect the means of coordination that are available to potential claimants. The rise of professional armies, industrial firms, schools, and associations, to take the obvious example, creates new sorts of claimants and connections within them that facilitate coordination of their members' actions.

Box 6.1 lists conditions and processes that promote salience and coordination of collective violence, as well as counterconditions and processes that inhibit salience and coordination. As the box illustrates, *salience* generally increases when participants in political interaction are themselves specialists in violence, when uncertainty about an interaction's outcome

BOX 6.1 Conditions and Processes Promoting Salience and Coordination of Collective Violence

Conditions and processes that promote salience include:

1. regime toleration of claim-making performances (e.g., of local vengeance) that involve direct application of force; regime repression of such performances reduces salience
2. regime narrowing of tolerated nonviolent performances (e.g. peaceful demonstrations), which increases the likelihood both that claimants will turn to violent performances and that governmental agents will use force to break up forbidden nonviolent performances; regime broadening of tolerated nonviolent performances reduces salience
3. frequent participation of violent specialists (troops, police, militia, gangs, etc.) in contention; withdrawal or disarming of violent specialists reduces salience
4. increasing uncertainty about the outcome of claims; routinization of outcomes (whether successful or otherwise) reduces salience
5. rising stakes of outcomes for the parties; reducing stakes inhibits salience
6. polarization across a single us/them identity boundary; conversely, deactivation of such a boundary and/or simultaneous activation of multiple boundaries reduces salience
7. absence of third parties to which participants in claim-making have stable relations; presence of such third parties reduces salience

Conditions and processes that promote coordination among violent actors:

1. increasing openness of political opportunity structure; closing of POS reduces coordination
2. authorities' control over the stakes of claim-making's outcomes for participants; where authorities lack control over stakes, coordination declines
3. brokerage: political entrepreneurs create connections among previously independent individuals and groups; dissolution of such connections inhibits coordination
4. categories dividing major blocs of political participants (e.g., gender, race, or nationality) figure widely in routine social life, and are therefore readily available for collective claim-making; nonroutine categories and ad hoc coalitions inhibit coordination
5. networks connecting members of political actors figure widely in routine social life, and are therefore readily available for collective claim-making; mobilization of externally unconnected persons and groups inhibits coordination
6. political actors organize and drill outside of public claim-making; if their only occasions of joint action occur in collective claim-making, coordination declines

increases, when stakes of the outcome for the parties increase, and/or when third parties to which the participants have stable relations are absent. *Coordination* generally rises when the costs of connection decline.

Some of these generalizations, though obvious, are still worth noting. As earlier vignettes of Peru, Uganda, and other relatively violent regimes have shown us, the freedom of action with which violent specialists operate strongly affects the salience of violence. Others are more subtle; item 11, for instance, notes that despite the strategic advantages of well-run conspiratorial organizations, on the whole correspondence of mobilized political divisions to such everyday boundaries as religion, ethnicity, and race facilitates the coordination of violence across the boundaries. If everyday boundaries crosscut each other, lower levels of coordination prevail. Clearly the relevant conditions and processes vary substantially from one type of regime to another.

The variable configuration of prescribed, tolerated, and forbidden performances in different sorts of regimes also affects processes 1 to 13 as listed in box 6.1. The tendency of low-capacity, nondemocratic regimes to repress forbidden performances incompletely and unpredictably, for instance, increases the salience of violence in their contentious interactions. Both forbidden performers and violent specialists reach out to damage each other more immediately than under other regimes. Because high-capacity, democratic regimes, in contrast, combine effective means of forbidding violent performances with toleration of extensive nonviolent performances, violence becomes much less salient in those regimes.

These regularities do, in their turn, have significant implications for a regime's extent of collective violence and for those who get involved in it. Leaving aside government-initiated warfare, overall levels of violence run higher in low-capacity regimes, whether nondemocratic or democratic. Democracy depresses violence within domestic politics, if not necessarily in relations among governments. The overall implications for levels of collective violence within regimes look as follows:

High violence: Low-capacity, nondemocratic regimes.

Medium violence: High-capacity, nondemocratic and low-capacity, democratic regimes.

Low violence: High-capacity, democratic regimes.

If substantial shifts from regime type to regime type occur in the world, we should expect them to affect overall levels of collective violence. If high-capacity, nondemocratic regimes lose capacity—as happened widely in the disintegrating Soviet Union after 1985—we should expect levels of violence to increase

(Beissinger 1998, 2001). If many regimes democratize without losing capacity, we can expect short-run increases in collective violence as struggles for control intensify, followed by long-term declines in violent encounters.

Type by type, we can identify some further regularities. In *low-capacity, nondemocratic* regimes such as Somalia and Sudan, petty tyrants use coercion freely, governmental officials deploy violent punishments when they can catch their enemies, and means of violence distribute widely across other political actors. In *low-capacity, democratic* regimes such as Belgium, Jamaica, and Switzerland, we see less involvement of governmental officials in violent repression. In such regimes, widespread spiraling of initially nonviolent conflicts into violence takes place because government agents in low-capacity, democratic regimes do not serve as effective third-party enforcers of agreements, much less inhibitors of escalation.

When it comes to *high-capacity, democratic* regimes such as Germany, Japan, India, and the United States, we generally find relatively low levels of violence in routine claim-making. We also discover highly selective—hence relatively rare—deployment of violent means by governmental agents. But in such regimes we also observe extensive involvement of government agents (as initiators, objects, or peacemakers) in such collective violence as does occur. Ironically, the net effect is to magnify the political impact of violence when it does happen in high-capacity, democratic regimes; each bit of damage dramatizes the significant political stakes over which participants are contending, more so than in regimes where collective violence occurs every day. Even in India, the great bulk of claim-making occurs without violence, and violence across religious boundaries calls up an immediate political outcry.

Finally, *high-capacity, nondemocratic* regimes such as Morocco, China, and Iran feature widespread threats of violence by governmental agents, frequent involvement of governmental agents in collective violence when it occurs, but great variability in the actual frequency of collective violence, depending on the opening and closing of opportunities for dissent. In such regimes, as in the case of high-capacity, democratic regimes, visible violence tends to broadcast the high political stakes of contention.

Boundaries and Violence

Notice one feature of the variations we have reviewed. A significant share of collective violence involves activation and reinforcement of boundaries. Claims to be or represent a certain "we" always identify a boundary separating us from "them," whoever they are. Any individual or population, however, always has multiple identities—and thus multiple boundaries—available (Tilly 2005d). In India, many of the very same people can on different occasions act together as workers, women, Hindus, Gujaratis, villagers, or members of certain castes. Boundary activation singles out one of these shared identities and its opposition to other identities.

Activation of we–they boundaries often promotes damaging interaction where social relations previously went on in a more or less peaceful fashion. As the mass killing of nonconforming Hutu by Hutu activists in 1994's Rwandan genocide indicates, furthermore, violence sometimes occurs in the course of power struggles *within* categories and around control over public representation of those categories (Dallaire 2003; Des Forges et al. 1999; Jones 1995; Mamdani 2001; Pillay 2001; Prunier 1995; 2001; Taylor 1999). The stronger the emphasis on a single we–they boundary, in general, the greater the salience of damage in all interactions and the more extensive the coordination among all violent actors.

The sorts of boundaries that are present and available for activation varies systematically by type of regime. High-capacity regimes generally limit drastically the range of categorical pairs—hence boundaries—in terms of which people can make claims. In the high-capacity, nondemocratic Soviet Union prior to 1989, for example, members of religious sects, women, ethnic groups outside the privileged number of titular nationalities, and even the informal mutual aid networks through which people actually conducted their daily affairs had no public standing as political actors, and little opportunity to gain that standing (Ledeneva 1998, 2004).

In high-capacity, democratic Canada, members of categories that can present themselves as certain kinds of citizens (including categories currently deprived of their proper citizenship rights) have a much greater chance of being heard than do kinship groups or religious sects. Yet, in general, democratic regimes erect fewer barriers to formation of new bounded groupings so long as those groupings model themselves on existing political actors. Thus boundaries of sexual preference become more available for public political action in democracies than in nondemocracies, insofar as the people involved make their claims as categories of citizens deprived of equal rights rather than as separatist communities.

What about activation of boundaries in collective violence? When violence swells rapidly from a small to a large scale, three processes are usually at work, albeit in varying sequences and combinations. First, political entrepreneurs are engaged in their work of activation, connection, coordination, and representation. Second, polarization—widening of political and social space between claimants in a contentious episode and the gravitation of previously uncommitted or moderate actors toward one, the other, or both extremes—commonly accompanies or results from the work of entrepreneurs. Finally (often as a result of political brokerage and polarization), uncertainty rises across the boundary, as actors on each side have less reliable information, and more exaggerated estimates, concerning the likely actions on the other side.

Violence generally increases, and becomes more salient, in situations of rising uncertainty across the boundary (Gould 2003). It increases because people respond to threats against weighty social arrangements they have built on such boundaries—social arrangements such as exploitation of others, property rights, in-group marriage, and power over local government. It becomes more salient among all interactions because existing nonviolent routines lose their guarantees of payoff. Uncertainty over identity boundaries can rise through a number of different processes:

- Overarching political authorities lose their ability to enforce previously constraining agreements binding actors on both sides of the boundary.
- Those same authorities take actions that threaten survival of crucial connecting structures within populations on one side of the boundary while appearing to spare or even benefit those on the other side.
- The declining capacity of authorities to police existing boundaries, control use of weapons, and contain individual aggression facilitates cross-boundary opportunism, including retaliation for earlier slights and injustices.
- Leaders on one side of the boundary or the other face resistance or competition from well-organized segments of their previous followers.
- External parties change, increase, or decrease their material, moral, and political support for actors on one side of the boundary or the other.

Change and variation in these circumstances help explain the surge in violence over nationality issues that occurred in Eurasia between 1986 and 1995. During those years, major powers including the United States and the United Nations responded to the weakening of central authority in the Warsaw Pact, the Soviet Union, and Yugoslavia by signaling increased support for claims of leaders to represent distinct nations currently under alien control. That signaling encouraged leaders to emphasize ethnic boundaries, compete for recognition as valid interlocutors for oppressed nations, attack their ostensible enemies, suppress their competitors for leadership, and make alliances with others who would supply them with resources to support their mobilization.

All those moves in turn generated what observers saw as ethno-political violence (Chirot and Seligman 2000; Olzak 2006). International authorities became less receptive to new claims for autonomy and independence as they saw how much violence attended those claims and how little formal autonomy reduced the violence. But by that time arms dealers, mercenaries, drug runners, diamond merchants, oil brokers, and others who benefited from weak central political control had moved in to take advantage of supposedly ethnic conflicts, and even to promote them.

These lessons will come across more clearly if we crank down the level of abstraction from coordination and salience in general to specific varieties of collective violence as conventionally defined. Let us apply the analysis so far to civil war and terror. Both civil war and terror include collective violence at several different locations within the coordination-salience space. Both typically range among coordinated destruction, broken negotiations, scattered attacks, and opportunism. The mix of those types provides much of the texture of particular episodes. Two conclusions follow immediately. First, because what happens within civil war and terror is causally heterogeneous, no single set of conditions or processes should suffice to explain all cases of either one. Second, both their frequency and their character vary significantly across different sorts of regimes. (In chapter 7, I reiterate both points in the case of revolutions.)

Civil War

Civil war occurs when two or more distinct military organizations, at least one of them attached to the previously existing government, battle each other for control of major governmental means within a single regime (Ghobarah, Huth, and Russett 2003; Henderson 1999; Hironaka 2005; Kaldor 1999; Licklider 1993; Walter and Snyder 1999). We have already glimpsed civil wars raging in Colombia, Iraq, Israel/Palestine, Kashmir, Nepal, Peru, and Uganda. In 2003 alone, Scandinavia's professional conflict-spotters identified civil wars above their twenty-five-dead threshold in Afghanistan, Algeria, Burma/Myanmar, Burundi, Chechnya, Colombia, Iraq, Israel/Palestine, Kashmir, Liberia, Nepal, the Philippines, Sri Lanka, Sudan, Turkey/Kurdistan, and Uganda (Eriksson and Wallensteen 2004, 632–35).

Over the years since World War II, a remarkable change in the world's armed conflicts, including civil wars, has occurred. During the two centuries prior to that war, most large-scale lethal conflicts had pitted states against each other. But in the immediate postwar period, European colonial powers faced resistance and insurrection in many of their colonies. Colonial wars surged before subsiding during the 1970s. As the Cold War prevailed between the 1960s and 1980s, great powers—especially the United States, the Soviet Union, and the former colonial masters—frequently intervened in postcolonial civil wars such as those that rent

Angola between 1975 and 2003 (Dunér 1985). But increasingly civil wars without direct military intervention by third parties became the main sites of large-scale killing conflict (Kaldor 1999; Tilly 2003, chap. 3).

Scandinavian specialists in the study of armed conflict divide those since World War II into several categories:

Extrasystemic: Between a state and a nonstate group outside its own territory, the most typical cases being colonial wars

Interstate: Between two or more states

Internal: Between the government of a state and internal opposition groups without intervention from other states—civil war, in short

Internationalized internal: Between the government of a state and internal opposition groups, with military intervention from other states (Strand, Wilhelmsen, and Gleditsch 2004, 11)

Figure 6.2 (adapted from Eriksson and Wallensteen 2004, and using data supplied by them) illustrates trends in the four categories of conflict from 1946 through 2004. The figure shows colonial wars declining, then disappearing after 1975, interstate wars fluctuating but never predominating, and internationalized civil wars reaching their maximum during the 1980s, then declining after 2000. In terms of sheer frequency of conflict, the big news comes from civil wars without foreign intervention. These

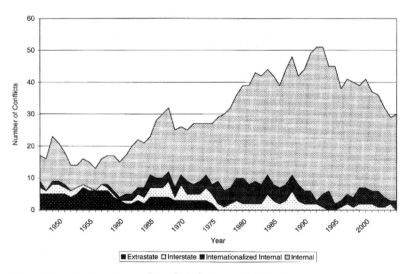

Figure 6.2. Number of armed conflicts by type, 1946–2004

internal armed conflicts climbed irregularly but dramatically from the 1950s to the 1990s, only to decline significantly in frequency from the mid-1990s. Soviet and Yugoslav disintegration contributed to the surge of the early 1990s (Beissinger 1998, 2001; Kaldor 1999).

During the later 1990s, despite such sore spots as Chechnya and Kosovo, most postsocialist regimes settled into more stable, less violent forms of rule. Partial democratization of previously divided regimes—South Africa is a case in point—also contributed to civil war's decline from 1994 onward (Piano and Puddington 2004). Despite continuing civil wars in Afghanistan, Algeria, Myanmar, Burundi, Chechnya, Colombia, Iraq, Israel/Palestine, Kashmir, Liberia, Nepal, the Philippines, Sri Lanka, Sudan, Turkey/Kurdistan, and Uganda, the scope of civil war has been shrinking.

Over the longer period since World War II, civil wars have concentrated in two kinds of regimes: (1) relatively high-capacity regimes, however democratic or nondemocratic, containing significant zones that escape central control (of recent cases, Israel/Palestine, Kashmir, Peru, Chechnya, the Philippines, Turkey, and possibly Colombia); (2) low-capacity, nondemocratic regimes (the rest).

Why should that be? The two sorts of regimes have in common a fundamental principle we have encountered before: controlling their own government gives rulers advantages denied to subjects of the government who lack that control. Even weak governments give rulers power over resources, activities, and populations—not to mention prestige and deference—ordinary citizens do not enjoy. In poor countries, control over governments and access to their benefits become even more valuable relative to lack of control and access: fewer alternative sources of support exist.

In poor countries, for example, service in the military typically looks much more attractive relative to other available livelihoods than it does in rich countries. Low-paying governmental jobs, with their opportunities for patronage, perquisites, and bribes, likewise often became more enticing than work in whatever private sector exists. Those facts alone help explain the survival of visibly corrupt and incompetent governments in many poor countries; they offer their clients little, but little is better than nothing.

Of course capacity and democracy make a difference. By definition, high-capacity governments exert more extensive control over resources, activities, and populations. High-capacity governments also generally limit independent access to coercive force and smash any group that starts to acquire lethal arms. Not quite by definition, democratic regimes not only greatly expand the ruling class and promote turnover in its membership, but also impose greater costs and constraints on rulers' disposition of government-controlled resources.

Hence a paradox: where the returns from gaining governmental power are lower, violent attempts to seize power occur more frequently. Armed struggle for control of an existing government becomes more attractive in low-capacity, nondemocratic regimes and in regions of higher-capacity regimes that operate like low-capacity, nondemocratic regimes: semicolonial outposts, porous frontiers, areas of inaccessible terrain. Since their populations often define themselves (or become defined) as ethnically distinct, civil wars based in such territories often acquire the false reputation of being ethnically motivated.

James Fearon and David Laitin have carried out one of the most revealing analyses of the conditions under which civil wars do and do not occur. They assembled their own data on 127 civil wars that began somewhere in the world between 1945 and 1999, then indexed characteristics of all existing regimes, including such frequently proposed candidates as ethnic and religious fragmentation. Multivariate analyses then indicated which of the characteristics actually coincided with extensive civil war.

Despite their plausibility and popularity, the fragmentation measures did not survive multivariate testing; they showed only weak, inconsistent associations with civil war. The robust associations were the following:

- Low per-capita income
- Large total population
- Mountainous terrain
- Exportation of oil
- State less than three years old
- Instability of governmental form (Fearon and Laitin 2003, 84)

Fearon and Laitin conclude reasonably that these conditions do not represent discontent or division in a national population. Previously existing grievances and ethnic or religious segmentation fall by the wayside.

But Fearon and Laitin also challenge the alternative view proposed by Paul Collier and Anke Hoeffler: namely, that the availability and marketability of valuable, portable natural resources such as diamonds promote civil war by making it feasible to support dissident military forces (Collier 2000b; Collier and Hoeffler 2001). Nevertheless, both analyses agree that the prevalence of antigovernmental grievances and the confrontation of ethnic or religious fragments have little effect on the likelihood of civil war. What matters is the ease with which armed insurgents can organize, challenge, and support themselves. In language none of these authors uses, political opportunity structures (POS) matter, and vary enormously from one sort of regime to another.

Nicholas Sambanis has pointed out the limits of the Fearon-Laitin/ Collier-Hoeffler line of explanation. Among other things, it assumes that civil wars are causally coherent—all the same thing, and therefore subject to the same explanation. It also equates causes with prior conditions:

> I argue that it is not as useful to view civil war outcomes as the result of deep-seated and hardly changing structural conditions as it is to observe the links among different forms of political violence and to analyze the dynamics of conflict escalation and the transition from one form of violence to another. (Sambanis 2004a, 260; see also Sambanis 2002, 2004b; Collier and Sambanis 2005, vol. 1, chap. 10)

Sambanis's critique joins with this book's main arguments. The South African struggles analyzed in chapter 5 came close enough to civil war for us to conclude that knowing the background conditions—at what point in time?—tells us little about the process by which South Africa divided into deeply hostile camps, then struggled its way to uneasy peace.

Initial conditions shape subsequent processes, but do not determine them. POS and repertoires vary in characteristic ways from one type of regime to another, and therefore produce differences in initial propensities to different forms of collective violence. Among other things, the availability of alternative paths to power affects the attractiveness of military insurgency even where material and organizational conditions make insurgency technically possible.

Once we have specified the relevant initial conditions, dynamic analysis begins. Peru's terrain and population distribution changed little between civil war and turbulent semi-democratic politics, but POS and repertoire shifted significantly. Changes in the salience and coordination of collective violence, including the violence of civil war, result from alterations in the conditions and processes named in box 6.1: rising or falling uncertainty about the outcomes of claims, shifts in the stakes of achieving control over the government, exercise or disruption of brokerage, and so on.

As it happens, David Laitin's own analysis of the Somalian civil war (1989–92) supports just such an argument. The Soviet Union's collapse ended the possibility for Somalian regimes to support themselves by playing off Soviet against U.S. aid; hence the parties who had been receiving payoffs for collaboration with the government entered a competitive situation. The competition resembled wars of attrition as often described in the biological, international relations, and industrial organization literatures: actors including the one that currently holds the advantage (controls what remains of the government) continue to fight their enemies despite diminishing means of supporting their own activity and paying off their followers.

The parties continue to fight in the hope that others will quit first, leaving them with the battered prize. In the Somali context, Laitin puts it this way:

> The logic of the model suggests that Aideed and Ali Mahdi continued fighting not so much because they feared being decimated by the other if they lost . . . but because each leader strategized, if the war was costing more for the opponents, that they would sue for peace first. If both leaders think this way, the war continues. I think the war of attrition model might also help explain post-cold war events in Liberia, Sierra Leone, Congo (former Zaire), Congo, and Uganda. As France is tentatively withdrawing from the use of military personnel to prop up dictators in its former colonies, my analysis suggests we will be seeing Somali-like civil wars in former French African colonies as well. (Laitin 1999, 159–60)

The strategic logic operates, however, within limits set by POS and established repertoires. It also depends on the availability and support of specialists in violence. After the Cold War ended, Laitin points out, small arms became much more widely and equally available to actors on both sides of African conflicts (Laitin 1999, 157; see also Boutwell, Klare, and Reed 1995). So, for that matter, did mercenary forces, available to those who could pay (or whose diasporas could pay) with resources drawn from the country and its external commerce (Davis and Pereira 2003; Singer 2003). Specifying the context takes us back to regimes, repertoires, and specialists in violence.

Terror

A similar set of lessons applies to terrorism.[2] The word "terror" does not appear in the salience-coordination typology, for good reason. As we will soon see, most terror does occur in the upper-right corner of the salience-coordination space as depicted in figure 6.1, high on salience and high on coordination. Suicide bombings belong in that territory. Many

---

2. For reviews, critiques, and syntheses, see Bloom 2005; Caddick-Adams and Holmes 2001; Crenshaw 1995; Enders and Sandler 2002; Farah 2004; Gambetta 2005; González Callejo 2002a; González Callejo, ed., 2002; Kushner 2001; Mazower 2002; Oliverio 1998; Pape 2003; della Porta and Pasquino 1983; Rapoport 1999; Schmid 2001; Senechal de la Roche 2004; Smelser and Mitchell 2002a, 2002b; Stern 2003; Tilly 2004c; Turk 2003.

attacks by Basque or Palestinian nationalists likewise embody high coordination and salience. But a significant minority of terrorist episodes involves less coordination despite the high salience of violence within them.

Throughout the twentieth century and beyond, for example, Northern Ireland experienced plenty of terror, but at times its violence has moved from high to low coordination (Hart 1998; Jarman 1997; Keogh 2001; Lavery 2001a, 2001b). In the widespread terror of Colombia and Chechnya, kidnapping for revenge or ransom has become a favorite tactic of clandestine actors that are also carrying on sustained military action; highly coordinated and less coordinated forms of violence complement each other (Ramirez 2001; Tishkov 2001). Both the organization and the personnel of terror vary widely.

Al-Qaeda's coordination of devastating attacks on New York's World Trade Center and Washington's Pentagon on September 11, 2001 fixed American awareness of terror on conspiratorial fanatics. Most terror does concentrate in the high-coordination/high-salience portion of our space. But confinement of terror to high-coordination/high-salience uses of violence or threats of violence by tightly organized conspirators misses the widespread presence of terror by other sorts of political actors in the course of other sorts of politics (Tilly 2002b, 2004c). Assassins, bombers, and hostage-takers also appear among the initiators of less highly coordinated varieties of terror (see, for example, Andreas 2004; Bayart, Ellis, and Hibou 1999; Briquet 2000; Derluguian 1999; Godoy 2004; Kalyvas 2003; Tishkov 2004).

Terror, then, is not a single form of violence but a strategy: deployment of violence or threats of violence against a very unequal target. Terror's inequality can run in either direction: a relatively weak political actor strikes against a very strong political actor, or a very strong political actor deploys violence and threats of violence against a relatively weak political actor. Terror matters politically when it dramatizes the target's vulnerability. By doing so, it broadcasts a threat not only to the target but also to third parties that have allied with the target, depended on the target for protection, or occupied positions similar to the target's. Terror therefore succeeds if it deters the target from acting in opposition to the perpetrators' interest, but also if it drives third parties away from collaboration with the target. Many different sorts of political actors engage in this sort of asymmetrical interchange.

What sorts of collective violence, for example, do those State Department reports on international terror I mentioned earlier in this chapter actually capture? Box 6.2 lists the incidents for January 2003. More than we might expect, the catalog overlaps with two lists we have seen before: (1) the contentious events we caught in our sweep of Reuters and the BBC on New Year's Day 2005, and (2) the sites of civil wars in 2003. All the events

BOX 6.2 Significant Terrorist Incidents, January 2003

1/5   *Kashmir, India:* In Kulgam, a hand grenade exploded at a bus station injuring 40 persons: 36 private citizens and four security personnel, according to press reports. No one claimed responsibility.

1/5   *Pakistan:* In Peshawar, armed terrorists fired on the residence of an Afghan diplomat, injuring a guard, according to press reports. The diplomat was not in his residence at the time of the incident. No one claimed responsibility.

1/5   *Israel:* In Tel Aviv, two suicide bombers attacked simultaneously, killing 23 persons including: 15 Israelis, two Romanians, one Ghanaian, one Bulgarian, three Chinese, and one Ukrainian and wounding 107 others—nationalities not specified—according to press reports. The attack took place in the vicinity of the old central bus station where foreign national workers live. The detonations took place within seconds of each other and were approximately 600 feet apart, in a pedestrian mall and in front of a bus stop. The al-Aqsa Martyrs Brigade was responsible.

1/12 *Pakistan:* In Hyderabad, authorities safely defused a bomb placed in a toilet of a Kentucky Fried Chicken restaurant, according to press reports. Two bomb explosions in Hyderabad in recent months have killed a total of four persons and injured 33 others, all Pakistanis. No one has claimed responsibility.

1/21 *Kuwait:* In Kuwait City, a gunman ambushed a vehicle at the intersection of al-Judayliyat and Adu Dhabi, killing one U.S. citizen and wounding another. The victims were civilian contractors working for the U.S. military. The incident took place close to Camp Doha, an installation housing approximately 17,000 U.S. troops. On January 23–24, a twenty-year-old Kuwaiti civil servant, Sami al-Mutayri, was apprehended attempting to cross the border from Kuwait to Saudi Arabia. Al-Mutayri confessed to the attack and stated that he embraces al-Qaida ideology and implements Usama Bin Ladin's instructions although there is no evidence of an organizational link. The assailant acted alone but had assistance in planning the ambush. No group has claimed responsibility.

1/22 *Colombia:* In Arauquita, military officials reported either the National Liberation Army (ELN) or the Revolutionary Armed Forces of Colombia (FARC) terrorists bombed a section of the Cano Limon-Covenas oil pipeline, causing an unknown amount of damage. The pipeline is owned by U.S. and Colombian oil companies.

1/24 *Colombia:* In Tame, rebels kidnapped two journalists working for the *Los Angeles Times.* One was a British reporter and the other a U.S. photographer. The ELN is responsible. The two journalists were released unharmed on 1 February 2003.

> 1/27 *Afghanistan:* In Nangarhar, two security officers escorting several United Nations vehicles were killed when armed terrorists attacked their convoy, according to press reports. No one claimed responsibility.
>
> 1/31 *Kashmir:* In Srinagar, armed terrorists killed a local journalist when they entered his office, according to press reports. No one claimed responsibility.
>
> *Source:* State 2004b, 95–96.

on the State Department roster involved physical violence or threats of violence, but otherwise they covered an impressive range of political purposes, from civil war to domestic oppositions. They also spread across Asia, the Middle East, and Latin America. In other months of 2003, Europe, Africa, the Pacific, and North America all show up in State Department inventories of terror.

For its 2003 report, the State Department defined terrorism as "politically motivated violence perpetrated against noncombatant targets by subnational groups or clandestine agents, usually intended to influence an audience" (Ruby 2002, 10). Any such definition has the disadvantage of requiring solid information on motivations and intentions, which rarely becomes available for collective violence. Still, the report's implicit selection principles single out attacks on noncombatant targets by other than regularly constituted national military forces, especially when someone broadcasts political claims on behalf of the attackers. The report narrows its focus further: in accordance with its congressional mandate, it singles out *international* terrorist incidents in which actors somehow identified with one regime attacked actors somehow identified with a different regime.

By definition, State's catalog excludes terror applied by national armies, including the U.S. forces that in 2003 were trying—rather unsuccessfully—to pacify Afghanistan and Iraq. It excludes terror employed by one side or another in civil wars, such as the attacks of Tamil and Sinhalese forces on each other that were occurring in Sri Lanka. An official 2005 statement of criteria declared:

> [Incidents] were judged to be significant if they involved the kidnapping, killing, or wounding of noncombatants, unless there was readily available evidence that injuries were minor. Kidnapped victims who were killed are counted as killed in the charts and graphs, and kidnapped victims either liberated or still in captivity are counted as

kidnapped in the charts and graphs. Incidents may also have been deemed significant if they resulted in physical or economic damage of approximately $10,000 or more. (National Counterterrorism Center 2005, viii)

In the reports for 2003 in box 6.2, the phrase "no one claimed responsibility" ironically identifies those situations in which State's analysts judged that the unknown actor represented some outside power.

Terror Counts

Where do the data come from? Since the 1980s, the U.S. State Department has, by congressional mandate, issued an annual report on global terrorism. Until 2003, State officials collected annual summaries from embassies across the world, compiling them into a global catalog with simple statistics. After the attacks of September 11 and shortly before the American invasion of Iraq, the Bush administration changed the reporting procedure. It created the (ominously named) Terrorist Threat Integration Center, which took over responsibility for preparation of the annual catalog and which, in turn, compiled reports from the Central Intelligence Agency (CIA), the Federal Bureau of Investigation (FBI), the Department of Homeland Security, and the Department of Defense. Descriptive details, nevertheless, seem to have come largely from press reports.

The new coordination did not work well. State's annual report for 2003, issued on April 29, 2004, stated that acts of terrorism had declined from 346 in 2001 to 198 in 2002 to a record low of 190 in 2003 (State 2004a, 1). Deputy Secretary of State Richard Armitage took credit for the decline on behalf of the Bush administration's antiterror efforts. "You will find in these pages," declared Armitage, "clear evidence that we are prevailing in the fight" (Associated Press 2004, 1). After prodding by Congressman Henry Waxman of California, however, on June 10 the department issued a retraction: the 2003 data from the CIA, FBI, Homeland Security Department, and Defense were "incomplete and in some cases incorrect" (State 2004b, 1). Between my consulting the 2003 report on June 20, 2004 and my follow-up the next day, the report disappeared from the State Department's web site.

By the morning of June 23, a "Year in Review (Revised)" had appeared at the web site. The revision not only raised the event count for 2003 from 190 to 208, but also increased some figures for earlier years (State 2004c). At the June 22 press conference releasing the new numbers, Secretary of State Colin Powell conducted an irritable exchange with reporters. "Asked if the new statistics meant that the United States was not "prevailing,"

Mr. Powell said that he had to leave for a meeting at the White House but that two specialists would explain. "Here are the experts," he said. "They will tell you" (Weisman 2004, A12).

Experts J. Cofer Black, coordinator for counterterrorism, and John O. Brennan, director of the Terrorist Threat Integration Center, blamed an obsolete database and a defective computer program for the previous undercount. More than one critic raised doubts about the explanation (for example, Krueger 2004; Krueger and Laitin 2004; Krugman 2004).

Within a year, in any case, the official story had changed considerably. Philip Zelikow had been executive director of the government's National Commission on Terrorist Attacks upon the United States, the September 11 Commission. He had largely authored the commission's widely read final report. Among a great many other changes in the gathering and dissemination of terror-related intelligence, the report recommended establishment of a National Counterterrorism Center (Commission 2004, 403–6). The government created its new terrorism data center a few months after the report's publication. By the spring of 2005, Zelikow had become counselor of the State Department. Meanwhile, John Brennan had become interim director of the National Counterterrorism Center (NCTC). The new center still reported to the State Department, but now lived a partly separate existence as custodian of a national database on terror.

To the surprise and consternation of many specialists in the study of terror, the NCTC abandoned the format and procedures of previous annual reports on terror. At a Zelikow-sponsored press conference unveiling the NCTC's new "Country Reports on Terrorism," Brennan made the following declaration to skeptical reporters:

> To ensure a more comprehensive accounting of terrorist incidents, we in the NCTC significantly increased the level of effort from three part-time individuals to 10 full-time analysts, and we took a number of other steps to improve quality control and database management. This increased level of effort allowed a much deeper review of far more information and, along with Iraq, are the primary reasons for the significant growth in a number of terrorist incidents being reported. (Zelikow 2005, 3)

As compared with the (upwardly revised) 208 incidents for 2003, the 2004 report enumerated a full 651 significant international terrorist incidents—a tripling of the count in a single year.

In response to reporters' questioning, Zelikow and Brennan denied that the numbers actually recorded an increase in worldwide terrorism, much less that the government's well-advertised war on terror was failing. They did not, oddly, take the obvious social scientific step: compare the number of events the previous year's procedures would have yielded with the number produced by the new, superior procedures. But they did concede in passing that in 2004 far more events had shown up from Iraq and Kashmir than State had reported in 2003. The number of Iraqi events rose from 22 to 201, the number of Kashmiri events from 50 to 284 (Zelikow 2005, 3, 5, plus my count from the 2003 report). Those two increases, totaling 413, account almost fully for the rise in total events from 210 to 651.

The numbers suggest an at least equally plausible alternative to the official explanation: Kashmir extremists stepped up their terror campaign as the Indian and Pakistani governments took steps toward rapprochement, while in Iraq insurgent attacks on noncombatant foreigners multiplied enormously. The fact that every single Iraqi incident reported for 2003 had already involved an attack on non-Iraqi noncombatants supports the alternative interpretation.

Box 6.3 presents the events reported for the first few days of 2004. As we might expect, they roughly tripled the frequency of events compared with the previous year, as recorded in box 6.2. Over the year as a whole, significant terrorist incidents increased from about 4 to 12.5 per week. In Kashmir, we see NCTC analysts qualifying a variety of violent attacks as foreign-initiated regardless of whether any group claimed responsibility. In Iraq, we see the first of the year's many attacks on foreigners working for the American-led coalition.

With the new numbers in place, figure 6.3 shows the trend in State's count of significant terrorist attacks from 1980 to 2004. Despite the 2004 uptick, the overall trend before 2004 ran downward. The total reached a high point in 1988, and generally declined thereafter. Contrary to widespread views of mounting terrorism across the world, the line zigzags downward. Attacks reached their peak in 1987, with 666 incidents in the State Department catalog. After an earlier wave of anticolonial and postcolonial terror as European states withdrew from their overseas empires, the terrorist attacks of the 1980s centered on struggles against the rulers of postcolonial states—civil wars, separatist mobilizations, or both at once. As the *Annual Register* editorialized in 1988:

> These were the internal wars, or warlike strife, which blazed or smouldered in many nations on all continents: in Central America, Lebanon, Iraq, Yugoslavia, Sudan, Ethiopia, Burundi, Indonesia, Sri Lanka, Kampuchea, New Caledonia, and other countries. Violent regional or

BOX 6.3 Significant Terrorist Incidents, January 1–9, 2004

1/1 *Kashmir, India:* In Srinagar, a militant on a bicycle was carrying a bomb, which prematurely exploded, injuring six civilians. No group claimed responsibility.

1/2 *Colombia:* Between Puerto Colon and San Miguel, 11 bombs exploded at different points along the Trans-Andean Pipeline, suspending Colombia's exports of petroleum. The bombs had been placed between the 20th and 29th kilometers of the pipeline. No group claimed responsibility, although local police blamed the Revolutionary Armed Forces of Colombia (FARC).

1/2 *Kashmir:* At about 6:30 p.m., two armed militants opened fire at a Jammu railway station, killing four Indian security personnel and wounding 17 civilians. This attack occurred one day before the Indian prime minister was due to make his first visit to Pakistan in four years. No group claimed responsibility.

1/2 *Kashmir:* In Bijbehara, militants threw a grenade at an armed convoy, killing one soldier and one civilian and wounding eight other civilians. No group claimed responsibility.

1/4 *Iraq:* In Mosul, an improvised explosive device exploded inside a taxicab, killing two Iraqis and wounding one Jordanian. It is unknown if the blast was premature or if the taxicab and its occupants were the intended targets. No group claimed responsibility.

1/5 *Bolivia:* In Oruro, a bomb exploded at a building of the National Telecommunications Enterprise (Entel), a telecom company under the management of Italian Telecom, injuring two security guards and a civilian. The explosion also shattered almost all of the windows on the north side of the building and partially collapsed several walls. No group claimed responsibility.

1/5 *Iraq:* Near Falluja, unknown attackers shot and killed two French nationals and wounded one other. The victims worked for a U.S. company contracted to repair Iraqi infrastructure. No group claimed responsibility.

1/5 *United Kingdom:* In Manchester, anarchists sent a letter bomb to the office of Gary Titley, leader of the Labor Party's members of the European Parliament. The device burst into flames when Titley's secretary opened the package, and a fire spread throughout the office. There were no reported injuries. This was the sixth bomb sent from Italy to European Union officials throughout Western Europe. A group calling itself the Informal Anarchic Federation claimed responsibility.

1/6 *Kashmir:* In Shopian, Islamic militants opened fire at a police patrol, killing one shopkeeper. This incident occurred as India and Pakistan resumed diplomatic talks. No group claimed responsibility.

1/9 *Kashmir:* In Srinagar, an Islamic militant threw a grenade at a crowded mosque during prayers, missing the intended target and hitting the roof of a shop, killing two civilians and injuring 18 others. The attack occurred after India and Pakistan agreed to resume bilateral talks, and Islamabad pledged it would not allow its soil to be used for terrorism. No group claimed responsibility, but police blamed the United Jihad Council.

1/9 *Kashmir:* In the Kupwara District, armed militants beheaded a police officer. No group claimed responsibility.

Source: National Counterterrorism Center 2005, 3–4.

communal revolts plagued yet more states, from the Balkans to India, not least the uprising of Arab people in the Israeli-occupied lands. Even the Soviet Union, with its massive central authority, was shaken by the rebellion of Armenians against their Azerbaijani neighbours and theretaliatory massacres—events of a different order from the calls by the Baltic states for autonomy within the Soviet Union.

The common character of those internal conflicts and revolts was that, unlike the political upheavals in such countries as Burma, Haiti or Algeria, they were primarily racial or tribal; those who leagued together, and likewise those against whom they leagued, were linked by race, religion or culture, not by political or economic

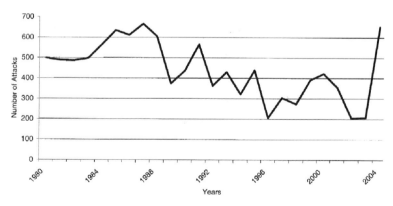

Figure 6.3. Total international terrorist attacks, 1980–2004
Source: U.S. State Department, *Patterns of Global Terrorism*, selected years; National Counterterrorism Center, *Chronology of Significant International Terrorism for 2004.*

philosophies, save in so far as the political and economic establishment was seen by dissidents as racially or culturally oppressive. (*Annual Register* 1988, 1–2)

Erratically and incompletely, demands for political autonomy backed by violent attacks have actually been declining since the 1980s. Despite the counterexamples of Palestine and the Basque Country, support by major powers for newly autonomous political entities and for forcible overturns of existing authorities has weakened dramatically since the Soviet Union's collapse and the Cold War's end. Collective violence, as we have seen, has by no means faded away across the world since then. With its program of clearing infidels from the Holy Land, al-Qaeda still exists. But the special version of collective violence captured by the State Department's catalogs of terrorist incidents dwindled significantly from 1988 onward.

However we interpret the upward spurt of 2004, the 208 attacks of 2003 lie far below the frequencies of the 1980s, when the numbers rarely fell below 500 reported terrorist attacks per year. Overall casualties fluctuated more from year to year than did number of attacks, but deaths generally declined as well from the 1980s onward (Enders and Sandler 2002). The years from 1999 to 2004 produced dramatic fluctuation in reported deaths from terrorist incidents:

1999	233 deaths
2000	405
2001	3,547 (including 3,000 assigned to September 11)
2002	725
2003	625
2004	1,907

Note, in any case, what these counts exclude, even if they get the trend right. The word "terror" took on a political meaning with the French Revolution's virtue-imposing dictatorship of 1793 (Gérard 1999; Greer 1935; Guenniffey 2000; Mayer 2000). From that point on, analysts often applied it to governments that enforced compliance by threat and deed. In the recent past, Stalin, Hitler, Pol Pot, and Saddam Hussein have all figured as men who ruled by terror, with the implication that except for fear their people would have rejected them. The State Department's definition of terror, however, excludes the threat or use of force by governments (Brockett 2005; Oliverio 1998; Stanley 1996; Tilly 1985). It also downplays the frequent employment of threat and coercion by armies and militias against civilian populations during civil wars (Berkeley 2001; Chesterman 2001; Davenport 2000; Ellis 1999; Tishkov 1997, 2004).

Excluding state-initiated terror against the state's own citizens eliminates a large part of the phenomenon. Acting by congressional mandate, however, the State Department's reporters focus on violence and threats of violence in which nongovernmental groups presumably backed by or based in one country aim at targets in a second country. Since they draw their data especially from far-flung members of the CIA, they give particular attention to the targeting of American property and personnel.

Whether backed by governments or not, genocide and ethnic cleansing likewise do not appear in the State Department's counts (Bax 2000; Brubaker and Laitin 1998; Harff 2003; Kakar 1996; Levin and Rabrenovic 2001; Mamdani 2001; Mazower 2002; Naimark 2001; Prunier 1995, 2001; Taylor 1999; Toft 2003; Uvin 2001). Although we might quibble over that unexploded bomb in a Pakistani toilet reported for January 2003, State Department listings generally omit threats to do harm unless someone had put lethal weapons in place, ready for use. Official U.S. government inventories of terrorism draw a rough circle around episodes in which politically identified actors other than governments or armies apply violent means to noncombatants, with special attention to episodes in which perpetrators and victims identify with different national governments.

In detail, the annual reports actually describe two kinds of events. First are what they call "significant terrorist incidents": attacks their specialists regard as crossing international lines because the attackers came from outside the country, received substantial backing from outside, or assaulted foreigners. The second kind comprises other attacks by domestic groups on domestic targets.

Using a fairly small scale, the State Department's locally knowledgeable observers probably report the bulk of qualifying actions in the first category for the world as a whole. Those are the events for which they supply synopses one by one and make annual counts. But they surely miss the vast majority of the world's violent events in the second category (Bonneuil and Auriat 2000; Davenport 2000; della Porta and Pasquino 1983; Furet, Liniers, and Raynaud 1985; Martínez 2001; Olzak 2006; Tilly 2003).

The following four steps might improve on the State Department's definitions:

1. Notice that a recurrent strategy of intimidation occurs widely in contentious politics, and corresponds approximately to what many people mean by terror: asymmetrical deployment of threats and violence against enemies.

2. Recognize that a wide variety of individuals, groups, and networks sometimes employ that strategy.
3. Connect the strategy systematically to other forms of political struggle proceeding in the same settings and populations.
4. Observe that violent specialists ranging from government employees to bandits sometimes deploy terror under certain political circumstances, usually with far more devastating effects than the terror operations of nonspecialists.

In short, locate terror in relation to regimes and repertoires, as an aspect of collective violence. The horrors of September 11 should not blind us to systematic variation in the character and origins of terror.

Even in the absence of reliable data, we can hazard some strong statements about terrorism in the contemporary world. Overall, political actors including governments use the strategy much more frequently in low-capacity, nondemocratic regimes than in other sorts of regime. Violent specialists employed or at least backed by governments regularly intimidate dissidents and enemies by means of asymmetrical applications and threats of violence in low-capacity, nondemocratic regimes. But in the same class of regimes dissidents and opponents also try their hands at terror in striking at governments and at civilian populations.

In Colombia (1989–2005), Liberia (1992–2003), Sierra Leone (1998–2000), and Chechnya (1995–2005), self-styled rebels who were engaged in civil war also terrorized civilian populations with killings, mutilations, and/or abductions. In all those war-torn countries, government forces replied in kind. In Congo-Kinshasa, Sudan, and Uganda, whole villages spend their nights away from home for fear of militia attacks. In Afghanistan and Iraq, Afghans and Iraqis deploy terror against each other daily. Most of these applications of terror disappear from U.S. State Department compilations because both perpetrators and victims come from the same regime. In most such cases, the users of terror are not long-distance conspirators in the style of al-Qaeda, but organized military units that employ terror as one of several strategies for maintaining or seizing political power. Terror attacks that strike targets in rich democratic countries such as the United States and Spain attract attention precisely because they are exceptional.

Why that concentration in low-capacity, nondemocratic regimes? The answer returns to regimes and repertoires. In high-capacity regimes, governments maintain extensive controls over coercive means including violent specialists. High-capacity governments exercise near-monopolies of the means of terror, but generally employ terror sparingly. In such regimes, it takes extensive clandestine preparation, most often with external support, to evade the government's preventive repression. The attacks of September 11, Morocco's suicide-bombings of 2003, and Spain's railway bombings of 2004 depended on small groups' underground assembly of lethal means, and almost instantly activated the repressive capacities of the three regimes.

In democratic regimes, furthermore, the availability of claim-making repertoires including extensive nonviolent performances channels political actors away from high-risk terror as a strategy. High-capacity democratic regimes regularly employ substantial security forces whose job includes blocking any move of claimants toward violent means, pushing claimants toward prescribed and tolerated means of claim-making, maintaining surveillance of potentially violent claimants, and breaking up any serious accumulations of coercive means outside of governmental control. On the whole, such measures work to make nongovernmental terror extremely rare in high-capacity, democratic regimes; relatively rare in high-capacity nondemocratic and low-capacity democratic regimes; but tragically common in low-capacity, nondemocratic regimes.

Considering all sorts of collective violence including civil war and terror, the most general relations run as shown below. All of these causal connections have by now become quite familiar. Even more so than earlier analyses, however, the study of collective violence brings out the importance of governmental control (or lack of control) over violent means. High-capacity, democratic regimes certainly have a capacity for violence. Even if they are less likely to fight each other, they engage in interstate war about as frequently as other regimes (Geller and Singer 1998; Gowa 1999; Hagan 1994; Olzak 2006; Ray 1998; Reiter and Stam 2002). But on the domestic scene, their powerful combination of governmental control over violent means, widely available nonviolent repertoires, and accountability of government agents for their uses of force produce a remarkable variety of contentious politics.

Here this chapter's arguments concerning collective violence and the earlier analyses of regimes converge. The public politics of high-capacity, democratic regimes brings together widespread collective claim-making; low salience, coordination, and overall levels of collective violence; and impressively restrained domestic use of the government's enormous coercive power. Less democratic and lower-capacity regimes experience more authoritarian and/or more violent forms of contentious politics. The relations illustrated in the chart above help us understand why.

As the next chapter shows, a similar analysis helps explain revolutions.

CHAPTER SEVEN >>
Revolutions

DURING THE BLOODY YEARS of 1993 and 1994, Canadian general Roméo Dallaire commanded the United Nations's small military force in Rwanda. Of that contingent, fourteen of his soldiers—ten Belgians, three Ghanaians, and one Senegalese—died in combat with the presidential guard and militias that spearheaded Rwanda's genocide. Dallaire tells the bitter story of his Rwandan experience in a memoir vividly titled *Shake Hands with the Devil*.

Dallaire's UN assignment followed decades of struggle in Rwanda. Germany had occupied and colonized the African nation during the 1890s, then lost the colony to Belgium during World War I. Belgium ruled Rwanda from 1916 until the colony's independence in 1962. For most of that time, Belgium relied on the minority Tutsi as their collaborators in the regime. But when Tutsi emerged as leaders of the independence movement, Belgium responded by redirecting its favor to the Hutu. In the process, Hutu massacres of the dethroned Tutsi began. Many Tutsi fled the country, especially to adjacent Uganda. After independence, Hutu politicians dominated the country.

In July 1973, Rwanda's senior military officer, General Juvénal Habyarimana, seized power by means of a relatively bloodless coup. He moved quickly to establish a one-party regime that lasted for two decades. A Hutu from the northwest, Habyarimana ruled with the help of his wife and her powerful family. But they faced opposition from

Tutsi-based military forces in Uganda and along Rwanda's northern border, as well as from Hutu political leaders based in the south.

Starting in 1990, the primarily Tutsi Rwanda Patriotic Front (RPF) advanced from its base near the Ugandan border, as Hutu peasants fled the Front's advance. Tutsi Paul Kagame led the RPF. Meanwhile, Hutu Power activists organized local massacres of Tutsi in response to the threatened return of the previously dominant Tutsis to power. In 1992, Habyarimana's political party organized its own militia, the Interahamwe. Something even larger was afoot: beginning in 1993, Rwanda imported about 580,000 machetes in addition to substantial small arms from France, the United States, and elsewhere.

International authorities, including representatives of the United Nations, sought to intervene. In August 1993, talks in Arusha, Tanzania that had begun in July 1992 produced a peace treaty between Habyarimana and the RPF. In November 1993, the United Nations sent in a small peacekeeping force under Dallaire's command. In April 1994, African leaders succeeded in bringing together Habyarimana, adjacent Burundi's president Cyprien Ntaryamira, and a number of other political potentates in Dar es Salaam, Tanzania to work out a peace plan for Rwanda. But Habyarimana felt threats from the RPF, Uganda, other foreign powers, and domestic enemies as well. So on his way to Tanzania the fourth of April, Habyarimana stopped in Gbadolite, Zaïre (ancestral home and rural capital of Zaïre's dictator Joseph Mobutu) and appealed to Mobutu for protection (Booh Booh 2005, 132).

Traveling on from Gbadolite to Dar es Salaam, Habyarimana joined talks that discussed, and perhaps agreed on, installation of a broad-based transitional Rwandan government. That prospect seems to have turned his former domestic allies, including members of the military, against him. At approximately 8:00 P.M. on the sixth, President Habyarimana's aircraft was approaching its landing at the Rwandan capital, Kigali, when someone using sophisticated missiles shot it down. In that crash, not only the Rwandan and Burundian presidents but also the Rwandan army chief of staff died.

An army-based Crisis Committee immediately took over what remained of government in Kigali. The committee utterly excluded the president's legal successor, Prime Minister Agathe Uwilingiyimana. Well-armed units of the presidential guard soon controlled the capital's center. Except for the absence of a declaration by an officers' junta, the maneuvers of April 6 and 7 followed the routines of a military coup. Colonel Théoneste Bagosora, a Hutu extremist who had been the chief advisor of the government's defense minister, appeared to lead the coup.

Whoever instigated Habyarimana's killing, within a day one of the twentieth century's bloodiest massacres had begun. It started with execution of previously prepared attacks on enemies of the ruling clique. The Interahamwe militia spearheaded those attacks. From the start, military men and Hutu Power activists targeted not only members of the Tutsi minority, but also prominent rivals among the Hutu. As Alison Des Forges recounted:

> At first assailants generally operated in small bands and killed their victims where they found them, in their homes, on the streets, at the barriers. But, as early as the evening of April 7, larger groups seized the opportunity for more intensive slaughter as frightened Tutsi—and some Hutu—fled to churches, schools, hospitals, and government offices that had offered refuge in the past. In the northwestern prefecture of Gisenyi, militia killed some fifty people at the Nyundo seminary, forty-three at the church of Busogo, and some 150 at the parish of Bursasamana. A large crowd including Burundian students and wounded soldiers took on the task of massacring hundreds of people at the campus of the Seventh Day Adventist University at Mudende to the east of Gisenyi town.
>
> In Kigali, soldiers and militia killed dozens at a church in Nyamirambo on April 8 and others at the mosque at Nyamirambo several days later. On the morning of April 9, some sixty Interahamwe led by Jean Ntawutagiripfa, known as "Congolais," and accompanied by four National Policemen, forced their way into the church at Gikondo, an industrial section of Kigali. They killed more than a hundred people that day, mostly with machetes and clubs. (Des Forges et al. 1999, 209–10)

Eventually several hundred thousand Rwandan civilians took part in massacres of Tutsi and of Hutu accused of siding with them. They used machetes, clubs, and other crude instruments to do most of the killing.

Between March and July of 1994, assailants slaughtered perhaps eight hundred thousand Tutsi as well as ten to fifty thousand Hutu. But the bloody victory of Hutu supremacists did not last long. Genocide mutated into civil war in Rwanda that spring; after the massacre, the RPF drove Hutu leaders out of the country or into hiding, then took over the government. Tutsi Paul Kagame became Rwanda's head of state. Box 7.1 presents an abbreviated chronology.[1]

---

1. For background, see Adelman and Suhrke 1996; Allen 2002; Amnesty International 1998; Bayart, Ellis, and Hibou 1999; Berkeley 2001; Chrétien 1997; Ellis 1999; Jones 1995; Mamdani 2001; Pillay 2001; Prunier 1995, 2001; Taylor 1999; Uvin 1998, 2001, 2002; de Waal 1997.

BOX 7.1 Selected Chronology of Rwandan Conflicts, 1990–1994

1 Oct 1990	(Predominantly Tutsi) Rwandan Patriotic Front (RPF), first organized in 1987 partly in response to Rwandan exiles' loss of property rights within Uganda, invades northwest from Uganda, suffers extensive losses, but then reorganizes under Paul Kagame, back from military training in the United States
1990–91	Scattered killings of Tutsi begin (for example 300 in Kibilira, October 1990)
1992–94	Extensive flight and expulsion of Hutu from regions captured by RPF, for a total of perhaps a million refugees
Mar–Apr 92	Hutu Power activists organize anti-Tutsi CDR (party) and Interahamwe (militia of governing party MRND)
12 Jul 92	Internationally sponsored peace talks begin in Arusha, Tanzania; killings of Tutsi accelerate thereafter
15 Oct 92	After demonstrations by Hutu activists, Rwandan government repudiates recently signed peace settlement
1/93–3/94	Rwanda imports about 580 thousand machetes in addition to substantial small arms from France, the Unites States, and elsewhere
8 Feb 93	In violation of ceasefire, major RPF offensive begins, reaching within 23 km. of Rwandan capital Kigali
4 Aug 93	In Arusha, Rwanda's president Habyarimana signs peace treaty with RPF, establishing parliamentary system in Rwanda and (under pressure from negotiators) excluding Hutu hardliners from power
8 Aug 93	Hutu Power radio-TV Milles Collines begins broadcasting anti-Tutsi messages
Oct 93	In neighboring Burundi, newly elected Hutu president and thousands of Hutu massacred, with Tutsi-dominated army heavily involved in killing
Nov 93	First battalion of UN peacekeeping mission, commanded by Canadian general Roméo Dallaire, arrives in Rwanda; Hutu Power forces begin systematic distribution of weapons to militants and militias; attacks on civilians and peacekeepers (especially Belgian) accelerate
6 Apr 94	Habyarimana's airplane downed by surface-to-air missile as it approaches Kigali airport, killing him, the army chief of staff, and the president of Burundi; Hutu-dominated military forces seize government, assassinating prime minister and opposition leaders; almost instantly, roadblocks appear around Kigali, attacks on Tutsi begin (20 thousand dead, mostly Tutsi, by April 11)

7 Apr 94	RPF resumes attacks on Rwandan government forces; widespread killing of Tutsis and unaligned Hutus in Kigali and elsewhere, eventually totaling between 500 and 800 thousand deaths, perhaps 75 percent men and boys; women and girls raped by the thousands
13 Apr 94	After the massacre of ten Belgian paratroopers on April 7, Belgium announces withdrawal of its troops from Rwanda
16–17 Apr 94	Coup leaders replace military chief of staff and regional prefects opposed to killings
May 94	As RPF continues to advance, increased killing of Tutsi women and children, often previously spared; Hutu militias prey increasingly on fellow Hutu
4 Jul 94	RPF, commanded by Paul Kagame, takes Kigali
18 Jul 1994	Mass killing ends

From his first visit to the Rwandan capital, Kigali, on August 17, 1993 until the explosion of genocide on April 6–7, 1994, General Dallaire had worked hard to create peacemaking connections among the deeply divided Rwandan parties. On the sixth and seventh of April, he repeatedly met with members of the army-linked Crisis Committee that seized power in Kigali, but failed completely to move them toward organizing peace. They asked him to recommend withdrawing the 450 extremely unpopular Belgian troops of his contingent. He refused. As Dallaire reflected later:

> The Belgian soldiers had become targets of the extremists who wanted to create a climate of fear. Their purpose was, first of all, to get rid of the Belgians and then of the UN. The fanatics had copied the text of the sinister comedies played in Bosnia and Somalia. They knew that western countries didn't want to lose soldiers in a peacekeeping operation taking place in a distant country without strategic value. When they face possible losses of life in their military, like the US in Somalia or the Belgians in Rwanda, westerners flee without considering the consequences for the population left behind. (Dallaire 2003, 311)

Dallaire's UN superiors ordered him not to let his troops use force except in self-defense. On April 7, during his frantic, risky attempts to knit his own command back together, Dallaire saw the corpses of ten Belgians from the UN contingent whom Rwanda's presidential guard had slaughtered. He also heard that the guard had killed Prime Minister Uwilingiyimana and her husband.

Dallaire still had under his protection Faustin Twagiramungu, a moderate leader who would become Rwanda's prime minister after the genocide ended. The general's narrative continues, however, at 1:00 A.M. on April 8:

> Before going to rest, I went to see Faustin, who had spent the day listening to the radio after his rescue. The station RTLM [Radio Télévision Libre des Mille Collines] had reported the murders of moderates and their families. Radio-Television Death encouraged its listeners to massacre Tutsis and asked for the heads of all moderate Hutus, which it considered to be traitors. Recorded music performed by popular singers accompanied these calls. The songs aimed to provoke violence with words such as "I hate the Hutus, hate the Hutus, I hate the Hutus who think that Tutsis aren't snakes." According to Faustin, the apocalypse had begun. What could I say to him? Simply that he was safe at our headquarters and that we would try to find the members of his family who had fled. Deeply upset, I left him. (Dallaire 2003, 335–36)

A slaughter that would eventually kill close to a million Rwandans was already well under way.

Was That a Revolution?

Unquestionably the Rwandan events of April to July 1994 qualify as collective violence (Tilly 2003, 136–42). Did the process as a whole also amount to a revolution? After all, a new Rwandan regime came to power through struggle that tore the entire country apart. The answer is that it depends on what you mean by revolution.[2]

Jeffery Paige, for example, has formulated a very strict definition of revolution:

> A revolution is a rapid and fundamental transformation in the categories of social life and consciousness, the metaphysical assumptions on which these categories are based, and the power relations in which they are expressed as a result of widespread popular acceptance of a utopian alternative to the current social order. (Paige 2003, 24)

---

2. For recent reviews and syntheses, see Barker 1998; Foran 2003; Goldstone and Useem 1999; Goodwin 2001, 2005; Halliday 1999; Katz 1997; Kurzman 2004; Mason 2004; Mayer 2000; Oberschall and Seidman 2005; Sanderson 2005; Schock 2005; Stinchcombe 1999.

If *that* is revolution, then Rwanda did not experience one in 1994 or at any other time. In fact, such a strict definition raises doubts whether any revolution has ever occurred anywhere. Although the French Revolution, an obviously relevant case, made a permanent difference to French politics, it surely did not produce a "rapid and fundamental transformation in the categories of social life and consciousness" (Woloch 1994).

For that matter, Rwanda 1994 did not qualify as revolutionary even by less utopian standards. "Most scholars," declares Misagh Parsa, "define social revolutions as rapid, basic transformations of a society's state and class structures that are carried through class-based revolts from below" (Parsa 2000, 6). Although we might squeeze some class content into the Hutu/Tutsi divide, we could hardly force Rwandan events of 1990–94 into rapid, basic state and class transformations, much less class-based revolts from below. Nor do observers ordinarily apply the word "revolution" to Rwanda's bloodletting. They usually call it genocide, civil war, or ethnic conflict.

I nevertheless argue that a revolution did, in fact, occur in Rwanda. I necessarily do so by expanding the definition of revolution and insisting that the expanded definition better serves this book's purposes of explanation. The definition matters for three reasons. First, asking whether Rwanda's lethal events add up to a revolution draws attention to what those events do and do not have in common with other violent transfers of power.

Second, answering the question returns us to the distinction between causal coherence and symbolic coherence. It brings out the importance of previously existing models for identification of a complex series of events as a revolution, a rebellion, a coup, civil war, or genocide. Those models affect both participants and analysts, as they compare the events at hand with previous events that might belong in the same category.

Third, given the change and variation of regimes we have already witnessed as well as the causal complexity of violent struggle, it is at best implausible that a single set of necessary conditions, not true by definition, exists for all revolutions. The implausibility remains regardless of whether we apply the strict utopianism of Paige's definition or the much broader criteria I set out below. As with wars, social movements, democratization processes, and other forms of contentious politics, causal regularities do not lie in necessary or sufficient conditions that apply to whole, complex historical episodes but in the mechanisms and processes that interlace within those episodes (Tilly 1995b, 1997b, 2001).

The distinction between causal and symbolic coherence matters crucially here. A similar set of problems came up in chapter 6's treatment of collective violence. On one side, I denied that violence constitutes a separate realm subject to *sui generis* laws. I claimed instead that the same cause-and-effect principles apply to violent political interactions as to nonviolent politics. I then identified causal principles governing change and variation in the forms of collective violence. The principles built on the ideas of earlier chapters concerning regimes and repertoires.

On the other side, however, I pointed out that terms such as "civil war" and "terror"—not part of my explanatory scheme—have political meaning despite lacking causal coherence. They have symbolic coherence. They have meaning both because labeling a form of politics as "civil war" or "terror" activates and justifies certain responses on the part of external actors and because each term calls up precedents that shape the behavior of participants, victims, and third parties. As we analyze repertoires and their variations across regimes, we are looking at that very accumulation of meanings.

Consider a telling parallel. When Raphael Lemkin coined the term "genocide" to describe fascist horrors in 1944, he opened the way to grouping terrible events together and to giving them a status in international law; the UN's designation of a government as genocidal increases the pressure on major powers to intervene against the aggressors (Grimshaw 1999, 54–55). Labeling a conflict as genocide means comparing it, at least implicitly, to the Holocaust that annihilated European Jews during World War II. But the existence of a well-defined, legal category provides no guarantee that the phenomena falling under the category all result from the same causes and produce the same effects. Just as homicides vary in their causes and effects despite belonging to a single legal category, so do episodes of genocide.

Similar reasoning applies to revolutions. In its modern sense, the term "revolution" gains part of its meaning from the upheavals that shook France between 1789 and 1799. Once those upheavals had occurred and participants had called what they were doing a revolution, historians sometimes applied the term retroactively to the sort of overturn that occurred in Great Britain as William and Mary displaced James II in 1688 and 1689. But historians, contemporary commentators, and political actors living after 1799 much more commonly applied the model of 1789–99 to programs and events of their own time. Twin ideas took root: (1) that opponents of existing regimes could use the French Revolution's experience as a guide to overturning those regimes, and (2) that analysts could specify the necessary or even the sufficient conditions for revolutions in general by shrewd comparison of existing cases.

The first idea is correct, the second idea wrong. Unquestionably the experiences of French revolutionaries, counterrevolutionaries, and power-holders between 1789 and 1799 supplied later contenders for

BOX 7.2 An All-Purpose Revolution Finder: Proximate Conditions

Revolution = forcible transfer of power over a state in the course of which at least two distinct blocs of contenders make incompatible claims to control the state, and some significant portion of the population subject to the state's jurisdiction acquiesces in the claims of each bloc.

A full revolution combines a *revolutionary situation with a revolutionary outcome:*

REVOLUTIONARY SITUATIONS

1. contenders or coalitions of contenders advancing exclusive competing claims to control of the state or some segment of it
2. commitment to those claims by a significant segment of the citizenry
3. incapacity or unwillingness of rulers to suppress the alternative coalition and / or commitment to its claims

REVOLUTIONARY OUTCOMES

1. defections of regime members
2. acquisition of armed force by revolutionary coalitions
3. neutralization or defection of the regime's armed force
4. acquisition of control over the state apparatus by members of the revolutionary coalition

---

power—including later French contenders for power—with images, models, vocabularies, and strategic lessons. At such high points of struggle as 1830, 1848, 1851, 1870, and 1871, nineteenth-century revolutionaries claimed to be applying, defending, or extending the ideals of 1789: liberty, equality, and fraternity. But regimes vary and change historically. As a result, so do the conditions for violent seizure of state power. No natural history of all revolutions, specifying necessary or sufficient conditions that are not true by definition, is possible.

Box 7.2 describes what is possible. It proposes a less demanding definition of revolution than Paige's or Parsa's. It then breaks the definition into components that are present by definition, but that discipline the work of explaining change and variation in revolutionary struggles. Conditions and processes that cause the listed components vary and change historically.

A revolution, according to this definition, involves a forcible transfer of power over a state in the course of which at least two distinct blocs of contenders make incompatible claims to control the state, and some significant portion of the population subject to the state's jurisdiction acquiesces in the claims of each bloc. A revolution thus defined combines a revolutionary situation with a revolutionary outcome.

A revolutionary *situation* splits a regime into two or more blocs, each one controlling some significant segment of state power and/or territory, and receiving significant popular support. Such was the case when RPF and Hutu Power forces each controlled part of Rwanda. A revolutionary *outcome* shifts control over a state to a new set of rulers. Because states always control concentrated means of coercion and rulers ordinarily deploy those means against their enemies, a revolutionary outcome necessarily includes defection or neutralization of those coercive means as well as acquisition of coercive means by the new rulers. Whether a revolutionary outcome occurred in Rwanda, according to these criteria, depends on how much the Tutsi-led ruling coalition of July 1994 (which by then unquestionably controlled the principal concentrated means of coercion in Rwanda) differed from the Hutu-led ruling coalition of April 1994. Verdict: by this less demanding definition, a revolutionary situation did lead to a revolutionary outcome in Rwanda, and thus a revolution did occur.

At this point, I imagine howls of protest from revolutionary analysts who insist on more change and/or a different kind of change. In particular, analysts of great revolutions typically stipulate a combination of class turnover and social transformation. Let me reply to these imagined protests with a simple claim: the less demanding definition of revolution is actually more useful for purposes of explanation. Its utility includes explanation of major social revolutions.

The proposed definition allows for the fact that major transfers of power vary and change as a function of variation and change in the organization of states and regimes. It blocks the easy, attractive, but fallacious presumption that if people desire a revolution passionately they will make one. It inhibits unproductive backward-reasoning from the fact of a revolutionary outcome to the presumed readiness of a people for revolution. It facilitates comparison among different sorts of shifts in control over states. It integrates the study of revolutions with the analysis of other contentious processes.

In the special case of great revolutions, the scheme turns a tautology—great revolutions involve class turnovers and produce extensive social transformations—into a trio of empirical questions:

1. Under what conditions and how do class actors and coalitions actually produce revolutionary situations?

2. Under what conditions and how do they produce revolutionary outcomes?

3. To what extent, under what conditions, and how do class-based revolutions—combinations of revolutionary situations and outcomes—generate large-scale social transformations?

When, How, and Why Do Revolutions Occur?

As box 7.2 indicates, the distinction between revolutionary situations and revolutionary outcomes facilitates the explanation of revolutions by specifying exactly what must be explained. In the case of revolutionary situations, we must explain the emergence of competing blocs of contenders, commitment of significant segments of the citizenry to each of the contenders, and failure of existing rulers to suppress the blocs and/or citizen commitment to them. In the case of revolutionary outcomes, we must explain defections of regime members, acquisition of armed force by revolutionary coalitions, neutralization or defection of the regime's armed force, and control of the state apparatus by members of the revolutionary coalition. In both cases, origins of the components involve causal regularities. But no grand law governs all components at once.

The crucial causal regularities connect revolutionary situations and outcomes to regimes and repertoires. The greater a regime's capacity and democracy, the more difficult it is for revolutionary contenders to form, for substantial segments of the citizenry to commit themselves on behalf of those contenders, and for those who do organize and commit themselves to escape suppression. Hence revolutionary situations occur much more frequently in low-capacity, nondemocratic regimes than in other types, especially high-capacity, democratic regimes.

As for revolutionary outcomes, the regularities are subtler. Defections of regime members, acquisition of armed force by revolutionary coalitions, and neutralization of a regime's armed force all happen more easily in low-capacity, nondemocratic regimes than others. Control of the state apparatus by members of revolutionary coalitions, however, faces severe obstacles in low-capacity, nondemocratic regimes, since the apparatus itself tends to fragment during such seizures of power. Hence medium-capacity, nondemocratic regimes foster more revolutionary outcomes than other types of regime.

Repertoires also shape revolutions. Chapter 3 laid out a distinction between two broad types of repertoires: parochial, particular, and bifurcated on one side; cosmopolitan, modular, and autonomous on the other. At that point, I insisted that neither type of repertoire was more "revolutionary" than the other. The rest of this chapter amply substantiates that claim. But the availability of one sort of repertoire or the other strongly affects how revolutionary processes occur. Parochial, particular, and bifurcated repertoires embed political actors, identities, and interactions in daily local routines. When everyday resistance to demands of governmental agents cascades across whole populations, for example, it typically does so through activation of previously existing ties in parochial and particular performances such as attacks on tax collectors or landlords.

Cosmopolitan, modular, and autonomous performances, in contrast, propagate across groups and localities even in the absence of dense interpersonal ties, just so long as linking organizations, media, and brokers make the crucial connections. The components of revolutionary situations and outcomes—formation of revolutionary coalitions, popular commitment to those coalitions, rulers' failure to suppress them, defections of regime members, and so on—happen differently according to the availability of different claim-making performances.

Consider just two important examples of repertoire effects. Despite the fact that workers had struggled with their masters for centuries long before, once the strike took shape as a mainly nonrevolutionary form of claim-making during the nineteenth century, it became available as a mighty instrument of revolutionary action thereafter (Haimson and Sapelli 1992; Haimson and Tilly 1989; Shorter and Tilly 1974). The worldwide diffusion of cosmopolitan, modular, autonomous demonstrations as a consequence of nonrevolutionary social movement activity has made the demonstration available as a twenty-first-century revolutionary vehicle in a way that was inconceivable anywhere during the eighteenth century (Tartakowsky 1997, 2004, Tilly 2004a).

These causal principles imply somewhat different distributions of revolutionary situations and revolutionary outcomes across time, space, and type of regime. Revolutionary situations occur frequently, especially in low-capacity regimes. In such regimes, contenders or coalitions of contenders often advance exclusive competing claims to control of some state segment, mobilize commitment to those claims from significant numbers of citizens, and brave rulers who (at least temporarily) lack the capacity and/or will to suppress them. Revolutionary outcomes occur much more rarely because existing rulers and their allies regularly end revolutionary situations by destroying or pacifying their opponents. But they sometimes emerge in the absence of revolutionary situations.

Historically, revolutionary outcomes have occurred without revolutionary situations chiefly in the course of five situations: (1) conquest of an existing state by another very different state; (2) a general war's settlement; (3) intervention of powerful outsiders in national politics; (4) a ruler's sudden, deliberate, and thorough top-down reorganization of power; and (5) a dominant class coalition's withdrawal of support from a state (Bermeo 2003; Bueno de Mesquita, Siverson, and Woller 1992; Lupher 1996; Mason 2004; Tilly 1992, 1993, 2004b; Trimberger 1978).

Unlike revolutionary situations, revolutionary outcomes concentrate in relatively high-capacity, nondemocratic regimes. Such regimes foster revolutionary outcomes because, once a new coalition seizes control of a high-capacity government, its actions produce more far-reaching effects than are possible in low-capacity regimes. But sometimes the revolutionary process itself creates an increase in capacity as compared with the outgoing regime. The first four situations listed above—all of the situations except a dominant class coalition's withdrawal of support—typically increase governmental capacity. The English, French, Russian, and Chinese revolutions all emerged from phases of debilitating civil war with enlarged governmental capacity. The RPF military conquest that subdued Rwanda had nothing near the scope of those earlier military efforts. Paul Kagame was no Leon Trotsky or Mao Zedong. But (with the backing of outside powers) the conquest gave Kagame's government capacities far greater than Habyarimana's had ever exercised.

The distinction between revolutionary situations and civil wars begins to dissolve before our eyes. If we want to maintain the distinction, we will do so by pointing out that they overlap a great deal, but still not perfectly. The elements of a revolutionary situation—contenders with competing claims, citizen commitment to each set of claims, and failed governmental suppression of claims—sometimes come together without constitution of separate armies on each side. Kurt Schock points out that what he calls "unarmed insurrections" (mass mobilizations without confrontations of opposing armies) split regimes in South Africa, the Philippines, Burma, China, Nepal, and Thailand (Schock 2005).

Competing armies, furthermore, sometimes battle for control of a government with little or no civilian support. Lack of widespread commitment to the revolutionary coalitions disqualifies these civil wars as revolutionary situations according to my proposed definition. At least in some phases, recent civil wars in Angola, Uganda, Liberia, Côte d'Ivoire, Sierra Leone, and Colombia have all pitted against each other armies that inspired more fear than love among reluctant civilians.

Oil-producing Angola, for example, experienced genuine revolutionary situations most of the time from the mobilization of independence movements against Portugal in the 1950s through independence (1975) up to the death of UNITA leader Jonas Savimbi in combat (2002). Competing regionally based, and often foreign-backed, armies commanded considerable popular support over much of the long struggle. But in Angola's Cabinda region (separated from the country's main territory by a segment of the Democratic Republic of the Congo), factions of the Front for the Liberation of the

Cabinda Enclave (FLEC) pursued guerrilla warfare against the Angolan government on behalf of the enclave's independence from the 1960s to 2003, when massive governmental forces annihilated the rebel militias. Whatever popular support FLEC enjoyed in the 1960s had long since disappeared.

Similarly, when the Peruvian army and its paramilitaries were battling Sendero Luminoso, Sendero soon lost its initial support from highland indigenous communities, but the national army also quickly wore out its welcome. A significant subset of civil wars lack the civilian support for opposition coalitions that might qualify them as revolutionary situations.

Europe's Revolutionary Situations, 1492–1991

For all the revolutionary richness of the last few decades, concentrating heavily on the recent past risks masking how much the conditions, forms, and processes of revolution vary and change. Let us step back for a longer comparative-historical look. The history of European revolutions over the last half-millennium underscores three points of great importance for the study of regimes and repertoires: (1) that close concentration on class-based revolutions from below introduces deep distortion into our perception of forcible shifts in control over governments; (2) that prevailing forms of those shifts vary and change historically; and (3) that variation and change in the organization of regimes and the character of contentious repertoires shapes what kinds of shifts actually occur.

For six major European regions—the Low Countries, Russia/Poland, France, the British Isles, Iberia, and the Balkans plus Hungary—I have assembled chronologies of revolutionary situations from 1492 to 1991 (Tilly 1993). Those five hundred years took Europe from what historians often call "feudal rebellions" and "Jacqueries" through all the great European revolutions to the breakup of Yugoslavia and the Soviet Union.

As a practical matter, the catalog of revolutionary situations included any episode in which some major segment, region, or city within a previously existing state lived for a month or more under the rule of a domestic opponent, or set of opponents, to the previously established ruler. (Clearly, all six regions, even Russia/Poland, included more than one state over most of the five hundred years, which means that many more than six regimes were at risk to revolutionary situations in any given year.) In the six regions over the five hundred years, the inventory identified 707 region-years in which revolutionary situations occurred, about twenty-four per century in the average region. Roughly translated, major European regions were hosting revolutionary situations in at least one of their regimes almost a quarter of the time during the half-millennium after 1492.

Our All-Purpose Revolution Finder (box 7.2) teaches that to explain the rise and fall of Europe's revolutionary situations over that long a period we must provide defensible accounts of (1) how contenders or coalitions of contenders came to advance exclusive competing claims to control of the state or some segment of it, (2) commitment to those claims by a significant segment of the citizenry, and (3) incapacity or unwillingness of rulers to suppress the alternative coalition and/or commitment to its claims. How each of these three elements of a revolutionary situation took shape varied and changed fundamentally over the course of the five hundred years. Transformations in the character of Europe's prevailing regimes and repertoires reshaped the processes that generated revolutionary situations.

Many different combinations of political actors created revolutionary situations by concerted opposition to existing states. Another two-dimensional classification clarifies the variation involved. One dimension runs from strictly territorial actors to those organized around interests that span multiple territories. At one end of the continuum, we find long-established local communities; at the other, occupational groups and trade diasporas. The other dimension runs from actors that drew from previously established direct connections to those brought into a revolutionary coalition through indirect connections. The dimension's direct end includes kinship groups that maintain continuous connections, while the indirect end includes armies in which individual fighting units remain segregated from each other and the main connections run through senior officers. Figure 7.1 describes the space and identifies six rather different types of revolutionary coalitions that formed recurrently in Europe over the half-millennium under study.

Here are more details on the types of revolutionary coalition depicted in figure 7.1:

- National coalitions activated territorially contiguous populations claiming rights due them as a distinct nation, as when Cossacks who had formed as largely autonomous frontier forces during the Russian empire's expansion rebelled against tightening central control from the Russian or Polish-Lithuanian state. Relations among the Cossacks prior to their rebellions qualify as indirect because most of the time they consisted of smaller bands that often did battle against one another except when they united against the imperial enemy. Within the Spanish empire, sustained demands for independence such as those of the Netherlands (1566–1609, ultimately successful), Catalonia (1640–59, finally defeated), and Portugal (1649–68, successful at last) all created revolutionary situations before their resolutions.

- Communal coalitions also built on territorial bases, but at a smaller scale. From the sixteenth to nineteenth centuries, as warmaking states

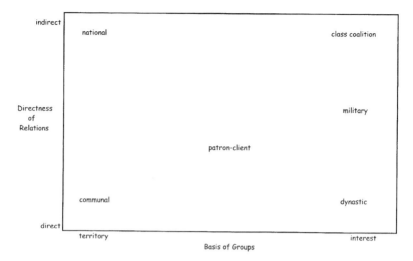

Figure 7.1. Types of revolutionary situation as a function of territory vs. interest and directness of relations among revolutionary actors

demanded increased taxes and manpower from local communities, sometimes those communities joined in massive risings against tax collectors and military recruiters. Religious communities, including those that converted to Protestantism, similarly resisted rapidly increasing top-down control, not to mention subjection to alien religious control. Here the more directly connected actors could build resistance on well-established local ties and daily interaction routines. Pitted against the vastly greater military power of states, communal coalitions never achieved their aims unless they connected with patron-client, national, or dynastic coalitions.

- Patron-client coalitions (common in the earlier centuries, but on their way out by the nineteenth) regularly brought together great lords who were defending their privileges and autonomies against royal encroachment with vassals, dependent communities, or other more localized actors. Communal coalitions sometimes became patron-client coalitions when a warlord responded to local rebellions in defense of his and their interests. Patron-client coalitions occupy a position closer to the space's midpoint, as shown in figure 7.1, because clusters of clients rarely connected directly with each other and typically spread across multiple territories.
- Karl Marx's brilliant analyses of revolution have led subsequent analysts to think of revolutions primarily in *class coalition* terms. English, French, Russian, and Chinese revolutions certainly did involve class coalitions that spanned multiple regions. Even in those cases, however, the class coalitions regularly called up more territorial actors. As

Britain's Glorious Revolution of 1688–89 unfolded, for example, the revolution's major violent struggles did not pit class against class in England, but resulted from William of Orange's finally successful effort to reconquer rebellious Ireland. Although local segments of class coalitions such as workers in a given shop often had a communal character, the coalition as a whole always relied heavily on leaders and brokers who connected members of different social classes across multiple locales.

- Coalitions centering on the *military* sometimes simply used arms to displace whatever military forces the previously established state commanded. But they often attracted communal or class allies. (In fact, early defection of a regime's armed forces has usually been crucial to the success of class-based revolutions [Russell 1974].) During the nineteenth century, Iberia repeatedly experienced revolutionary situations in which military officers issued *pronunciamientos* calling for reform with the backing of powerful landlords, merchants, or other civilian political actors. Military coalitions clearly represented interests rather than territories, but they generally relied in part on indirect connections, with conspiratorial officers bringing in separate units of troops that did not initially belong to the conspiracy.

- Finally, dynastic coalitions seem alien to revolution in the Paige-Parsa conception, yet once played large parts in Europe's revolutionary situations. In Russia and Poland, notably, sixteenth- and seventeenth-century pretenders to the throne (whether authentic royalty or not) regularly joined, led, or even initiated rebellions against the established authority. Some dynastic coalitions more closely resembled patron-client chains than the diagram indicates, yet on the whole loyalty to a given claimant connected followers more closely than in the contingent alliances that underlay Europe's great tax rebellions.

Over the whole period from 1492 to 1991, the relative prevalence of these different coalition types altered dramatically in Europe. One trend follows obviously from our earlier analyses of regimes. As states and therefore regimes increased in geographic scale, coalitions consisting mainly of directly connected political actors became less and less prominent. Revolutionary situations based on communal, dynastic, and patron-client coalitions recurred during the sixteenth and seventeenth centuries, but faded away thereafter. Less directly connected military, class coalition, and national networks of regime opponents took their places.

The second trend—or rather lack of trend—is more surprising. Following theorists who have identified true revolutions as modern phenomena involving bottom-up class coalitions, we might have expected the long-term specialization of state structures and the growth of interest-group politics to produce a decisive shift from territorial to interest-based coalitions. The decline of communal and patron-client coalitions reinforces such an expectation. Contrary to that expectation, however, national coalitions changed character, but remained prominent into the twentieth century.

Between 1570 and 1598, for example, struggles for territorial control among Poland-Lithuania, the Habsburgs, the Ottomans, and their regional allies opened up revolutionary situations in Croatia, Moldavia, Wallachia, and Transylvania. Those revolutionary situations brought together national, communal, patron-client, and dynastic coalitions. Yet national revolutionary situations did not then disappear definitively from the Balkans or Hungary. In the same broad region after 1988, the collapse of state socialist regimes in Albania, Bulgaria, Hungary, Romania, and Yugoslavia (especially the latter) promoted national revolutionary situations galore. Divided sovereignty leading to vicious civil war in Croatia and Bosnia-Herzegovina marked the low point of that process.

Nevertheless, the stakes of national revolutionary coalitions changed fundamentally from the sixteenth to the twenty-first century. In sixteenth-century Europe, rulers and their rivals sought to control low-capacity states with the modest revenues, intermittent military support, and prestige that rule provided. Powerful rulers did not run unitary states, but governed patchworks of segmented states (te Brake 1998; Tilly 1992). Every state above a very small scale depended on indirect rule, in which intermediaries enjoying substantial autonomy retained control over their own territories, clients, and military means, but collaborated with nominal national rulers' military, fiscal, and religious programs at a price. Hence revolutionary situations always involved the breaking of vertical ties, as multiple communities banded together in resistance to top-down demands, warlords withdrew their contingent support from rulers, and dynastic rivals of current incumbents drummed up followings.

By the twentieth century, the growth of territorially extensive high-capacity states with their own programs of cultural homogenization through education, the media, and ritual representation of their histories had produced a paradoxical situation. On one side, every regime above a very small scale actually contained a wide variety of populations, cultures, and territories; international migration and the expansion of states from core areas into new territories limited the effects of top-down homogenization. On the other side, state-led efforts fortified two nationalistic claims that often contradicted each other:

> We control the state, and therefore we have the right to define the nation.

versus

We are a separate nation, and therefore we have the right to our own state.

When well-connected, culturally distinct minorities occupied contiguous territories, the second claim often justified demands for autonomy or secession. The Soviet Union's breakup featured a sensational series of nationalist demands, based largely on the titular nationalities around which Communist leaders had built their Moscow-centered rule (Beissinger 1993,

---

BOX 7.3 Revolutionary Situations in the Balkans and Hungary, 1892–1991

1896–98	Independence war in Crete, Greek and British intervention
1902–3	Independence war in Macedonia
1905	Independence war in Crete (finally annexed to Greece, 1910)
1907	Peasant insurrection in Moldavia
1907–9	**Young Turks' revolution in Ottoman empire, including insurrection in Macedonia**
1907	**Albanian insurrection, independence war, independence**
1918–19	**Bloodless revolution in Hungary, ending in foreign military intervention**
1923	Overthrow and assassination of Stamboliski in Bulgaria
1935	Venezelist rising in Greece
1938	Revolt in Crete
1943–45	**Anti-fascist resistance in Yugoslavia**
1944–45	Greek civil war
1949	Greek civil war
1955–56	Enosis struggle in Cyprus, with British intervention
1956	Attempted revolution in Hungary ended by Soviet intervention
1963–64	Civil war in Cyprus
1974	**Turko-Cypriot war, including guerrilla warfare in Cyprus**
1989–91	**overturning of communist regimes in Albania, Bulgaria, Hungary, Romania, and Yugoslavia**
1991–93	**Civil war in Croatia, Bosnia-Herzegovina**

Note: Bold denotes revolutionary situations that produced revolutionary outcomes lasting a year or more.

2001; Kaiser 1994; Khazanov 1995; Tishkov 1997, 1999). In the Soviet Union, in Soviet satellite states, and in Yugoslavia, nationalist coalitions regularly produced revolutionary situations from 1989 through the early 1990s.

Box 7.3 illustrates how seriously and persistently national revolutionary coalitions formed during the twentieth century. For the Balkans and Hungary, it lists each revolutionary situation in my catalog over the century beginning in 1892, marking those with revolutionary outcomes in bold type. The list makes clear how extensively interstate war, civil war, and revolutionary situations entangled in the region. In the Balkans, most of the century's revolutionary situations had a significant national component. Before World War I, they concentrated in the disintegrating Ottoman Empire. Although they continued in former Ottoman territories thereafter, national revolutionary situations also occurred frequently in the lands that had once belonged to the Austro-Hungarian empire as well as the perilously independent countries between the two empires. They produced frequent revolutionary outcomes, most sensationally in the overthrow of state socialist governments between 1989 and 1991.

Lest we think nationalism a Balkan peculiarity, however, remember the Basques and Catalans in Spain, the Irish in the British Isles, the great civil wars of the Soviet Union between 1918 and 1921, and the new surge of nationalism that finally broke apart the Soviet Union between 1987 and 1992. The (ironically named) United Kingdom alone faced deep revolutionary situations in Ireland in 1916 and 1919–23, then again in Northern Ireland from 1969 to the recent past. The struggle of 1919–23 created an independent Irish state. National revolutionary situations and outcomes did not disappear in the twentieth century.

Change and Variation in Europe's Revolutionary Coalitions

As the recent history just canvassed suggests, however, changes in the prevalent forms of revolutionary coalitions followed contrasting rhythms in different regions. Regions of relatively early state consolidation included the Low Countries, France, and the British Isles. Those regions saw early peaks of communal, patron-client, and dynastic revolutionary coalitions in reaction to that very consolidation. But once fairly high-capacity governments took control of the same regions, revolutionary coalitions formed less frequently and shifted toward the national and class coalition types.

In Iberia, Napoleon's partial conquest left behind governments of middling capacity with substantial, rather autonomous armed forces. As a result, for more than a century after the French Revolution, Iberia's political history featured multiple revolutionary situations involving

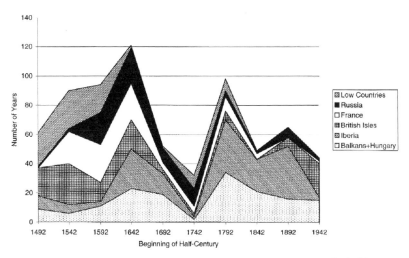

Figure 7.2. Years in revolutionary situations for European regions by half-century, 1492–1991

either reformist or conservative military coalitions. More generally, comparisons among the six European regions reinforce the main point of my argument: the changing structure of regimes largely determined the frequency and character of revolutionary situations.

As figure 7.2 shows, these diverse regional histories summed into striking fluctuations in the overall frequency of revolutionary situations in Europe from 1492 to 1991. Remember what the figure does *not* tell us. It does not record the overall frequency or intensity of violent conflicts, the timing of revolutionary outcomes, or even the extent of destruction in the course of revolutionary situations. It represents the number of years a region's regimes faced at least one revolutionary situation: opponents of the previously existing authorities controlled some substantial segment of the state for a month or more. It therefore tells us about long-run changes in the relative vulnerability of different regions' regimes to the formation of effective revolutionary coalitions.

The high point of revolutionary activity by this measure took place between 1642 and 1691. During that half-century, the array of revolutionary situations was as follows:

Low Countries: struggles between municipal federations and supporters of the Princes of Orange for control of the Netherlands

Russia/Poland: cossack, noble, and municipal rebellions against Russian and Polish rulers

France: the Fronde (1648–53), plus numerous regional rebellions, typically initiated by the state's increased fiscal demands

British Isles: multiple civil wars, terminating with the Glorious Revolution of 1687–92

Iberia: continuation of the Catalan and Portuguese revolts (begun in 1640), compounded by revolutionary struggles within Portugal

Balkans and Hungary: repeated wartime rebellions in Wallachia, Transylvania, Moldavia, and Hungary

By that time a division had already opened up between states that consolidated early and late. In early consolidators the Dutch Republic, France, and England revolutionary situations regularly accompanied the efforts of rulers to establish central control before 1650. Despite France's vast divisions in the Fronde, for example, Louis XIV (1643–1715) faced nothing like the many years of revolutionary situations confronted by his royal predecessors during the sixteenth and early seventeenth centuries.

Over the century following 1691, the frequency of revolutionary situations declined across Europe as the early consolidators strengthened their top-down controls. Then the French Revolution of 1789–99 provided a new model (and, temporarily, a new sponsor) of revolutionary mobilizations elsewhere on the continent. After 1800, the bulk of revolutionary situations arose in the Balkans, Hungary, and Iberia. During the twentieth century, struggles over Ireland brought revolutionary situations back to the British Isles. But revolution never again returned to its seventeenth-century peak.

The data show us three half-century high points of revolutionary situations, in descending order: 1642–91, 1792–1841, and 1892–1941. Each accompanied a burst of international warfare: the first an amazing proliferation of wars on the European continent, around the Mediterranean, and on the high seas; the second especially the wars of the French Revolution and Napoleon; the third a series of Balkan wars leading up to World War I. Although the scale of wars increased, the overall frequency of revolutionary situations declined from one high point to the next.

That decline resulted from the net movement of regimes out of the low-capacity, nondemocratic quadrant into higher capacity and/or more democratic forms of rule. By the nineteenth century, according to this measure, revolutionary mobilization concentrated in Iberia and the Balkans, where low-capacity, nondemocratic regimes still prevailed. Over the long run, communal, patron-client, and (more slowly) military revolutionary coalitions became less common in Europe as national and class coalition situations came to dominate the revolutionary scene. Even after World War II, nevertheless, every one of our six European regions hosted at least a few revolutionary situations.

A trustworthy trio of truisms emerges from this survey of Europe's revolutionary situations. First, the character, loci, and frequency of revolutionary situations varied and changed fundamentally as a function of regime transformations. At least half of what revolution could mean depended on the organization of states and their regimes. In that sense, the history of revolutions tracks the histories of states and regimes. Second, general explanations of revolutions in terms of favorable, necessary, or sufficient conditions might possibly work for a single era and region, but have no chance of validity for all European revolutions, much less all revolutions everywhere. Third, the decomposition of revolutionary situations into formation of contenders, commitment to contenders' claims, and failures of rulers to suppress the first two disciplines the search for valid explanations, and holds some hope of identifying processes—not prior conditions—that recur in a wide variety of revolutions.

Beyond truisms, some broad processes did promote revolutionary situations over most of the period under study. When discrepancies increased sharply and visibly between what states demanded of their best-organized citizens and what they could induce those citizens to deliver, revolutionary situations became more likely. In Europe, pressures of external wars recurrently caused rulers to make such excessive demands, and thus to crystallize widespread resistance. When states made demands on their citizens that threatened widely shared collective identities or violated rights attached to those identities, holders of those identities often formed revolutionary coalitions, acquired broad commitment to those coalitions, and resisted immediate suppression. Communal and national revolutionary actors repeatedly formed through just such processes.

In another recurrent process, when the power of rulers visibly diminished in the presence of strong competitors, groups of citizens that had previously complied with hated demands acquired the opportunity to organize more open and widespread resistance to existing regimes. If rulers lost major wars after exacting great sacrifices from citizens as they pursued those wars, all three conditions sometimes converged in powerful stimuli to revolutionary situations. As a consequence of losses in World War I, the Austro-Hungarian, Ottoman, Russian, and German empires all faced revolutionary situations that either exploded or overturned their previously existing regimes.

Finally, as European-wide openings of 1945, 1968, and 1989 indicate, revolutionary situations became more frequent when international models and signs of external support for revolutionaries became more visible. At those points, revolutionary coalitions not only emulated each other, but often communicated and collaborated (Horn and Kenney 2004; Suri 2003). Those momentous events, however, turn our attention to the second half of our problem: revolutionary outcomes.

Revolutionary Outcomes

Let me suppress my urge to present an equally detailed survey of Europe's revolutionary outcomes from 1492 to 1991. Although revolutionary outcomes occurred much less frequently than revolutionary situations, they offer their own fascinating complexities. They require us to explain how defections of regime members occur, by what means revolutionary coalitions acquire armed force, what processes neutralize the regime's armed force or cause its specialists in violence to defect, and how revolutionary coalitions actually take control of an existing state apparatus. Again we discover that the conditions and processes promoting these outcomes vary and change as a function of prevailing regimes and repertoires.

In the case of Europe, the overall rise of governmental capacity profoundly transformed the prospects for revolutionary outcomes. Rising capacity meant that the stakes of revolution increased; it became less and less likely that a revolutionary coalition would walk away from an unsuccessful bid for power retaining control of its own region or segment of government. It reduced the frequency with which the very revolutionary seizure of power would fragment that power into partly autonomous segments, only some of them under command of the putative revolutionaries. But it also greatly increased the social impact of any revolutionary outcome that actually did occur. In the hands of Lenin and Trotsky, even the ramshackle apparatus of the Russian imperial state became an instrument of fundamental social transformation.

The changing relation of military to civilian power in European states greatly affected the prospects, conditions, processes, and effects of revolutionary outcomes. Over the long run of 1492 to 1991, Europe moved, broadly speaking, through three contrasting military eras: (1) a time in which relatively autonomous military forces such as great lords' private armies and municipal militias occasionally joined the equally limited forces of nominal rulers in making war and putting down rebellion; (2) a period in which commercially organized mercenaries, hired with borrowed money and eventually paid from tax revenues, became Europe's dominant national military forces; and (3) the displacement of mercenaries by standing armies operating under central civilian control and dependent on national fiscal establishments.

How early and effectively these changes occurred largely determined changes in regime capacity (Tilly 1992, chap. 3). We have already seen Iberia and the Balkans struggling with incomplete subordination of their military forces at a time when Western Europe's states had long since suppressed significant autonomous military forces and placed state armed forces under firm fiscal and administrative restraints. As a result, effective seizures of state power by military-led revolutionary coalitions persisted in Iberia and the Balkans into the twentieth century when they had faded from memory in France, Italy, the United Kingdom, the Low Countries, Scandinavia, and Germany. Outside of Iberia and the Balkans, even the major authoritarian regimes of the 1920s and 1930s came to power led by civilians with military ambitions rather than by professional military officers.

Changing repertoires also exerted some independent influence on the prospects, conditions, processes, and impacts of revolutionary outcomes in Europe. As chapter 8 shows in much greater detail, the emergence of partially democratic, high-capacity regimes promoted the formation of a distinctive social-movement repertoire. That repertoire included a package of claim-making performances all of which had precedents, but none of which had ever previously been widely available in one another's company: formation of special-purpose associations and named public coalitions; petition drives; public meetings, rallies, demonstrations, strikes, public statements; and lobbying.

Once in place, those performances facilitated creation of temporary political actors across the boundaries of class, gender, ethnicity, and region; promoted coordination of simultaneous action spanning whole regimes; and connected national mobilizations with local bases of recruitment and support. In high-capacity, semi-democratic regimes such as those of France, the repertoire became the means by which nineteenth- and twentieth-century revolutionaries pressed the bulk of their claims. Social-movement revolutionaries sometimes even won. For all their later reversals, French revolutions of 1830, 1848, and 1870 became European-wide models for elite-led but popularly based transfers of national power.

Non-European Revolutions since 1945

Most of the 127 civil wars James Fearon and David Laitin identified across the world from 1945 to 1999 involved revolutionary situations, at least for part of their duration. Each armed group attracted enough popular support to produce a sharp divide within the regime (Fearon and Laitin 2003). But, like most revolutionary situations elsewhere and before, most of them ended without revolutionary transfers of power. As in Europe from 1492 to 1991, far fewer revolutionary outcomes occurred than revolutionary situations.

Even by Misagh Parsa's demanding definition of revolutions as "rapid, basic transformations of a society's state and class structures that are carried through class-based revolts from below," however, a number of postwar revolutions occurred outside of Europe. Parsa himself identifies Iran

(1979) and Nicaragua (1979) as genuine social revolutions, and treats the overthrow of Philippine president Ferdinand Marcos (1986) as a "political" revolution that consequently produced less change than occurred in Iran and Nicaragua (Parsa 2000, 26–28).

Other analysts of postwar revolutions have included these sets from outside of Europe:

Vietnam, Nicaragua, Iran, Poland, Afghanistan, the Philippines, Cambodia, Zimbabwe, South Africa, Palestine (Goldstone, Gurr, and Moshiri 1991)

China, Vietnam, Cuba, Nicaragua, Iran, South Africa (DeFronzo 1991)

China, North Vietnam, Cuba, Congo, South Yemen, Benin, Ethiopia, Guinea-Bissau, Cambodia, South Vietnam, Laos, Madagascar, Cape Verde, Mozambique, Angola, Afghanistan, Grenada, Nicaragua, Egypt, Syria, Iraq, Algeria, North Yemen, Sudan, Libya (Katz 1997, 25–26)

Vietnam, China, Bolivia, Cuba, Algeria, Ethiopia, Angola, Mozambique, Cambodia, South Vietnam, Iran, Nicaragua, Grenada (Goodwin 2001, 4)

The rosters vary chiefly because criteria differ; Goodwin's, for example, only includes "major social revolutions," while Katz's covers all seizures of power he regards as emulating the models of Russia (1917), Egypt (1952), and Iran (1979). Yet all agree that genuine revolutions—in this book's terms, combinations of revolutionary situations with revolutionary outcomes—took place in Asia, Africa, and South America as well as Europe during the post-World War II years.

These various analysts also agree that the possibility of revolution depended heavily on the organization of regimes. Speaking of Central America, for example, Goodwin argues:

[R]evolutionary movements became strong only where militarized yet infrastructurally weak states were consistently exclusionary, antireformist, and more or less indiscriminately repressive of their political opponents (moderates and reformists as well as revolutionaries) throughout the 1960s and 1970s. This formula applies to Nicaragua, El Salvador, and Guatemala, but *not* to Honduras, where the military was more tolerant of politically moderate labor and peasant unions and even introduced a significant, if limited, agrarian reform "from above" during the early 1970s. (Goodwin 2001, 143)

Although this passage describes conditions rather than processes, elsewhere Goodwin makes clear that in such states the very application of repression generated resistance rather than compliance (see also Brockett 2005; Francisco 2005; Mason 2004).

By now we understand that revolutionary movements arise all over the world, and have been arising for centuries, but that most of them fail to produce revolutionary transfers of power. The question we must answer is, given a revolutionary situation, what processes cause defections of regime members, acquisition of armed force by revolutionary coalitions, neutralization or defection of the regime's armed force, and acquisition of control over the state apparatus by members of a revolutionary coalition? By now we also know the most general answer: that it depends on prevailing regimes and repertoires. Which processes produce these outcomes therefore vary and change historically.

For the postwar period outside of Europe, nevertheless, some general principles seem to hold. Most notably, the international connections of regimes have played even more potent parts in the success or failure of revolutionary bids for power than they did before World War II. Revolutionary success has always depended on the ability of dissidents to amass coercive force, overcome the regime's coercive force, and use force to take over governmental organization. Defection of regime members has always facilitated these moves. Some of the other general principles include the following:

- Except for decolonization, great powers and their agent, the United Nations, have resisted alterations of state boundaries with unprecedented tenacity and effectiveness.
- As a consequence, secessionist and irredentist movements have seen their chances of success plummet, but a revolutionary coalition that established military superiority within an existing state's territory faced increasing prospects of external recognition, financial aid, and international help with postwar reconstruction.
- How the great powers reacted to bids for revolutionary power shifted significantly from decolonization to the Cold War to the postsocialist period.
- After the Cold War ended, great powers including the United States became increasingly reluctant to intervene in revolutionary situations unless the conflict threatened to expand into adjacent regimes or hinder access to precious resources such as oil.
- In contrast, international nongovernmental organizations greatly increased their advice and aid on behalf of revolutionary challengers that made appropriate displays of their commitment to human rights, democracy, and development. To some extent, international institutions such as the United Nations, the International Labor Organization, and the World Bank supported those interventions.

- Global trade—both licit and contraband—in oil, diamonds, other minerals, timber, drugs, sexual services, weapons, and other high-value commodities greatly increased.
- The trade made low-capacity, nondemocratic regimes that exported or transported such high-value commodities increasingly vulnerable to economic fluctuations over which they had little control, and thus more subject to revolutionary challenges when their sources of revenue and support declined.
- The trade also made it increasingly feasible, even attractive, for rebel forces to support themselves by dealing in high-value commodities or forming alliances with gangsters and merchants dealing in those commodities. Contraband for arms became a common exchange.
- In some cases (Chechnya, Liberia, and Colombia come to mind) the exchange became so easy and lucrative that putative revolutionaries gave up serious attempts to seize central power in favor of profiteering.
- Yet elsewhere (as Angola's history illustrates), disciplined revolutionaries used similar resources to seize power and destroy their enemies.

Together, these major changes transformed the world's low-capacity regimes and their claim-making repertoires. Always important, international responses and economic support for competing military organizations came to dominate the prospects for revolution during the late twentieth century.

On balance, these changing revolutionary processes give democrats and capitalists plenty of room for worry. They increase the possibility that twenty-first-century revolutions will bring to power warlords who rely on criminal activity and resource monopolies rather than popular consent for the viability of their governments; that new rulers will fail to establish regimes in collaboration with their citizens; that their citizens will remain poor as rulers enrich themselves; and that their low-capacity, nondemocratic regimes will remain vulnerable to challenge from the next contraband-wielding military entrepreneur that comes along. Such regimes will resist the relatively peaceful, relatively democratic contentious politics of social movements. To clarify what their citizens will miss thereby, the chapter 8 examines how social movements work.

CHAPTER EIGHT >>
Social Movements

THE VISUALLY VIBRANT FRENCH SPA TOWN of Evian-les-Bains spills down from the Alps to the south shore of Lake Geneva—Lac Léman in French. It commands a beautiful slope across the lake from Switzerland's Lausanne and east of Switzerland's Geneva. Evian's seventy-five hundred inhabitants often see their streets fill with tourists, conventioneers, and aficionados of mineral water. From June 1–3, 2003, the small city hosted a summit meeting of the G8, eight of the world's leading economic powers. On Sunday morning, the first of June, delegation heads from across the world arrived in Evian by helicopter and boat. Because demonstrators blocked the way from Geneva, lesser members of delegations and the press had more trouble getting to the conclave.

The G8 heads of delegation included Jacques Chirac (France), Vladimir Putin (Russia), George W. Bush (United States), Jean Chrétien (Canada), Tony Blair (United Kingdom), Gerhard Schröder (Germany), Junichiro Koizumi (Japan), and Silvio Berlusconi (Italy). Other participants in the summit included Konstantinos Simitis (president of the European Council); Romano Prodi (president of the European Commission); Kofi Annan (secretary general of the United Nations); James Wolfensohn (president of the World Bank); Horst Köhler (managing director of the International Monetary Fund); Supachai Panitchpakdi (director general of the World Trade Organization); plus the chief executives of Egypt, Algeria, Nigeria, South Africa,

Morocco, Senegal, Mexico, Switzerland, Brazil, China, Saudi Arabia, Malaysia, and India (G8 2003, delegations).

In his summit summary, meeting chair Jacques Chirac announced that the august group had reached agreements on (1) strengthening growth worldwide, (2) enhancing sustainable development, (3) improving security, and (4) regional issues concerning Iraq, Israel, Palestine, North Korea, Afghanistan, Iran, Algeria, and Zimbabwe (G8 2003, chair's summary). This was no lightweight assembly.

Meanwhile, between 100 and 150 thousand demonstrators gathered on both sides of the nearby French/Swiss border to hold their own countersummit in response to Evian's great power deliberations. About a third each of the demonstrators came from Switzerland, France, and the rest of Europe. They stated their opposition to multinational corporations, to the indebtedness of poor countries, and to world financial institutions. But they also brought more particular national issues to the table. Looking back a month later, activists from Geneva complained that "[t]he big French organizations were not enthusiastic and [were] totally tied up in the massive mobilizations and general strike to save the pension system and public education" (APCM 2003, 2). Protest organizers had announced their intention of shutting down the summit by blocking access to Evian. But they settled for shows of numbers, unity, and commitment.

Days before the G8 opened, counterdelegations started gathering in separate camps, clustered by political tendency:

> On the French side, the Communist League's outlook dominated the Intergalactic Village, while libertarians assembled a short distance away in the Anti-Capitalist Anti-War Alternative Village. On their side, activists of ATTAC [Association for a Tobin Tax to Aid Citizens] joined a number of non-governmental organizations, the French Communist Party and the Greens in fields adjacent to the landing strips of the Annemasse airport. On the Swiss side, a more heterogeneous campground formed on land near the Lausanne University campus. During the morning [of June 1], after blocking roads at dawn, two processions converged at the frontier. (Agrikoliansky, Fillieule, and Mayer 2005, 9)

French police did not let demonstrators anywhere near Evian. Some clashes between police and activists occurred on the road from Geneva to Evian as well as at the return of demonstrators to Geneva. In Geneva itself, small groups of protesters broke windows, smashed cars, and torched shops. Mostly, however, thousands of Europeans stood together, lofted banners, chanted slogans, and demonstrated their united opposition to global capital.

The flurry of coordinated interactions around the shores of Lac Léman at the start of June 2003 belonged to a much larger series of transnational mobilizations. Since the 1990s, antiglobalization activists had regularly shadowed international financial and political summits with countersummits. The December 1999 meeting of the World Trade Organization brought something like fifty thousand demonstrators to Seattle, and drew worldwide attention to antiglobalization organizing.

In January 2001, when a World Economic Forum of great powers was meeting in well-guarded Davos, Switzerland, an international conference called the World Social Forum convened in Porto Alegre, Brazil. That countersummit had legs: it became a model not only for later worldwide gatherings but also for regional and local antiglobalization organizations as well. A week after the Evian protest, for example, the first-ever Portuguese Social Forum met in Lisbon. One major organizer of the Evian demonstrations, indeed, called itself the Léman Social Forum.

Mobilization against the representatives of global capital overlapped with organized opposition to American military interventions in Afghanistan and Iraq. Millions of people across the world, for instance, joined the antiwar demonstrations taking place on February 15, 2003. (In Paris alone, from 100 to 250 thousand demonstrators—depending on whether you believe the police or the organizers—marched on that day.) Organizers and optimists spoke hopefully of a "global civil society" that would take action against the ravages of globalization. This new burst of transnational activism during the 1990s and the early twenty-first century marked the latest phase of a two-hundred-year-old form of contentious politics: the social movement.[1]

The Distinctions of Social Movements

People often use the term "social movement" loosely for all sorts of popular causes, as well as for the organizations and people participating in them. That happens in part because social movements have become so ubiquitous—at least in relatively democratic countries—that we simply

1. For surveys, syntheses, and critiques on social movements, see Banaszak, Beckwith, and Rucht 2003; Beckwith 2001; Buechler 2000; Casquette 1998; Diani and McAdam 2003; Fillieule 2005; Goldstone 2003; Goodwin and Jasper 2004; Ibarra 2003; Koopmans 2005; Markoff 1996; Mathieu 2004; McAdam, McCarthy, and Zald 1988; McAdam, Tarrow, and Tilly 2001; Meyer 2004; Meyer and Minkoff 2004; Pichardo 1997. For transnational social movements and the idea of global civil society, see Anheier and Themudo 2002; Bandy and Smith 2004; Barrett and Kurzman 2004; Beyeler and Kriesi 2005; Bob 2005; Chandhoke 2002; Deibert 2000; Edelman 2001, 2003; Giugni 2004; Granjon 2002; Keck and Sikkink 1998; Langman 2005; Maiba 2005; Mertes 2004; Murphy and Pfaff 2005; Oleson 2005; Pianta 2001; della Porta 2005; della Porta and Tarrow 2004; Rucht 2004; Smith and Johnston 2002; Tarrow 2005; Wainright 2005; Wood 2004.

take them for granted as the natural form of popular claim-making. As we know them, however, social movements had never existed anywhere in the world three centuries ago. Then, during the later eighteenth century, Western Europeans and North Americans began putting together the elements of a new political form. During the first half of the nineteenth century, the social movement became widely available to ordinary people in North America and Western Europe as it began spreading to other parts of the world (Tilly 2004a).

From that point on, the social movement followed quite a different historical trajectory from military coups, civil wars, and revolutions. It also acquired features distinguishing it from other vehicles of contentious politics that expanded more or less simultaneously and in interaction with social movements. Those companion forms included electoral campaigns, interest-group activity, and labor-union struggles. Social movements stood out from other varieties of contentious politics: they involved sustained challenges to power-holders in the name of one or more populations living under the jurisdiction of those power-holders by means of public displays dramatizing those populations' worthiness, unity, numbers, and commitment.

We have encountered social movements frequently in previous chapters under the headings of "repertoires," "regimes," and "regime change." Here, however, I take up the distinctive properties of social movements as a form of contentious politics. The chapter's organizing arguments are as follows:

- Social movements differ from other forms of contentious politics in their combination of sustained campaigns of claim-making, an exceptional array of claim-making performances, and concerted displays of supporters' worthiness, unity, numbers, and commitment.

- From their eighteenth-century origins onward, social movements have proceeded not as solo acts but as interactive campaigns.

- Those campaigns target specific objects, most often holders of power, but they also address other political actors and general publics.

- Social movements combine three kinds of claims: claims to identity, standing, and specific programs.

- The relative salience of identity, standing, and program claims varies significantly among social movements, among claimants within movements, and among phases of movements.

- Democratization promotes the formation of social movements, but by no means do all social movements advocate or promote democracy.

- Nevertheless, social movements assert popular sovereignty—the right of ordinary people to hold power and limit the actions of rulers.

- As compared with locally grounded forms of popular politics, social movements depend heavily on political entrepreneurs for their scale, durability, and effectiveness.
- Once social movements establish themselves in one political setting, modeling, communication, coalitions, and collaboration facilitate their adoption in other connected settings.
- The forms, personnel, and claims of social movements vary and evolve historically.
- Although many social movements established international connections from the form's first emergence, the later twentieth century brought a remarkable proliferation of transnational movements and connections among movements.
- The social movement, as an invented institution, could disappear or mutate into some quite different form of politics. In fact, the partial detachment of demonstrations from other elements of the social-movement repertoire, the rise of such performances as the counter-summit, and the shifting organizational bases of mobilizations like the Evian event of 2003 hint at the possibility of a split between national and international versions of future social movements.

Put together, these principles imply that within any given era and region social movements follow some empirical regularities because of mutual influence and modeling. They exhibit symbolic coherence: naming a campaign as a social movement (rather than, say, as an instance of terrorism) influences the reactions of both participants and other political actors as it brings relevant models of action into play. But they do not exhibit causal coherence in the sense of conforming to *sui generis* laws. Instead, the causal regularities of social movements are those of contentious politics in general.

Elements of Social Movements

As they evolved in Western countries, social movements combined three major elements: (1) sustained campaigns of claim-making; (2) an array of public performances including marches, rallies, processions, demonstrations, occupations, picket lines, blockades, public meetings, delegations, statements to and in public media, petition drives, letter-writing, pamphleteering, lobbying, and creation of specialized associations, coalitions, or fronts—in short, the social movement repertoire; and (3) repeated public displays of worthiness, unity, numbers, and commitment (WUNC) by such means as wearing colors, marching in disciplined ranks, sporting badges that advertise the cause, displaying signs, chanting slogans, singing militant songs, and picketing public buildings.

Unlike a demonstration, a petition, a declaration, or a mass meeting, a *campaign* extends beyond any single event—although social movements often include petitions, declarations, and mass meetings. A campaign always links at least three parties: a group of self-designated claimants, some object(s) of claims, and a public of some kind. Even if a few zealots commit themselves to the movement night and day, most participants move back and forth between public claim-making and other activities, including the day-to-day organizing that sustains a campaign. Participants in Evian's countersummit returned to other lives after the third of June, 2003.

The social-movement *repertoire* overlaps with such other repertoires of political phenomena as trade-union activity and electoral campaigns. During the twentieth century, special-purpose associations and coalitions in particular began to have an enormous impact on political work throughout the world. They operated both inside and well outside the zone of social movements. But the integration of most or all of these performances into sustained campaigns marks off social movements from other varieties of politics.

That brings us back to WUNC. Worthiness, unity, numbers, and commitment characterize effective demonstrations. But they also characterize other activities of an effective social movement: participants' petitions, press interviews, pamphlets, ribbon-tying, badge-wearing, flag-displaying, and just plain attendance at meeting after meeting after meeting (Polletta 2002). WUNC matters politically because it conveys crucial political messages. Geneva's 2003 activists worried about the self-styled anarchists who burned cars and smashed shops precisely because those actions subverted their movement's claims to worthy unity.

As chapter 3 indicated, we can distinguish roughly among three sorts of political claims that people make by means of WUNC displays: identity claims, standing claims, and program claims.

1. *Identity* claims declare that "we"—the claimants—constitute a unified force to be reckoned with. Such claims commonly include a name for "us," such as "Cherokees," "Diamond Cutters," "Southsiders," or "Citizens United against X."
2. *Standing* claims assert ties and similarities to other political actors, for example as excluded minorities, established trades, properly constituted citizens' groups, or loyal supporters of the regime.
3. *Program* claims involve stated support for or opposition to actual or proposed actions by the objects of movement claims.

On the whole, the three sorts of claims reinforce each other: a distinctive identity makes it easier to claim public standing, and standing gives credence to public support for a program. Now and then, nevertheless, a loose and temporary front, coalition, or alliance forms around some program (for example, calls on public officials to intervene in a case of police brutality) without much insistence on identity or standing. The three types of claims vary and change in partial independence of each other.

Put together and backed by WUNC displays, identity, standing, and program claims convey the message that a distinct political actor has marched onto the scene. That actor may simply represent a public conscience to which officials ought to pay attention. But under the right circumstances it could also form a voting bloc, create a new political party, organize a boycott, provide forces for an uprising, or otherwise interfere with politics as usual. WUNC says: pay attention to us; we matter.

Taken singly, each of these elements exists separately and in combination with other forms of contention. Military parades, religious processions, and fraternal order celebrations, for instance, often present their own versions of WUNC displays. Sustained campaigns frequently enliven contested elections, and social-movement performances such as public meetings also take place outside of movements. The *combination* of sustained campaigns, public performances, and WUNC displays, however, sets off the social movement from other forms of contentious politics. Participants in the Evian protests of June 2003 were clearly carrying on social-movement activity rather than performing a coup d'état, pursuing an election campaign, striking against employers, making a revolution, or exercising interest-group politics.

Antiglobalization activists of the 1990s and thereafter put their own stamps on social-movement campaigns, performances, and WUNC displays. They used the Internet, cellular telephones, and other electronic means of communication expertly, kept world-spanning coordination networks in action, played to world television, and invented such forms as Intergalactic and Anti-Capitalist Anti-War Alternative Villages. Yet their transnational connections as such did not distinguish them sharply from their predecessors. More likely the new forms and scales of those connections bear the seeds of longer-term change.

From the start, social movements have often connected across national borders and even across oceans. The venerable eighteenth-century international mobilization against the slave trade has a claim to be the first major social movement anywhere (d'Anjou 1996; Drescher 1994; Eltis 1993). During the nineteenth century, social-movement politics frequently went international over such issues as Irish independence and workers' rights (Hanagan 1999, 2003; Keck and Sikkink 2000). Evian's agitators were packing new connections, techniques, and programs into their own versions of a well-worn contentious routine. It remains to be seen whether a deeper split will open up between the character of local, regional, and national social movements, on one side, and the transnational arena, on the other.

Regimes and Social Movements

Regimes necessarily shape social movements, including the sheer possibility that social movements can occur at all. Regimes shape repertoires in three distinct ways:

1. By means of controls over claim-making repertoires—not only the broad division among prescribed, tolerated, and forbidden performances, but also the historical development that gives organized workers' gatherings greater scope in one regime, religious processions greater standing in another, and so on; in Evian, French and Swiss authorities had little choice but to tolerate activists' gatherings, meetings, and marches, but the Swiss authorities stepped in when anarchists started breaking and smashing both public and private property in Geneva.

2. By constituting both potential claimants and potential objects of claims; the Evian mobilization brought together a variety of constituted French and Swiss political groupings as well as the G8 participants, the press, and local authorities.

3. By producing streams of issues, events, and governmental actions around which social-movement campaigns rise and fall; we have already seen Geneva's activists complaining that their French allies were preoccupied with French disputes concerning pensions and public education.

The shaping of social movements by regimes operates both across regimes and within regimes. Across regimes, previous histories lay down different webs of issues, performances, symbols, and political alignments that significantly affect the conduct of social movements. As we have seen, some contemporary Indian social movements proceed with an array of chariots, religious symbols, and rituals that seem exotic to Western eyes. With equal clarity, Evian's Intergalactic Village, Greens, and ATTAC mark the 2003 mobilization as belonging to the twenty-first-century Western European world of social movements.

Within regimes, both long-term change and short-term variation affect the rise, fall, and mutation of social movements. Chapter 3 linked the long-term rise of British social movements to deep transformations of the British regime after 1750. In chapter 4, we caught sight of shorter-term changes in the Indian regime as the Hindu nationalist party BJP benefited from national rejection of the previously dominant Congress party in the parliamentary elections of 1989. The BJP rose from just two parliamentary seats in 1984 to eighty-eight in 1989, then to 119 in 1991. Buoyed by that move of political opportunity in their direction, Hindu activists renewed their campaign to destroy Ayodhya's Babri Masjid mosque, staged large pilgrimages to the site, confronted Indian authorities, and finally demolished the offending structure in December 1992. Similarly, fluctuations in French national politics, including Jacques Chirac's troubled presidency, shaped French activists' participation in the confrontations of Evian.

Changes in political opportunity structure (POS) made the difference. In static terms, POS consists of (a) the multiplicity of independent centers of power within the regime, (b) the openness of the regime to new actors, (c) the instability of current political alignments, (d) the availability of influential allies or supporters, and (e) the extent to which the regime represses or facilitates collective claim-making. Dynamically, it consists of decisive change in any or all of these elements. In India, Congress's losses in the 1989 election produced changes in all five elements that favored BJP activism. New centers of power were emerging within the regime; Congress's decline opened the regime somewhat to new actors; the political scene was clearly becoming more unstable; at least for Hindu activists, influential allies and supporters were becoming more readily available; and (again at least for Hindu activists) the regime was moving toward facilitation of collective claim-making. Although the BJP did not yet dominate the government, its members of parliament provided new allies, however reluctant, to anti-Muslim activists.

Regime variations in POS largely explain an otherwise puzzling fact—namely, the enormous concentration of social movements in democratic regimes, especially high-capacity, democratic regimes. From the start, social movements have occurred mainly in democratic regimes and have multiplied with democratization. But by no means does that follow as a matter of definition. As India's Hindu–Muslim conflicts should remind us, social movements have often mounted antidemocratic campaigns, especially nativistic and nationalistic campaigns. European fascists generally began their drives for power in the social-movement mode, creating or infiltrating special-purpose associations, holding meetings and demonstrations, and making public statements on behalf of their causes (Paxton 1995). Once democratic regimes come into play, they facilitate democratic, nondemocratic, antidemocratic, and narrowly interested social-movement campaigns alike. As with extremist parties in the electoral arena, democracies face a dilemma with antidemocratic social movements: does repressing them protect or damage democratic institutions?

Concretely, social-movement campaigns, performances, and WUNC displays depend on regime-backed rights, notably rights of association, assembly, and speech. Without sturdy defenses for such rights, powerful objects of unwelcome claims regularly retaliate against the claimants, call down governmental repression on the performances, and break up displays of WUNC. The Freedom House ratings of regimes' political rights and civil liberties reviewed in chapter 4 underline a point that should be obvious to any observer of contemporary regimes: those rights concentrate heavily in democratic regimes, especially high-capacity, democratic regimes. (Low-capacity, democratic regimes such as Jamaica and the Philippines more often feature divisions between zones in which the state actually enforces rights and others in which those rights have little sway.) Broad, equal, binding consultation and protection both build on and promote rights of association, assembly, and speech.

Nevertheless, when democratic and nondemocratic regimes connect closely with each other, claimants in the nondemocratic regimes more frequently borrow social-movement forms in making their own claims. Colonial India provides a striking case in point: for all the distinctiveness of India's contentious repertoires, from late in the nineteenth century the subcontinent's nationalist leaders organized associations, meetings, demonstrations, delegations, and petitions. The Indian National Congress (INC, founded in 1885) originated in just such an effort. During its early years, the INC made its claims in the manner of an orderly British pressure group, by meeting, lobbying, petitioning, and drafting addresses; it acted as a social-movement organization (Bose and Jalal 1998, 116–17; Johnson 1996, 156–62). Today, mass media have made the performances of social movements—especially their demonstrations—so visible throughout the world that dissidents in nondemocratic regimes often emulate their forms.

Demonstrations

Of all the events that recur in social movements, demonstrations best illustrate the synthesis of campaigns, performances, and WUNC displays. Among other things, they combine local symbols, practices, issues, and personnel with forms of interaction that are visible and meaningful well outside of any particular locality.

Before social movements existed, Europe's and North America's recognized corporate groups sometimes carried out performances that shared properties with demonstrations as they took shape during the nineteenth and twentieth centuries. Military units strutted their stuff in blatant displays of worthiness, unity, numbers, and commitment. But when authorized by local officials, guild workers, fraternal orders, and religious processions did the same. From those authorized marches and assemblies, social-movement activists took both their models of action and their legal precedents.

The *Oxford English Dictionary (OED)* nicely juxtaposes two meanings of the word "demonstration," with their first reported uses of the word in these two different senses, both dating from the late 1830s:

> A show of military force or of offensive movement, especially in the course of active hostilities to engage the enemy's attention while other operations are going on elsewhere, or in time of peace to indicate readiness for active hostilities.
>
> A public manifestation, by a number of persons, of interest in some public question, or sympathy with some political or other cause; usually taking the form of a procession and mass-meeting.

Both definitions imply a synthesis between a campaign and displays of unity, numbers, and commitment, if not necessarily of worthiness.

As the *OED* definition hints, political demonstrations involve more flexibility than do religious processions or military parades. Some center on a march through public thoroughfares, others consist mainly of a gathering in a field, square, or park, while still others combine a public meeting with marches to and/or from the meeting. Where demonstrations take place depends on a combination of local symbolic geography, governmental control over public space, and convenience in accommodating large numbers of people safely. But organizers of demonstrations do not, on the whole, hide them from public view. On the contrary, they make a deliberate effort to impress their WUNC displays on authorities, audiences, and media.

Whether directed by authorities, staged in support of authorities, or mounted against authorities, the demonstration has a remarkable dual character that it shares with few other contentious performances. It shows rather different internal and external faces. Internally, assembling, marching, giving voice, and displaying common membership through costumes, badges, and banners signal to participants that they belong to a disciplined, formidable force. William H. McNeill calls the process "muscular bonding" (McNeill 1995). Externally, the same collective acts project WUNC: worthiness, unity, numbers, and commitment. Moreover, they match WUNC with specific programs, typically through visible and audible presentation of demands, slogans, and self-descriptions: "We, People

United on Behalf of *X*, demand that authorities accept, defend, or enact *X* and that you onlookers support *X*."

Eventually WUNC display via demonstrations turned out to be an extraordinarily flexible and effective form of claim-making. In its pristine form as a march to or from a public meeting it advertised the presence of a determined political force far more dramatically than any gathering in a closed space alone could do. As it developed over time, it became a means of massing people adjacent to major sites of power such as parliaments, capital buildings, stock exchanges, and central squares. It ramified into powerful variants such as the petition march, the silent vigil, the blockade of a city street or major highway, the ostentatious destruction of symbolically significant goods, and the occupation of factories, schools, or public buildings. More so than the public meeting or the petition drive, it took on a wide variety of forms and underwent extensive historical evolution. Small wonder that police forces created special units and tactics to control demonstrations (Fillieule 1997b).

In Western Europe and North America, the effort to marry WUNC displays with sustained campaigns took decades, and faced serious legal obstacles. As England's Chartists launched their national campaign on behalf of workers' political rights in 1838, they energetically organized processions and mass meetings to galvanize and publicize their cause (Goodway 1982, 24–37). In August 1838, a provincial magistrate complained of the local Chartists:

> Their meetings are called together by a public bellman who goes through the streets giving notice "that a public meeting of the Working Men's Association will be held at half-past eight o'clock in the Evening at the Chartists' Hall." . . . At the time appointed, a drummer and fifer frequently go through the streets to assemble the Chartists, who proceed to the place of meeting in great numbers, to the terror of the peaceable inhabitants. (Thompson 1984, 70)

By that time, however, English authorities had grudgingly acknowledged the legality of such demonstrations, so long as they did not violate the Riot Act by actively threatening further illegal behavior such as property destruction or sedition (Thompson 1984, 71).

Scholars have most carefully traced the demonstration's emergence in England, France, and Ireland (Blackstock 2000; Farrell 2000; Favre 1990; Fillieule 1997a; Jarman 1997; Mirala 2000; Pigenet and Tartakowsky 2003; Robert 1996; Tartakowsky 1997, 1999; Tilly 1986, 1995a). In those countries, struggles for legal toleration of demonstrations lasted half a century or so. The struggles proceeded along three lines: extending to ordinary people the right of association that members of the ruling classes had long since enjoyed; expanding the right to hold public meetings from authorized bodies such as religious congregations, fraternal orders, workers' guilds, militias, and parish councils to self-directed groups of citizens; and bargaining out the right of large self-directed groups to walk through the streets on the way to or from an assembly.

Demonstrations and Political Rights

To this day, national authorities throughout the world generally resist granting a legal right to demonstrate as such. Democratic governments usually put rights to associate, to form labor unions, and to strike explicitly into their legal codes. Demonstrations do not receive that treatment. Instead, both democratic and nondemocratic governments typically control demonstrations through legislation governing freedom of assembly, freedom of speech, and public order, with police as the main enforcers (Fillieule 1997b; Lindenberger 1995; della Porta and Reiter 1998).

Avoidance of specific jurisprudence for demonstrations has an interesting pair of effects. When states create special legal regimes for strikes, trade unions, professional societies, or voluntary associations, to some extent they segregate the particular institution from more general definitions of rights and obligations. That under specified legal conditions organized industrial workers have the right to lay down their tools does not necessarily authorize farm laborers, government employees, or university students to strike against farms, governments, or universities.

What is more, creation of specialized legal status for unions and strikes means that government officials play a significant part in determining which workers have the right to strike, whether a striking union actually represents the workers in a given plant, whether a strike constitutes a threat to national interests, and what actions strikers do and do not have the right to perform. As a result, establishment of the right to strike regularly forced workers to abandon forms of collective action (for example, attacks on employers' property) they had previously used quite effectively (Perrot 1974).

The more general attachment of demonstrations to citizens' rights and obligations with regard to speech, association, and assembly, in contrast, produces effects in two directions. First, expansions or contractions of rights to speech, association, and assembly inevitably impinge on demonstrations whether or not they begin with demonstrations. But second, by their incorporation of claims to identity, standing, and program, demonstrations challenge authorities to resist or recognize shifts in boundaries between tolerated and forbidden political actors, actions, and claims.

As a result, demonstrations involve consequential assertions of more general rights. In many contemporary, predominantly Muslim countries, for example, students have limited rights to demonstrate, while committed Islamists enjoy no such rights (Wiktorowicz 2003). In chapter 4 we saw that very distinction at work in Morocco, where the nominally Muslim state cracked down on Islamists hard after 2001, but left some space for students and secular human-rights activists.

Because of the intimate ties between political rights and demonstrations, shifting frequencies and characteristics of demonstrations provide important clues of alterations in regimes, including boundaries between tolerated and forbidden political actors, actions, and claims. We can see shifting boundaries at work in Gita Deneckere's outstanding analysis of contentious actions during the nearly ninety years between Belgium's independence (1830) and 1918. Deneckere assembled a catalog of "collective actions" in Antwerp, Brussels, Ghent, and Liège spanning 1831 to 1918 from a wide range of archives, official publications, periodicals, and historical works. It shows us how the demonstration's rise tracked the expansion of political rights and civil liberties, but also helped drive that very expansion.

Deneckere's catalog includes about 440 occasions on which people gathered and made collective demands "in the socio-economic field of conflict," which means largely workers' actions and actions concerning work (Deneckere 1997, 10). Her narratives actually overflow the definition, however, since they include such events as patriotic resistance to the creation of a separate Grand Duchy of Luxemburg as part of Belgium's independence settlement of 1838–39 (Deneckere 1997, 66–68).

Deneckere's selection principle still excludes widespread violence surrounding the Netherlands's separation of church and state in 1834, just as the uneasy union of north and south was breaking up. Similarly, it omits extensive struggles over relations between church and state within Belgium between 1879 and 1884. Intense competition between organized French- and Dutch-speakers over language rights and political power likewise casts only faint shadows over Deneckere's chronology of collective actions (Carter 2003; Zolberg 1978). Within Deneckere's chosen field, nevertheless, her evidence demonstrates a great increase in performances attached to the social-movement repertoire, in particular demonstrations.

Her evidence reveals significant alterations between 1830 and 1918. Before the semi-revolutionary mobilizations of 1847–48, Deneckere's contentious events feature workers' assemblies and marches to present petitions, attacks on the goods or persons of high-priced food merchants, and work stoppages by people in multiple shops of the same craft. During the earlier nineteenth century, few junctions formed between ardent democrats and workers.

Workers' actions then frequently took the form of turnouts: occasions on which a small number of initiators from a local craft went from shop to shop demanding that fellow craft workers leave their employment to join the swelling crowd. The round completed, turnout participants assembled in some safe place (often a field at the edge of town), aired their grievances, formulated demands, and presented those demands to masters in the trade. Negotiations often took place in meetings of delegations from both sides. Turned-out workers then stayed away from their shops until the masters had replied satisfactorily or forced them to return. Before 1848, we see little of the social-movement repertoire in play.

Immediately after the outbreak of the 1848 revolution in France, Belgian republicans and radicals began calling for a fraternal revolution in their own country. But the government reacted quickly, among other measures by expelling Karl Marx from the country on March 4. By the time of Marx's hasty exit, the liberal-dominated Belgian government had already taken steps to forestall revolutionary mobilization in Belgium. It did so chiefly by reducing wealth requirements for voting and office holding, nearly doubling the Belgian franchise. The split between French and Dutch speakers worked to the government's advantage, since republicans and advocates of the French model came disproportionately from among the Francophones. That fact raised doubts about democratic programs on the Flemish side, ever wary of plots to incorporate Belgium into France (Dumont 2002, chap. 3). After all, the French *had* conquered and incorporated Belgium in 1795, only half a century earlier.

Between the political reforms of 1848 and the 1890s, the character of Belgian contention, as registered in Deneckere's catalog, altered considerably. Turnouts practically disappeared, for example, as demonstrations and large-firm strikes became much more frequent and prominent. In the 1890s, regionally and nationally coordinated general strikes emerged as major forms of contentious action. During the later decades of the nineteenth century, Deneckere's catalog also reveals a significant shift toward the demonstration as a site of public claim-making. Crude counts from the catalog of Belgian public meetings, demonstrations, strikes, and petitions by decade indicate the extent of change, as shown in figure 8.1. (I have included turnouts, coalitions, and general strikes in the tallies for strikes.)

As the figure makes clear, a great wave of demonstrations swept over Brussels, Ghent, and Liège during the 1880s and 1890s. Organized workers and democratic activists were arriving on the Belgian national scene as formidable actors. The founding of the Workers' Party (1885) brought new focus to democratic demands. In response to organized pressure, the Belgian Parliament adopted modified manhood suffrage in 1893 and

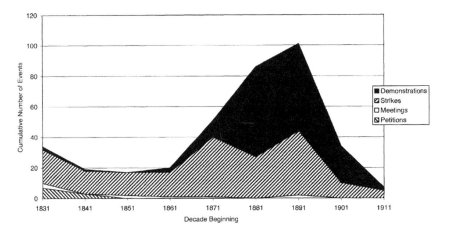

Figure 8.1. Petitions, meetings, strikes, and demonstrations in Belgium, 1831–1918

proportional representation in 1898. Then, as figure 8.1 shows, a partial demobilization occurred after century's end. Despite another general strike in 1913, the German occupation of 1914–18 made the period after 1910 a low point for demonstrations, meetings, and strikes in Belgium.

Working-class organizations mounted far more than strikes. They lay behind a great many of the meetings, demonstrations, and petitions. Petition delegations soon disappeared as ways of making public claims, in favor of autonomously organized meetings and, especially, demonstrations. (The measureable decline of public meetings, however, results in part from an illusion: Belgian demonstrations, as we might expect, often started from or included public meetings, but this tabulation accepts Deneckere's designation of a gathering as mainly meeting or mainly demonstration.) Organized workers increasingly made international connections: we first encounter the International Working Men's Association in Ghent, for example, during a demonstration in 1876.

Many of the later demonstrations occurred in the course of attempts to organize general strikes. As Deneckere says, workers and socialist leaders designed general strikes to be large, standard in form, coordinated across multiple localities, and oriented toward national holders of power. Instead of particular localities and trades, participants commonly represented themselves generally as socialists or as workers at large. Belgian workers began making nationwide program claims for socialism at large, identity claims as coherently connected workers, and standing claims that emphasized their improper exclusion from power.

These new activities signaled a significant shift of repertoire, offering evidence that social movements established themselves in Belgian popular politics between 1848 and 1900. There, street politics and parliamentary politics came to depend on each other. Social movements provided a significant portion of the connective tissue.

French Demonstrations

Demonstrations have inevitably figured in major catalogs of contentious events for a number of different countries. When it comes to catalogs focusing more specifically on demonstrations, however, the United States and France have predominated.[2] While scholars' largest, most detailed demonstration catalogs concern the recent experience of American cities, specialists in French history have assembled the fullest long series of demonstrations. Vincent Robert has done ground-breaking work on nineteenth-century Lyon; Danielle Tartakowsky has inventoried demonstrations throughout France as a whole from 1919 to 1968; Olivier Fillieule for Nantes from 1975 to 1990 and Marseille from 1980 to 1993; and Jan-Willem Duyvendak for France as a whole (but drawing events from just one newspaper issue per week) from 1975 to 1990.

Tartakowsky has also drawn counts of demonstrations for Paris alone from annual reports of the Police Prefecture, warning that police counts include "many very small mobilizations and festive gatherings that posed the same sorts of problems for the office of Order and Traffic as did more directly political mobilizations" (Tartakowsky 2004, 14). Figure 8.2 groups all of these authors' findings together.

Tartakowsky's fifteen thousand catalogued events and the smaller collections of Fillieule and Duyvendak establish that after World War I the demonstration became a major means of advertising political identities and programs in France. The police counts for Paris describe an enormous increase during the 1990s. Every major political controversy produced its own surge of demonstrators—and often of counterdemonsrators as well.

Both right-wing (for example, Croix de Feu) and left-wing (for example, Communist) groups initiated disproportionate shares of demonstrations;

2. For catalogs and analyses of demonstrations, see Barber 2002; Beissinger 2002; Deneckere 1997; Duyvendak 1994; Favre 1990; Favre, Fillieule, and Mayer 1997; Fillieule 1997a, 1997b; Giugni 1995; Hug and Wisler 1998; Imig and Tarrow 2001; Kriesi et al. 1995; McCarthy, McPhail, and Smith 1996; Mueller 1997, 1999; Oberschall 1994; Oliver and Maney 2000; Oliver and Myers 1999; Olivier 1991; Olzak 1989; della Porta 1995; della Porta and Reiter 1998; Robert 1996; Rucht and Koopmans 1999; Rucht, Koopmans, and Neidhardt 1998; Sugimoto 1981; Tarrow 1989; Tartakowsky 1997, 1999, 2004; Tilly, Tilly, and Tilly 1975; Titarenko et al. 2001.

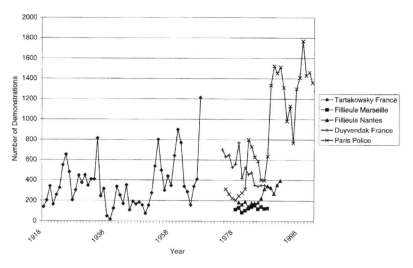

Figure 8.2. Number of demonstrations in France and selected French cities, 1919–2002

more often than groups in the center of the right–left continuum, they were the political groupings that recurrently asserted their identities as significant actors and sought to place forbidden issues on local or national agendas. Demonstrations served both purposes in France. World War II and the German occupation, as we might expect, produced the low point of demonstration activity registered by these series. During that exceptional period, women complaining to authorities about food shortages and high prices became the most frequent initiators of the rare demonstrations.

Although differences in method and geographic scope forbid strict comparisons, the data also make clear that demonstrations became far more common after World War II than they had been before. Even the 814 demonstrations Tartakowsky identified during the great Popular Front mobilization of 1936 did not match the 899 demonstrations of 1961 (massive conflict around the Algerian war) or the 1,213 of 1968 (immense movement activity mostly opposing the de Gaulle regime). As students of new social movements will not be surprised to learn, the all-time peak up to that point took place in 1968.

Although the series of Fillieule, Duyvendak, and the police point in somewhat different directions, put together they indicate that the demonstration continued to thrive in France after 1968. In 2002 and 2003 alone, France mounted some huge demonstrations:

- May 1, 2002, in Paris and elsewhere, 1.7 to 2.6 million people (depending on whether you believe the police or the organizers) marched against the presidential candidacy of right-winger Jean-Marie Le Pen.
- February 15, 2003, in Paris, 100 to 250 thousand marched against the imminent American invasion of Iraq.
- May 25, 2003, in Paris, 150 to 600 thousand demonstrated against proposed retirement reforms.
- June 10, 2003 (France as a whole), 440 thousand to 1.5 million demonstrated against the same reforms (Tartakowsky 2004, 15).

We begin to understand why the Evian organizers of June 1, 2003 might have found their French collaborators distracted by domestic campaigns.

In France, the broad correspondence between periods of relative democratization and periods of frequent demonstrations comes across vividly. The demonstration came into its own during the early Third Republic, declined during World War I and (especially) the German occupation of World War II, then flowered as never before during the postwar years. Tartakowsky herself worries that early twenty-first-century demonstrations are losing their cross-class, revolutionary character and that their connections with fundamental political issues as single-issue groups makes them more effective at bringing huge forces to the street for one day at a time. Even those that campaign for changes in legislation, she complains, "no longer confront public authorities in their established locations; they substitute spectacular displays for shows of force, and detach their actions from the rhythms of parliamentary activity. Demonstrations that are less attached to the center of the political system, furthermore, rarely draw on the historical precedents available to them" (Tartakowsky 2004, 79).

Elsewhere, Tartakowsky signals the substitution of literary, popular culture, and foreign models for the classic May Day image of *le peuple en marche*.

Having gone to the streets for many a great Parisian demonstration, I can empathize with Tartakowsky's nostalgia. But as observers of demonstrations at large, we should consider another interpretation of what is going on: that shifts in the paths, forms, and occasions of French demonstrations reflect alterations in the politics of French social movements in general. Single-issue organizations that specialize in displaying WUNC on behalf of their issues alone, and draw on international connections as they do so, occupy more and more of the social movement space. Mutations of the demonstration continue as social movement politics continue to change.

The Soviet Union's Collapse

Although demonstrations have played significant parts in social movements from early in the nineteenth century, during the later twentieth century they began to detach from full-fledged social movements in a spectacular series of mobilizations within and against high-capacity, nondemocratic regimes. The highly visible social-movement mobilizations of 1968 provided images and models that spread throughout the world (Horn and Kenney 2004; Suri 2003). Having seen demonstrations in the media or having participated in them while abroad, activists—especially students—well outside of established democracies began assembling to offer WUNC displays in symbolically important locations. During the fateful year 1989, students at Beijing's Tienanmen Square provided the most dramatic example (Zhao 2001). But prodemocracy demonstrations also grabbed headlines and television screens that year in Budapest, Berlin, Prague, and Warsaw.

Behind many of 1989's demonstrations lay political changes in the Soviet Union. After a quick shuffle of leaders, liberalizer Mikhail Gorbachev arrived at the Soviet Communist Party's head in 1985. Gorbachev soon began promoting *perestroika,* a shift of the economy from military to civilian production, toward better and more abundant consumer goods, and in the direction of higher productivity. He began withdrawing Soviet troops from the quagmire of Afghanistan. He also moved hesitantly forward with *glasnost,* a program that was meant to open up public life by releasing political prisoners; accelerating exit visas for Jews; shrinking the military; reducing the Soviet Union's external military involvement; and ending violent repression of demands for political, ethnic, and religious autonomy. When it came to the detailed components of democratization, Gorbachev concentrated on increasing protection more than on securing breadth, equality, or binding consultation.

All this happened as the Soviet government was attempting to generalize and liberate national markets. That meant reducing government involvement in production and distribution of goods and services. As a result, the central government's capacity to deliver rewards to its followers declined visibly from one month to the next. In response, officials and managers engaged in a sort of run on the bank: wherever they could divert fungible assets to their own advantage, they increasingly did so. They started stealing the state (Solnick 1998). The more one person stole, the more reason the next person had to steal before no assets remained. Soon a large share of government resources had moved into private hands.

On the political front, a parallel and interdependent collapse of central authority occurred. The results of Gorbachev's economic program alienated three different groups: (1) producers who had benefited from the previous regime's emphasis on military enterprise, (2) consumers who lacked ready access to one of the new distribution networks, and (3) officials whose previous powers were now under attack. The new political program opened up space for critics and rivals such as Boris Yeltsin. From his base in Moscow, Yeltsin rose to control the Russian federation. He promoted Russian nationalism with apparent disregard for the Soviet regime, including Gorbachev.

Gorbachev himself tried to check the threatened but still intact military and intelligence establishments through conciliation, caution, and equivocation. That effort, however, alienated reformers without gaining him solid conservative support. Simultaneously, he asked the legislature for emergency powers that would free him to promote economic transformation. His bid for independent authority brought him into conflict with rival reformers, political libertarians, and defenders of the old regime alike.

Opportunism channeled by the old regime's own institutions undid the regime. Russia's Communists had long dealt with non-Russian regions by co-opting regional leaders who were loyal to their cause. The regime had integrated such leaders into the Communist party, recruited their successors from among the most promising members of designated nationalities, but trained them in Russia and accustomed them to doing business in Russian. Candidates for regional leadership made long stays in Moscow under close supervision. The ones who proved smart, tough, and reliable returned to their respective homelands to lead the Communist parties.

At the same time, the Soviet government had dispatched many Russians to staff new industries, professions, and administrations, promoting Russian language and culture as media of administration and interregional communication. In that system of rule, the central government granted regional power-holders substantial autonomy and military support within their own territories so long as they ensured supplies of government revenue, goods, and conscripts. The regime struck immediately against any individual or group that called for liberties outside of this system. Such a system could operate effectively under two conditions: first, that regional leaders receive powerful support from the center and, second, that their local rivals have no means or hope of appealing for popular backing. Those conditions held most of the time from the 1930s to the early 1980s. The system survived.

Yet the system's strength also proved to be its downfall. Gorbachev and collaborators actively promoted opening of political discussion, reduced military involvement in political control, tolerated alternatives to the Communist connecting structure, and made gestures toward truly contested elections. At the same time, they acknowledged their reduced capacity to reward faithful followers. They asked Soviet citizens to remain loyal through hard times, but provided few guarantees of future rewards for loyalty.

Widespread popular demands for guarantees of religious and political liberties arose in 1987. But disintegration really began during the next two years, as nationalist and nationalizing leaders rushed to seize assets and autonomy that would fortify their positions in the new regime. Most of those who came to power in the Soviet Union's successor states had already held important positions under the Soviet regime. But even politicians who had long served as party functionaries began portraying themselves as independents, reformers, or nationalists. Many of them actually succeeded.

As the USSR disintegrated, accordingly, both regional power-holders and their rivals suddenly acquired strong incentives to distance themselves from the center. Most of them started recruiting popular followings. Ambitious regional leaders established credentials as authentic representatives of the local people, urged priority of their own nationalities within territorial subdivisions of the USSR they happened to occupy, and pressed for new forms of autonomy. In the Baltic republics and those along the USSR's western or southern tiers, new nationalists capitalized on the possibility of special relations with kindred states and authorities outside the Soviet Union—Sweden, Finland, Turkey, Iran, the European Community, and NATO. Those relations offered political leverage and economic opportunity that the Soviet Union itself was increasingly incapable of providing.

Time horizons contracted rapidly. On the large scale and the small, people could no longer count on payoffs from long-term investment in the existing system; they reoriented to short-term gains and exit strategies. In a referendum of March 1991, Gorbachev sought a new Union treaty, with greater scope for the fifteen republics but preservation of a federal government's military, diplomatic, and economic priority. Six republics (Latvia, Lithuania, Estonia, Moldavia, Armenia, and Georgia) had already started the process of declaring themselves independent. Their leaders boycotted the referendum. Results for the other republics confirmed the division between Russia and non-Russian portions of the tottering federation. From outside, venture capitalists, development economists, world financial institutions, and powers such as the United States, Turkey, Iran, and the European Union all grabbed for their pieces of the action. At the same time, they tried to contain ugly spillover from Soviet turmoil.

Ethnic segmentation, economic collapse, undermining of the old regime's powers, and Gorbachev's principled refusal to engage in that regime's customary vigorous, violent repression transformed public politics. Among other things, they combined to open opportunities for right-wing movements. Many observers and participants on the Soviet scene feared a bid of the military, intelligence, and Communist Party establishment to reverse the flow of events. History proved them right to worry. In August 1991, a self-identified Emergency Committee sequestered Gorbachev. The committee failed to accomplish a coup, however, as Yeltsin led resistance in Moscow.

Over the next four months, Yeltsin sought to succeed Gorbachev. He proposed to take power not as party secretary but as chief of a confederation maintaining a measure of economic, military, and diplomatic authority over its component states. Even that effort ended with dissolution of the Soviet Union into an ill-defined and conflict-ridden commonwealth. The Baltic states absented themselves entirely from the commonwealth, while other Soviet republics rushed for the exits.

Although momentous political struggles were tearing the Soviet Union apart, most of them did not resemble social movements. Even today, through most of the former Soviet space, the full combination of campaigns, performances, and WUNC displays has failed to gain the political standing that it rapidly acquired in such former Soviet satellites as Poland (Ekiert and Kubik 1999; Glenn 2001; Osa 2003). Only as relatively democratic regimes develop should we expect social movements to multiply. Yet one performance from the social-movement repertoire— the street demonstration—figured importantly in the Soviet collapse, and continues to produce political consequences through much of the former Soviet zone.

Demonstrations in the Disintegrating USSR

What part did demonstrations play in the Soviet Union's disintegration? In a massive, close investigation of the years between 1987 and 1992, Mark Beissinger has shown how widely Soviet claimants adopted demonstrations as their means of broadcasting their demands, how those demands shifted from calls for reform to calls for political autonomy, and how demonstrations led increasingly to violent encounters over time. Beissinger centered his analysis on two large catalogs of episodes from the beginning of 1987 to August of 1991: one of 5,067 protest demonstrations with at least a hundred participants, the other of 2,173 incidents in which at least fifteen people attacked persons or property (Beissinger 2002, 462–65). Beissinger also prepared catalogs of strikes and of demonstrations before 1987, but concentrated his analysis on the two large files. In preparing the two, he and his collaborators consulted 150 different sources including Russian-language newspapers, wire services, compilations by Soviet dissidents, émigré publications, and reports of foreign monitoring services.

Beissinger points out that demonstrations and attacks did occur occasionally in the Soviet Union before Mikhail Gorbachev began his reform programs. In April 1965, for example, one hundred thousand people gathered in Yerevan, Armenia to commemorate victims of the Ottoman expulsion and massacre of Armenians fifty years earlier (Beissinger 2002, 71). But under that repressive regime both demonstrations and collective attacks by anyone other than state authorities remained very rare. The script ran differently after 1985. Once such Soviet Republics as Estonia and Armenia started edging toward independence with foreign support, leaders of titular nationalities across the Soviet Union began making demands for autonomy or independence. Figure 8.3 describes monthly changes from 1987 through 1992.

Setting his catalogs beside his own deep knowledge of Soviet politics, Beissinger was able to show how initial demands for internal reforms of the Soviet Union gave way to bids for regional autonomy and independence, by no means all of them successful. Early successes of demands for independence in such places as Estonia and Latvia encouraged further demands across a wide range of republics, which resulted in increasing violence as unsuccessful claimants faced competition and repression.

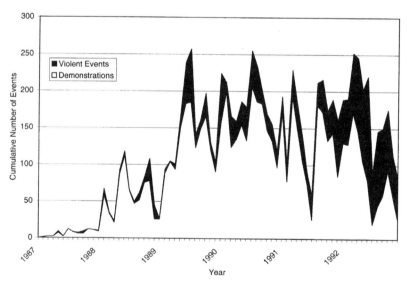

Figure 8.3. Demonstrations and violent events in the Soviet Union and successor states, 19987–1992
Source: Data supplied by Mark Beissinger

What began as a largely peaceful process soon radicalized and escalated. In principle, a straightforward cycle could have occurred: a decentralized USSR could have granted partial autonomy to a certain number of titular nationalities, incorporated them into its governing structure, repressed the more unruly and threatening claimants, and returned to a revised version of Soviet business as usual. Instead, fifteen nationalities gained total independence, others acquired rights they had never enjoyed under Soviet rule, and what Beissinger calls a "tide of nationalism" emerged. In the process, the Soviet regime disappeared.

Beissinger explains the sequence as a consequence of a modified political cycle: early risers, on the average, either gained some advantages or demobilized peacefully, but those who persisted despite previous failures or arrived on the scene late—especially if their program centered on political autonomy or independence—encountered rising resistance and engaged increasingly in claim-making that incited or entailed violence.

Beissinger's data take us only to the end of 1992. By then, some demobilization had already occurred among the early risers that gained the autonomies they were seeking. For the full story of mobilization and demobilization in Soviet space, however, we would have to separately follow newly independent countries such as Georgia, Kazakhstan, Estonia, Armenia, Azerbaijan, and Ukraine. Most of these regimes mounted new waves of mobilization and demobilization in their post-Soviet phases. Struggles for power within titular nationalities did not end with the Soviet collapse. In fact, the great tide of mobilization that swept over the Soviet Union after Mikhail Gorbachev's arrival in power provided models for renewed claim-making through most of the post-Soviet space.

It actually spilled over into postsocialist Yugoslavia as well. In 2000, Slobodan Milosevic's botched attempt to steal the Serbian presidential election produced mass demonstrations by hundreds of thousands that toppled Milosevic in two tumultuous days. In Georgia three years later, the attempt of president (and former Soviet foreign minister) Eduard Shevardnadze to cook parliamentary elections stirred demonstrations led by the opposition parties. When demonstrators handed out roses to government troops, participants began to call their movement the "Rose Revolution."

Although Georgia's opposition leader Mikhail Saakashvili called his successful ouster of Shevardnadze a "velvet revolution," in an echo of the Czechoslovak exit from state socialism from 1989 onward, the international press continued to emphasize the color rose. Over the next two years, opposition movements in postsocialist regimes and elsewhere in the world took to wearing uniform colors and waving banners in the same colors as WUNC displays.

An "orange revolution" overthrew Ukraine's president in 2004. Leonid Kuchma (former Soviet director of military production) had come to power more or less democratically in 1994. In 2004, however, his regime's agents stole a national election from the opposition party and poisoned its candidate, Victor Yushchenko, with dioxin. In November, supported by foreign observers and neighboring states, thousands of demonstrators occupied the public squares of Kiev, the capital. Wearing orange and carrying orange flags, they sang and chanted, blocked entry to government buildings, and overthrew Kuchma.

Colors caught on. In Kyrgyzstan, opponents who drove out Askar Akaev in 2005 divided between tulip and lemon, but the term "tulip revolution" finally stuck. Even authoritarian Belarus had its cautious color coordinators. As writer Thomas Vinciguerra comments:

> All this political peacockery has its detractors. President Aleksandr G. Lukashenko of Belarus is appalled that one of his country's beloved totems, the cornflower, might be used against him. It's all part of a plot by the West, he said.
>
> "They consider that Belarus is ripe for some sort of an orange, or—I'm terrified to utter it out loud—some blue or cornflower revolution," he was quoted as saying recently. "Such blue revolutions are the last thing we need." (Vinciguerra 2005, 12)

At this writing, Lukashenko's regime remains in power. But a new sort of demonstration, underlining the unity of its WUNC with a distinctive color, has clearly become part of the international social-movement repertoire.

Transnational Social Movements

For the time being, however, the greater surprise runs in the opposite direction: in how little change of the repertoire has occurred as social movements have become increasingly transnational in scope. Long-term alterations in claim-making repertoires that occurred in such countries as France, Great Britain, the United States, and South Africa authorize us to expect that if regimes change significantly, so will repertoires. So, for that matter, does the emergence of the demonstration itself with partial democratization of Western countries. If the World Bank, the World Trade Organization, the International Monetary Fund, the United Nations, transnational corporations, the global scientific community, and international nongovernmental organizations are creating a new political environment less attached to any single national regime (Tarrow 2005), we might reasonably expect new political opportunity structures (POS) to transform social movements, or even to drive them out of business.

Yet recall the lesson from this chapter's opening vignette of Evian in 2003. For all the change in issues, slogans, symbols, and objects of claims, the standard combination of social-movement performances remains in place: marches; rallies; processions; demonstrations; occupations; picket lines; blockades; public meetings; delegations; statements to and in public media; petition drives; letter-writing; pamphleteering; lobbying; and creating specialized associations, coalitions, or fronts. In advance of the social movement's institutionalization, the demonstration itself is spreading well beyond democratic regimes as a means of challenging corrupt and authoritarian rulers.

On the single ordinary day of July 20, 2005, the Reuters newswire reported major demonstrations in Yemen, Peru, Kenya, and Cambodia. In the Cambodian case:

> Around 30 Montagnards, the mainly Christian tribespeople from Vietnam's Central Highlands, staged a brief demonstration outside offices of the United Nations High Commissioner for Refugees (UNHCR) in Phnom Penh. But their protest against Wednesday morning's repatriation of 101 Montagnards to Vietnam, where human rights workers say they face persecution, was cut short by the arrival of riot police. "Some of them got upset about the return of these people to Vietnam and they got out of the (asylum seekers' holding) center," Inna Gladkova, a UNHCR official [reported]. "But police escorted them back to the shelter. They are fine now." (Reuters 2005, 1)

Where nongovernmental organizations (NGOs) (in this case human-rights groups) intersect with international organizations (in this case the United Nations), demonstrations are becoming a favored means of attracting global attention to a local cause. But the routines of demonstrations differ little from those that emerged with the social movement two centuries ago.

Is nothing new? Some students of transnational movements (for example, Bennett 2003, 2004) reply that electronic communication is facilitating the formation of virtual political communities capable of nearly instantaneous international mobilization, and that the counter-summits, social forums, antiwar demonstrations, and similar phenomena of recent years constitute dramatic new forms of claim-making. Yet if (as Tartakowsky fears for France) the large but short-lived, single-issue demonstration is gaining ground, it has not driven out or much transformed the other standard social-movement performances at the national scale. So far, the organizational bases of social movements have shifted far more than their repertoires.

Enthusiasts for global civil society see it as growing up in reaction and opposition to the formation of the international power networks represented by international financial institutions and multinational corporations (Kaldor, Anheier, and Glasius 2005). The geographic distribution of international nongovernmental organizations (INGOs) devoted to such causes as human rights and environmental defense suggests that some such correspondence is emerging, As of 2001, the world capital of INGOs was Brussels, seat of the European Union's major administrative organs. In order, the top twenty cities (number of INGOs headquartered there in parenthesis) were Brussels (1,392), London (807), Paris (729), Washington (487), New York (390), Geneva (272), Rome (228), Vienna (190), Tokyo (174), Amsterdam (162), Madrid (140), Stockholm (133), Buenos Aires (110), Copenhagen (108), Berlin (101), Nairobi (100), Oslo (95), Mexico City (87), Montréal (86), and Milan (82) (Glasius, Kaldor, and Anheier 2002, 6).

Events highlighted by professional observers of global civil society likewise testify to the importance of international campaigns in recent social movements. Box 8.1 draws from a yearbook's chronology the "global civil society events" occurring during the two months of 2003 beginning with the Evian demonstrations. If we take the chronology as representative of recent transnational claim-making, it suggests that some changes in repertoire may yet be in the offing.

Three trends merit close watching. One is the emergence of countersummits closely tied to international financial gatherings. A second (and closely related) is the creation of international forums and conferences as vehicles for projecting claims. The third is the rapid intervention of externally based NGOs in political conflicts and mobilizations throughout across the world. Huge internationally coordinated demonstrations in multiple locations do not appear in box 8.1's compilation, but they are surely becoming more frequent. Although Socialist and Communist Internationals offered foretastes of these sorts of international connections many decades ago, international networks of activists and nongovernmental organizations are creating transcontinental connections among mobilizations over a wide variety of issues (Caniglia and Carmin 2005).

Yet most social-movement activity across the world occurs within local, regional, and national frames. Claimants, objects of claims, and relevant audiences come from within the same national regimes and share the same understandings concerning the meanings of the campaigns, performances, and WUNC displays involved. As Sidney Tarrow (2005) puts it, "rooted cosmopolitans" who remain attached to local, regional, and national political settings continue to provide most of the energy that

BOX 8.1 Global Civil Society Events, June–July 2003

6/1–3   *Evian, France:* 150,000 protesters demonstrate against the G8 meeting.

6/7–10   *Lisbon, Portugal:* First Portuguese Social Forum

6/16   *China:* In response to international anti-dam campaign, government admits that cracks have appeared in controversial Three Gorges Dam

6/16–29   *Cartagena de Indias, Colombia:* Following up Third World Social Forum, activists stage a forum on democracy, human rights, war, and drug trafficking

6/20–22   *Thessaloniki, Greece:* First Greek Social Forum, marking culmination of protests during Greek presidency of the European Union

6/20–25   *Sacramento, U.S.:* Activists demonstrate at World Trade Organization (WTO) ministerial conference on agricultural science and technology.

6/21–23   *Cairo, Egypt:* International women's and children's rights groups hold a three-day conference on legal instruments for the prevention of female genital mutilation.

6/26   *Sharm al Shaikh, Egypt:* WTO holds unofficial ministerial meeting, with NGO representatives (Greenpeace among them) excluded from closed sessions but present in public

6/29   *Calcutta, India:* First gay pride march in India

7/1   *Hong Kong, China:* 500,000 people march against new national security legislation for the region

7/6   *Reading, England:* After worldwide controversy, Canon Jeffery John, a gay celibate priest, withdraws his nomination as Anglican Bishop of Reading; later appointed Dean of Reading Cathedral

7/15   *Damascus, Syria:* Following human rights and civil liberties campaign, Syrian president pardons hundreds of prisoners and orders end of judicial pursuit for head of Syrian Human Rights Organization.

7/16   *Internet:* Site launched for World Campaign for In-depth Reform of the System of International Institutions

7/18   *São Paulo, Brazil:* Judge suspends eviction of 4,000 members of Workers Without a Roof, who are squatting on a plot owned by Volkswagen

7/21–24   *Tegucigalpa, Honduras:* Fourth Foro Mesoamericano meets, campaigning against Free Trade Area of Americas and neoliberalism

7/23   *Colombia:* Trade union members call for worldwide boycott of Coca-Cola, alleged to have employed militias for the murder of union members

7/23	*Juarez, Mexico*: Mexican and international NGOs plus UN observers meet with government officials to demand end of violence including murders of women and children in Juarez.
7/28–30	*Montréal, Canada*: Furing a WTO pre-meeting, hundreds of protesters demonstrate, some smashing storefront windows of multinational brands

Note: summarized from Anheier et al. 2005, 354–355.

goes into transnational claims-making. The greatest possibility for the future, indeed, is not that social movements as such will globalize, but that a split will occur between the forms of contention that people employ when engaged in local, regional, or national struggles, and those that prevail in the world of international institutions and multinational firms. Watch the international space closely for something new.

CHAPTER NINE >>
Conclusions

IN 2005, PERU STILL PERCHED precariously at a crucial boundary. Within regime space, Peru had still not established a visibly viable location firmly inside the high-capacity, democratic quadrant. Alejandro Toledo, elected president in 2001 after Alberto Fujimori's disgrace and exile, had soon stumbled over troubles of his own. Critics soon accused him of getting his wife a cushy job in a big bank and of fathering a child out of wedlock. Toledo shook off the first charge, but admitted to the second. He also faced violent opposition to his privatization of state-owned companies, saw a resurgence of Shining Path attacks, and lost badly in 2002 regional elections that he had himself precipitated by decentralizing the national government.

In 2003, anti-Toledo demonstrators blocked the country's major highways until the president declared a state of emergency and sent out the military to control half of the country's administrative regions. That same year, his first vice president had to resign his post as foreign commerce minister with apologies as the press broadcast revelations of government-expense favors his young girlfriend had received. In 2005, Toledo survived an impeachment vote after a congressional panel reported that he had sponsored the forgery of signatures during the 1998 registration of his Peru Possible Party.

The report of Peru's truth commission, issued in August 2003, revealed the extent of state-backed violence between 1980 and 2000, before Toledo's tenure. It established, among other things, how much the violence from both state forces and Shining Path had victimized highland indigenous people. But under Toledo government prosecutors only acted slowly and hesitantly against any of the perpetrators. Meanwhile, Peruvians took the law into their own hands:

> In April 2004, a furious mob lynched Cirilo Robles, the major of Ilave, Puno, who was accused of corruption. Another government official was seriously injured. During the same month, men armed with planks, machetes, and other weapons attacked townspeople in Lagunas, on the Peruvian Amazon, injuring more than forty, some seriously. The townspeople had surrounded the town hall to prevent the mayor from evading an accounting audit. (Human Rights Watch 2005, 230)

Elsewhere, discharged military officers took hostages to demand Toledo's resignation, highland farmers attacked American-owned gold mines, and opposition politicians staged street protests to publicize their causes. Addressing a military gathering on Air Force Day, Toledo himself ominously described Peru as "a country without democratic public institutions in a regime that is fragmenting," and declared that "[n]o one benefits from a nation with weak institutions" (*El Comercio* 2005, 1). Nothing like the relatively peaceful politics of social movements had yet become routine in Peru.

Whatever else this book has established, it has shown amply that contentious repertoires differ dramatically from one type of regime to another. Both governmental capacity and extent of democracy strongly affect the ways that people make collective claims on each other and how authorities respond to those claims. Among nondemocratic regimes, we begin to see the very different disadvantages of high-capacity and low-capacity governments. High-capacity, nondemocratic regimes give arbitrary power to a single tyrant, while low-capacity, nondemocratic regimes open the way to many small tyrants. As a result, civil wars concentrate in low-capacity, nondemocratic regimes, while successful revolutions concentrate in (relatively) high-capacity, nondemocratic regimes.

On the democratic side, the choice is not so stark. Low-capacity, democratic regimes gather more than their share of collective violence, and often harbor zones of extensive lawlessness. But at their centers they install some minimum of political rights and civil liberties. High-capacity, democracies endure relatively little collective violence in their domestic politics, even if they sometimes make up for it by their violence in external wars. Citizens of high-capacity democracies, furthermore, are now participating increasingly in coordinated transnational claim-making. That new arena, with international institutions and multinational corporations frequently its favored targets, promises to generate new forms of contentious politics.

We have witnessed broad correspondence between regimes and repertoires. We have regularly noticed differences in the prevailing forms of collective claims among low-capacity, nondemocratic; high-capacity, nondemocratic; low-capacity, democratic; and high-capacity, democratic regimes. As a result, those differences have started to look natural, even inevitable. Yet the correspondence goes beyond mere tautology: we can establish a regime's degree of democracy and check the capacity of its government without knowing the extensiveness of its collective violence or the frequency of its social movements.

The causal connections, nevertheless, remain harder to observe. With extensive illustrations but nothing like definitive proof, this book has argued that a regime's political history generates both a claim-making repertoire and a political opportunity structure. It has gone on to claim that, in the short run, the repertoire and opportunity structure interact to constrain the frequency, location, and character of collective claims. But in the medium run, claim-making alters the regime. It does so by shaping arrays of effective political actors, political alliances, public programs, governmental personnel, and even forms of government.

How do these complicated relations work? Let us return to this book's main arguments for a last look at how they have fared.

▸ THE LOCATION OF A REGIME *within the capacity-democracy space strongly affects its rulers' approach to generating and controlling contentious politics.*

Starting and ending with Peru, we have observed enormous variations in how rulers have prescribed, tolerated, and forbidden different varieties and locations of claim-making. Broadly speaking, we have seen capacity as governing the actual reach of governmental authorities: low-capacity governments, for example, exert significant control close to their operating bases, but intervene in contention much less vigorously, effectively, and continuously outside of that zone. The weak grip of Peruvian government on the highlands, as compared with coastal lowland Lima, illustrates the point. High-capacity governments, on the average, exert more energetic, effective, and continuous control over public claim-making throughout their territories. This is no tautology, since we can judge capacity quite outside the realm of contentious politics by the effectiveness with which government agents intervene in social life at large. Change and variation in governmental capacity cause change and variation in the character of contentious politics.

As for democracy, it operates simultaneously as a facilitator and a constraint. Given consent of citizens, it facilitates the carrying out of large collective programs such as health care and education. But it limits the ability of rulers and their agents to intervene arbitrarily and without fear of retaliation. Much more direct bargaining over the boundaries among prescribed, tolerated, and forbidden forms of claim-making therefore occurs in democracies than in nondemocracies. A significant share of that bargaining occurs within the campaigns, performances, and WUNC displays of social movements. Again this is no tautology, since (as illustrated by Freedom House ratings) we can judge democracy quite independently of social-movement activity. Change and variation in democracy cause change and variation in the character of contentious politics.

These regime differences involve subtle but powerful variation in the place of military specialists: frequently autonomous and dangerous in low-capacity, nondemocratic regimes; usually under tight central control (although sometimes ruling or sharing rule) in high-capacity, nondemocratic regimes; generally subordinate to civilian control and little involved in the domestic contentious politics of high-capacity, democratic regimes; and sometimes acquiring risky autonomy in low-capacity, democratic regimes. Democratization usually involves and depends in part on subordination of previously autonomous military specialists to civilian rule. We have repeatedly watched Peruvian regimes dividing and faltering over that subordination of the military.

▶ THE PREVIOUS TRAJECTORY OF A REGIME *within the same space, however, supplies much of the concrete means by which rulers and citizens engage in contentious politics.*

As we have seen repeatedly, regimes that locate in fairly similar positions within the capacity-democracy space nonetheless feature significantly different repertoires and campaigns. The contrast between India and the United States—both large, high-capacity, democratic regimes—makes the point dramatically. Although both regimes emerged from anticolonial rebellions and civil wars, the inscription of religious differences into Indian public politics (as compared with the racial differences that have long shaped U.S. politics) resulted from the trajectory out of colonialism and through civil war.

Consider a smaller but still significant difference between France and Great Britain. In France, police generally carry lethal arms. In Great Britain (with the exception of such special forces as antiterror squads) police usually carry batons, but not lethal arms. That difference emerged early in the nineteenth century, as a democratizing British regime created specialized but unarmed police forces for urban patrol and crowd control.

French police operated much longer and more extensively as part of the national military, and retained their arms. As a consequence, British claim-makers suffered plenty of bruises but few deaths as compared with their French counterparts.

- IN PARTICULAR, *changes in the multiplicity of independent centers of power within the regime, openness of the regime to new actors, instability of current political alignments, availability of influential allies or supporters, and the extent to which the regime represses or facilitates collective claim-making (which together comprise political opportunity structure, or POS) strongly affect the levels and loci of claim-making within the regime.*

After periods of severely restricted opportunity, we have seen POS becoming more favorable to popular claimants in such disparate cases as Great Britain after the Napoleonic Wars, South Africa as apartheid began to crack, and the Soviet Union as a reforming Gorbachev government unleashed far more opportunities than Gorbachev himself intended. In all these instances and more, concerted popular claim-making itself initiated or accelerated expansion of POS: multiplying independent centers of power within the regime, opening the regime to new actors, rendering political alignments more unstable, bringing out influential allies and supporters, and blunting governmental repression while stimulating facilitation by some sectors of government.

- RULERS AND CITIZENS *bargain out a set of understandings concerning possible and effective means of making collective claims within the regime.*

- THE "BARGAINING" *often involves vigorous, violent struggle, especially in nondemocratic regimes.*

- FROM THE TOP DOWN, *those understandings identify sets of prescribed, tolerated, and forbidden claim-making performances, with likely governmental responses to each of them.*

The emergence of the demonstration as an established claim-making performance has shown us a bargain that no ruler initially wanted to make nonetheless becoming powerful. Where rulers had once tolerated or even prescribed public displays of WUNC by acceptable groups of citizens, regimes moved through struggle to rights of assembly, association, and speech on the part of claimants that were often hostile to current governments. At first broken up, shot down, and prosecuted as riots, demonstrations acquired a quasi-legal standing in all democratic regimes. Indeed, the demonstration became such an effective way of displaying WUNC that during the later twentieth century it began to diffuse widely into semi-democratic regimes and the less repressed segments of nondemocratic regimes as well. At the same time, however, regimes created police forces that contained most demonstrations within tolerated limits. As a result, domestic claim-making became simultaneously less violent, more frequent, and larger in scale.

- FROM THE BOTTOM UP, *the performances clump into repertoires that describe the forms of claim-making available to any particular set of political actors, including the government, and the likely consequences of making such claims.*

- BOTH INTERNAL MUTATIONS *within contentious politics and external alterations of regimes and ruler–citizen relations create the repertoires that prevail in any particular time and place.*

The demonstration again provides a dramatic example. Organizers of demonstrations constantly innovate within the stringent limits set by the form; bargain with authorities about locations, itineraries, and actions; police their own ranks by means of marshals; strive to limit breaking and smashing performed by their more aggressive adherents; and, after the fact, argue publicly with authorities, rivals, and media about the worthiness, unity, numbers, and commitment of their participants. But (as the necklacing and bus-burning of Alexandra during the 1980s should remind us) performances that frighten and attack authorities also clump into repertoires where governments lack the capacity to prevent or repress them. On the whole, low-capacity regimes, especially nondemocratic ones, generate a wider range of performances that authorities would forbid if they had the means, and do repress seriously when and where they do have the means.

- CONTENTION ITSELF *reshapes regimes both incrementally and in bursts of struggle.*

For incremental effects, India's militant Hindus provide remarkable examples. The campaign to destroy the Uttar Pradesh mosque of Babri Masjid, for example, helped bring the Bharatiya Janata Party (BJP) to national power. The actual destruction of Babri Masjid during a Hindu demonstration of 1992 drummed up support for the party; electoral gains meant that the BJP actually led national coalition governments in 1996 and 1998, with the second government lasting until 2004. In Gujarat, government-backed Hindu attacks on Muslims brought the BJP a landslide victory in the 2002 elections. Although neither the national nor the Gujarati government succeeded in implementing religious rule, the BJP's rise weakened the already threatened position of Muslims within the Indian regime.

For the impact on regimes by bursts of struggle, the civil wars and revolutions of chapter 7 provide multiple examples over centuries of upheaval. So does the drama of South Africa in chapter 5. Against long odds, black militants and their few white allies brought down an apartheid regime that had seemed cruelly invulnerable. In 1994, long-time prisoner Nelson Mandela actually became South African president. Contentious politics sometimes fizzles and sometimes reproduces the status quo, but now and then produces profound alterations in regimes.

▸ NOT ALL CONTENTIOUS PERFORMANCES, *repertoires, and episodes are causally coherent in the sense that systematic regularities across time and place govern their existence, change, and variation.*

▸ SOME CONTENTIOUS PERFORMANCES, *repertoires, and episodes, however, have symbolic coherence in the sense that naming them is a consequential political act, classifying a new instance as like its predecessors has political impact, and their existence provides models for claim-making even if they are not causally coherent.*

▸ ANY ANALYSIS OF REGIMES AND REPERTOIRES *must both distinguish causal from symbolic coherence, and examine their interplay with care.*

Both revolution and riot illustrate these points clearly. Revolutions do not conform to general laws, but once someone has identified a proposed or actual turnover of governmental power as revolutionary, the identification has powerful symbolic significance, and participants' actions provide models for would-be revolutionaries elsewhere. Similarly, the events people call "riots" result from a wide variety of conditions and causes. But labeling a crowd action as a riot authorizes repressive forces to intervene against the crowd. It also provides a possible model for future crowd action—depending on the reactions of authorities, observers, media, and members of the general public. In both cases, whatever causal coherence the contention displays does not reside in the distinctive character of revolutions and riots, but in the mechanisms and processes that produce political contention in general.

▸ THESE LESSONS APPLY TO COLLECTIVE VIOLENCE, *revolutions, and social movements.*

The same sorts of causes that produce social movements also produce revolutions and collective violence. This book has concentrated on identifying causes that belong to change and variation in the organization of national regimes. So doing, it has clarified and made more urgent three questions that it nevertheless repeatedly brushed aside: Exactly how does contention itself transform regimes? What causes regimes to vary and change from low capacity to high capacity and back again? What causes democratization and democratization? This book underlines why we need better answers to all three questions. The future of popular politics is at stake.

REFERENCES >>

ADELMAN, HOWARD, AND ASTRI SUHRKE. 1996. *Early Warning and Conflict Management*. Vol. 2: *The International Response to Conflict and Genocide: Lessons from the Rwanda Experience*. Copenhagen: Danida [Danish International Development Agency].

AGRIKOLIANSKY, ÉRIC, OLIVIER FILLIEULE, AND NONNA MAYER, EDS. 2005. *L'Altermondialisme en France. La longue histoire d'une nouvelle cause*. Paris: Flammarion.

ALLEN, TERRY J. 2002. "The General and the Genocide." *Amnesty Now* (Winter): 18–22.

ALMEIDA, PAUL D., AND MARK IRVING LICHBACH. 2003. "To the Internet, From the Internet: Comparative Media Coverage of Transnational Protests." *Mobilization* 8:249–72.

AMNESTY INTERNATIONAL. 1998. "Rwanda, the Hidden Violence: 'Disappearances' and Killings Continue." Available at www.amnesty.org/ailib/ intcam/rwanda/repintro.htm, viewed September 2, 2001.

———. 2000. "A Summary of Concerns: A Briefing for the United Nations Human Rights Committee." Available at www.amnesty.org/library/print/ENGAMR460232000, viewed January 22, 2005.

———. 2001a. "Alberto Fujimori Ex-President of Peru Must Be Brought to Justice." Available at www.amnesty.org/library/print/ENGAMR460172001, viewed January 22, 2005.

———. 2001b. "Morocco: Intimidatory Measures against the Right to Freedom of Expression." Available at www.amnesty.org/library/print/ENGMDE290022001, viewed January 22, 2005.

———. 2001c. "Jamaica. Police Killings: Appeals against Impunity." Available at www.amnesty.org/library/print/ENAMR380122001, viewed April 5, 2005.

———. 2003a. "Amnesty International India." Available at www.amnesty. org/web/web.nsf/print/427E1B8D90F8C32180, viewed January 22, 2005.

———. 2003b. "United States of America. The Threat of a Bad Example—Undermining International Standards as 'War on Terror' Detentions Continue."

Available at www.amnesty.org/library/print/ENGAMR5111142003, viewed January 23, 2005.

———. 2004a. "Amnesty International Uganda." Available at www.amnesty.org/web/webnsf/print/5492971EE19957A9802, viewed January 22, 2005.

———. (2004b): "Jamaica: 'Let us kill him.'" Available at www.amnesty.org/web/wire.nsf/print/June 2004/Jamaica, viewed April 5, 2005.

ANDERSON, PERRY. 1974a. *Passages from Antiquity to Feudalism.* London: NLB.

———. *Lineages of the Absolutist State.* London: NLB.

ANDERSON JR., RICHARD D., M. STEVEN FISH, STEPHEN E. HANSON, AND PHILIP G. ROEDER. 2001. *Postcommunism and the Theory of Democracy.* Princeton: Princeton University Press.

ANDREAS, PETER. 2004. "The Clandestine Political Economy of War and Peace in Bosnia." *International Studies Quarterly* 48:29–52.

ANDREWS, GEORGE REID, AND HERRICK CHAPMAN, EDS. 1995. *The Social Construction of Democracy, 1870–1990.* New York: New York University Press.

ANHEIER, HELMUT, MARLIES GLASIUS, MARY KALDOR, AND FIONA HOLLAND, EDS. 2005. *Global Civil Society 2004/5.* London: Sage Publications.

ANHEIER, HELMUT, AND NUNO THEMUDO. 2002. "Organisational Forms of Global Civil Society: Implications of Going Global." In Marlies Glasius, Mary Kaldor, and Helmut Anheier, eds., *Global Civil Society 2002.* Oxford: Oxford University Press, 191–216.

D'ANJOU, LEO. 1996. *Social Movements and Cultural Change: The First Abolition Campaign Revisited.* New York: Aldine de Gruyter.

APCM [ACTION POPULAIRE CONTRE LA MONDIALISATION, GENEVA]. 2003. "Evaluation of the G8-Evian Mobilization and a Debate to Be Had on Violence." Available at www.indymedia.org.uk/en/2003/08/275043.html, viewed July 11, 2005.

APSA TASK FORCE. 2004. "American Democracy in an Age of Rising Inequality." *Perspectives on Politics* 2:651–66.

ARAT, ZEHRA F. 1991. *Democracy and Human Rights in Developing Countries.* Boulder: Lynne Rienner.

ARCHER, JOHN E. 1990. *By a Flash and a Scare: Incendiarism, Animal Maiming, and Poaching in East Anglia, 1815–1870.* Oxford: Clarendon Press.

ASHFORTH, ADAM. 1990. *The Politics of Official Discourse in Twentieth-Century South Africa.* Oxford: Clarendon Press.

———. 2005. *Witchcraft, Violence, and Democracy in South Africa.* Chicago: University of Chicago Press.

ASSOCIATED PRESS. 2004. "U.S. Wrongly Reported Drop in World Terrorism in 2003." *New York Times,* June 11, online edition.

BAGLA, PALLAVA. 2003. "Ayodhya Ruins Yield More Fuel for Ongoing Religious Fight." *Science* 301 (September 5): 1305.

BANASZAK, LEE ANN, KAREN BECKWITH, AND DIETER RUCHT, EDS. 2003. *Women's Movements Facing the Reconfigured State.* Cambridge: Cambridge University Press.

BANDY, JOE, AND JACKIE SMITH, EDS. 2004. *Coalitions across Borders: Transnational Protest and the Neoliberal Order.* Lanham, Md.: Rowman and Littlefield.

BARBALET, J. M. 1988. *Citizenship.* Minneapolis: University of Minnesota Press.

BARBER, LUCY G. 2002. *Marching on Washington: The Forging of an American Political Tradition.* Berkeley: University of California Press.
BARKAN, STEVE E., AND LYNNE L. SNOWDEN. 2001. *Collective Violence.* Boston: Allyn and Bacon.
BARKER, COLIN. 1998. "Some Notes on 20th Century Revolution." *Journal of Area Studies* 13:143–83.
BARNES, JONATHAN, ED. 1984. *The Complete Works of Aristotle.* Princeton: Princeton University Press. 2 vols.
BARRETT, DEBORAH, AND CHARLES KURZMAN. 2004. "Globalizing Social Movement Theory: The Case of Eugenics." *Theory and Society* 33:487–527.
BAX, MART. 2000. "Holy Mary and Medjugorje's Rocketeers: The Local Logic of an Ethnic Cleansing Process in Bosnia." *Ethnologia Europaea* 30:45–58.
BAYART, JEAN-FRANÇOIS, STEPHEN ELLIS, AND BÉATRICE HIBOU. 1999. *The Criminalization of the State in Africa.* Oxford: James Currey.
BECKWITH, KAREN. 2000. "Hinges in Collective Action: Strategic Innovation in the Pittston Coal Strike." *Mobilization* 5:179–200.
———. 2001. "Women's Movements at Century's End: Excavation and Advances in Political Science." *Annual Review of Political Science* 4:371–90.
BEISSINGER, MARK. 1993. "Demise of an Empire-State: Identity, Legitimacy, and the Deconstruction of Soviet Politics." In Crawford Young, ed., *The Rising Tide of Cultural Pluralism.* Madison: University of Wisconsin Press.
———. 1998. *Nationalist Mobilization and the Collapse of the Soviet State.* Cambridge: Cambridge University Press.
———. 2002. "Nationalist Violence and the State: Political Authority and Contentious Repertoires in the Former USSR." *Comparative Politics* 30:401–33.
BELAND, DANIEL. 2005. "Insecurity, Citizenship, and Globalization: The Multiple Faces of State Protection." *Sociological Theory* 23:25–41.
BENNETT, LANCE. 2003. "Communicating Global Activism." *Information, Communication, and Society* 6:143–68.
———. 2004. "Social Movements beyond Borders: Understanding Two Eras of Transnational Activism." In Donatella della Porta and Sidney Tarrow, eds., *Transnational Protest and Global Activism.* Lanham, Md.: Rowman and Littlefield.
BERKELEY, BILL. 2001. *The Graves Are Not Yet Full: Race, Tribe and Power in the Heart of Africa.* New York: Basic Books.
BERMEO, NANCY. 2003. *Ordinary People in Extraordinary Times: The Citizenry and the Breakdown of Democracy.* Princeton: Princeton University Press.
BEYELER, MICHELLE, AND HANSPETER KRIESI. 2005. "Transnational Protest and the Public Sphere." *Mobilization* 10:95–110.
BIGGS, MICHAEL. 2002. "Strikes as Sequences of Interaction: The American Strike Wave of 1886." *Social Science History* 26:583–617.
BLACKSTOCK, ALLAN. 2000. " 'The Invincible Mass': Loyal Crowds in Mid Ulster, 1795–96." In Peter Jupp and Eoin Magennis, eds., *Crowds in Ireland c. 1720–1920.* London: Macmillan.
BLOOM, MIA. 2005. *Dying to Kill: The Allure of Suicide Terror.* New York: Columbia University Press.
BOB, CLIFFORD. 2005. *The Marketing of Rebellion: Insurgents, Media, and International Activism.* Cambridge: Cambridge University Press.

BOHSTEDT, JOHN. 1983. *Riots and Community Politics in England and Wales, 1790–1810*. Cambridge: Harvard University Press.
BONNEUIL, NOËL, AND NADIA AURIAT. 2000. "Fifty Years of Ethnic Conflict and Cohesion, 1945–94." *Journal of Peace Research* 37:563–81.
BOOH BOOH, JACQUES-ROGER. 2005. *Le patron de Dallaire parle: Révélations sur les dérives d'un général de l'ONU au Rwanda*. Paris: Éditions Duboiris.
BORLAND, ELIZABETH. 2004. "Cultural Opportunity and Tactical Choice in the Argentine and Chilean Reproductive Rights Movements." *Mobilization* 9:327–40.
BOSE, SUGATA, AND AYESHA JALAL. 1998. *Modern South Asia: History, Culture, Political Economy*. London: Routledge.
BOURGUINAT, NICOLAS. 2002. *Les Grains du désordre: L'État face aux violences frumentaires dans la première moitié du XIXe siècle*. Paris: Éditions de l'École des Hautes Études en Sciences Sociales.
BOUTWELL, JEFFREY, MICHAEL T. KLARE, AND LAURA W. REED. 1995. *Lethal Commerce: The Global Trade in Small Arms and Light Weapons*. Cambridge, Mass.: American Academy of Arts and Sciences.
BOZZOLI, BELINDA. 2004. *Theatres of Struggle and the End of Apartheid*. Edinburgh: Edinburgh University Press for the International African Institute, London.
TE BRAKE, WAYNE. 1998. *Shaping History: Ordinary People in European Politics 1500–1700*. Berkeley: University of California Press.
BRASS, PAUL R. 1994. *The Politics of India since Independence*. Cambridge: Cambridge University Press. The New Cambridge History of India, IV-1, rev. ed.
———. 2003. *The Production of Hindu-Muslim Violence in Contemporary India*. Seattle: University of Washington Press.
BRATTON, MICHAEL, AND NICOLAS VAN DE WALLE. 1997. *Democratic Experiments in Africa: Regime Transitions in Comparative Perspective*. Cambridge: Cambridge University Press.
BREWER, JOHN. 1976. *Party Ideology and Popular Politics at the Accession of George III*. Cambridge: Cambridge University Press.
BREWER, JOHN, AND JOHN STYLES, EDS. 1980. *An Ungovernable People: The English and Their Law in the Seventeenth and Eighteenth Centuries*. New Brunswick: Rutgers University Press.
BRIQUET, JEAN-LOUIS, ED. 2000. "Les Mafias." *Politix* 49, entire issue.
BROCKETT, CHARLES D. 2005. *Political Movements and Violence in Central America*. Cambridge: Cambridge University Press.
BRUBAKER, ROGERS, AND DAVID D. LAITIN. 1998. "Ethnic and Nationalist Violence." *Annual Review of Sociology* 24: 423–52.
BUECHLER, STEVEN M. 2000. *Social Movements in Advanced Capitalism: The Political Economy and Cultural Construction of Social Activism*. New York: Oxford University Press.
BUENDE, KAIRE. 1995. "Social Movements and the Demise of Apartheid Colonialism in Namibia." In Mahmood Mamdani and Ernest Wamba-dia-Wamba, eds., *African Studies in Social Movements and Democracy*. Dakar: CODESRIA.
BUENO DE MESQUITA, BRUCE, RANDOLPH M. SIVERSON, AND GARRY WOLLER. 1992. "War and the Fate of Regimes: A Comparative Analysis." *American Political Science Review* 86:638–46.

BURKHART, ROSS E., AND MICHAEL S. LEWIS-BECK. 1994. "Comparative Democracy: The Economic Development Thesis." *American Political Science Review* 88:903–10.
BURT, JO-MARIE. 1997. Political Violence and the Grassroots in Lima, Peru." In Douglas A. Chalmers, Carlos M. Vilas, Katherine Hite, Scott B. Martin, Kerianne Piester, and Monique Sergarra, eds., *The New Politics of Inequality in Latin America: Rethinking Participation and Representation*. New York: Oxford University Press.
BURTON, JOHN W. 1997. *Violence Explained: The Sources of Conflict, Violence and Crime and Their Prevention*. Manchester: Manchester University Press.
CADDICK-ADAMS, PETER, AND RICHARD HOLMES. 2001. "Terrorism." In Richard Holmes, ed., *The Oxford Companion to Military History*. Oxford: Oxford University Press, 906–7.
CANIGLIA, BETH SCHAEFER, AND JOANN CARMIN, EDS. 2005. "Focus Issue on Social Movement Organizations." *Mobilization* 10:201–308.
CARTER, NEAL ALLAN. 2003. "Political Identity, Territory, and Institutional Change: The Case of Belgium." *Mobilization* 8:205–20.
CASQUETTE, JESÚS. 1998. *Política, cultura y movimientos sociales*. Bilbao: Bakeaz.
CHABOT, SEAN. 2000. "Transnational Diffusion and the African American Reinvention of the Gandhian Repertoire." *Mobilization* 5:201–16.
CHABOT, SEAN, AND JAN WILLEM DUYVENDAK. 2002. "Globalization and Transnational Diffusion between Social Movements: Reconceptualizing the Dissemination of the Gandhian Repertoire and the 'Coming Out' Routine." *Theory and Society* 31:697–740.
CHALOM, MAURICE, AND LUCE LÉONARD. 2001. *Insécurité, Police de proximité et Gouvernance locale*. Paris: l'Harmattan.
CHANDHOKE, NEERA. 2002. "The Limits of Global Civil Society." In Marlies Glasius, Mary Kaldor, and Helmut Anheier, eds., *Global Civil Society 2002*. Oxford: Oxford University Press, 35–53.
CHARLESWORTH, ANDREW, ED. 1983. *An Atlas of Rural Protest in Britain 1548–1900*. London: Croom Helm.
CHARNEY, CRAIG. 1999. "Civil Society, Political Violence, and Democratic Transitions: Business and the Peace Process in South Africa 1990 to 1994." *Comparative Studies in Society and History* 41:182–206.
CHATURVEDI, JAYATI, AND GYANESHWAR CHATURVEDI. 1996. "Dharma Yudh: Communal Violence, Riots, and Public Space in Ayodhya and Agra City: 1990 and 1992." In Paul R. Brass, ed., *Riots and Pogroms*. New York: New York University Press.
CHESTERMAN, SIMON, ED. 2001. *Civilians in War*. Boulder: Lynne Rienner.
CHIROT, DANIEL, AND MARTIN E. P. SELIGMAN, EDS. 2000. *Ethnopolitical Warfare: Causes, Consequences, and Possible Solutions*. Washington: American Psychological Association.
CHRÉTIEN, JEAN-PIERRE. 1997. "Interprétations du génocide de 1994 dans l'histoire contemporaine du Rwanda." *Clio en Afrique*. Available at www.up.univ-mrs.fr/~welio-af/numéro/2/sources, viewed September 2, 2001.
CHURCH, ROY, AND QUENTIN OUTRAM. 1998. *Strikes and Solidarity: Coalfield Conflict in Britain 1889–1966*. Cambridge: Cambridge University Press.
CIOFFI-REVILLA, CLAUDIO. 1990. *The Scientific Measurement of International Conflict: Handbook of Datasets on Crises and Wars, 1495–1988 A.D.* Boulder: Lynne Rienner.

COHN, SAMUEL R. 1993. *When Strikes Make Sense—And Why*. New York: Plenum.
COLLIER, DAVID, AND STEVEN LEVITSKY. 1997. "Democracy with Adjectives: Conceptual Innovation in Comparative Research." *World Politics* 49:430–51.
COLLIER, PAUL. 2000a. "Rebellion as a Quasi-Criminal Activity." *Journal of Conflict Resolution* 44:839–53.
———. 2000b. "Economic Causes of Civil Conflict and Their Implications for Policy." Paper prepared for United Nations Security Council Global Policy Forum. Available at www.igc.org/globalpolicy/security/issues/diamond/wb.htm, viewed August 7, 2000.
COLLIER, PAUL, AND ANKE HOEFFLER. 2001. "Greed and Grievance in Civil War." Unpublished paper, World Bank.
COLLIER, PAUL, AND NICHOLAS SAMBANIS, EDS. 2005. *Understanding Civil War*. Washington D.C.: World Bank. 2 vols.
COLLIER, RUTH BERINS. 1999. *Paths toward Democracy: The Working Class and Elites in Western Europe and South America*. Cambridge: Cambridge University Press.
COLLIER, RUTH BERINS, AND DAVID COLLIER. 1991. *Shaping the Political Arena: Critical Junctures, the Labor Movement, and Regime Dynamics in Latin America*. Princeton: Princeton University Press.
Commission [National Commission on Terrorist Attacks upon the United States]. 2004. *The 9/11 Commission Report*. New York: Norton.
CRENSHAW, MARTHA, ED. 1995. *Terrorism in Context*. University Park: Penn State University Press.
DAHL, ROBERT A. 1975. "Governments and Political Oppositions." In Fred I. Greenstein and Nelson W. Polsby, eds., *Handbook of Political Science*. Vol. 3: *Macropolitical Theory*. Reading, Mass.: Addison-Wesley.
———. *On Democracy*. New Haven: Yale University Press.
DALLAIRE, ROMÉO. 2003. *J'ai serré la main du diable. La faillite de l'humanité au Rwanda*. Outremont, Québec: Libre Expression.
DAVENPORT, CHRISTIAN. 2004. "Human Rights and the Promise of Democratic Pacification." *International Studies Quarterly* 48:539–60.
DAVENPORT, CHRISTIAN, ED. 2000. *Paths to State Repression: Human Rights Violations and Contentious Politics*. Lanham, Md.: Rowman and Littlefield.
DAVENPORT, CHRISTIAN, HANK JOHNSTON, AND CAROL MUELLER, EDS. 2005. *Repression and Mobilization*. Minneapolis: University of Minnesota Press.
DAVIS, DIANE E., AND ANTHONY W. PEREIRA, EDS. 2003. *Irregular Armed Forces and Their Role in Politics and State Formation*. Cambridge: Cambridge University Press.
DAWISHA, KAREN, AND BRUCE PARROTT, EDS. 1997. *The Consolidation of Democracy in East-Central Europe*. Cambridge: Cambridge University Press.
DEFLEM, MATHIEU. 2002. *Policing World Society: Historical Foundations of International Police Cooperation*. Oxford: Oxford University Press.
DEFRONZO, JAMES. 1991. *Revolutions and Revolutionary Movements*. Boulder: Westview.
DEIBERT, RONALD J. 2000. "International Plug 'n Play? Citizen Activism, the Internet, and Global Public Policy." *International Studies Perspectives* 1:255–72.
DENECKERE, GITA. 1997. *Sire, het volk mort. Sociaal protest in België (1831–1918)*. Antwerp: Baarn.

DERLUGUIAN, GEORGI. 1999. "Che Guevaras in Turbans." *New Left Review* 237:3–27.
DES FORGES, ALISON, ET AL. 1999. *Leave None to Tell the Story: Genocide in Rwanda*. New York: Human Rights Watch.
DIAMOND, LARRY. 1999. *Developing Democracy: Toward Consolidation*. Baltimore: Johns Hopkins University Press.
———. 2002. "Elections without Democracy: Thinking about Hybrid Regimes." *Journal of Democracy* 13(2):21–35.
DIAMOND, LARRY, ET AL. 2004. "The Quality of Democracy." *Journal of Democracy* 15:20–109.
DIANI, MARIO, AND DOUG MCADAM, EDS. 2003. *Social Movements and Networks: Relational Approaches to Collective Action*. Oxford: Oxford University Press.
DOGAN, MATTEI, AND JOHN HIGLEY. 1998. "Elites, Crises, and Regimes in Comparative Analysis." In Mattei Dogan and John Higley, eds., *Elites, Crises, and the Origins of Regimes*. Lanham, Md.: Rowman and Littlefield.
DOGAN, MATTEI, AND DOMINIQUE PELASSY. 1984. *How to Compare Nations: Strategies in Comparative Politics*. Chatham, N.J.: Chatham House.
DOWNING, BRIAN M. 1992. *The Military Revolution and Political Change: Origins of Democracy and Autocracy in Early Modern Europe*. Princeton: Princeton University Press.
DRESCHER, SEYMOUR. 1994. "Whose Abolition? Popular Pressure and the Ending of the British Slave Trade." *Past and Present* 143:136–66.
DUMONT, GEORGES-HENRI. 2002. *Le miracle belge de 1848*. Brussels: Le Cri.
DUNÉR, BERTIL. 1985. *Military Intervention in Civil Wars: The 1970s*. Aldershot: Gower.
DUYVENDAK, JAN WILLEM. 1994. *Le poids du politique. Nouveaux mouvements sociaux en France*. Paris: L'Harmattan.
EARL, JENNIFER, ANDREW MARTIN, JOHN D. MCCARTHY, AND SARAH A. SOULE. 2004. "The Use of Newspaper Data in the Study of Collective Action." *Annual Review of Sociology* 30:65–80.
Economist. 2005. "Tragi-comic Farce." *Economist*, January 8, 38.
EDELMAN, MARC. 2001. "Social Movements: Changing Paradigms and Forms of Politics." *Annual Review of Anthropology* 30:285–317.
———. 2003. "Transnational Peasant and Farmer Movements and Networks." In Mary Kaldor, Helmut Anheier, and Marlies Glasius, eds., *Global Civil Society 2003*. Oxford: Oxford University Press, 185–220.
EKIERT, GRZEGORZ, AND JAN KUBIK. 1999. *Rebellious Civil Society: Popular Protest and Democratic Consolidation in Poland, 1989–1993*. Ann Arbor: University of Michigan Press.
El Comercio. 2005. "Toledo pide contribuir al fortalecimiento de instituciones." *El Comercio* (Lima), July 24, online ed. Available at www.elcomercioperu.com, viewed July 24, 2005.
ELLINGSON, STEPHEN. 1995. "Understanding the Dialectic of Discourse and Collective Action: Public Debate and Rioting in Antebellum Cincinnati." *American Journal of Sociology* 101:100–44.
ELLIS, STEPHEN. 1999. *The Mask of Anarchy: The Destruction of Liberia and the Religious Dimension of an African Civil War*. New York: New York University Press.

ELTIS, DAVID. 1993. "Europeans and the Rise and Fall of African Slavery in the Americas: An Interpretation." *American Historical Review* 98:1399–1423.

ENDERS, WALTER, AND TODD SANDLER. 2002. "Patterns of Transnational Terrorism, 1970–1999: Alternative Time-Series Estimates." *International Studies Quarterly* 46:145–65.

ENGELSTAD, FREDRIK, AND ØYVIND ØSTERUD, EDS. 2004. *Power and Democracy: Critical Interventions*. Aldershot: Ashgate.

ENNIS, JAMES G. 1987. "Fields of Action: Structure in Movements' Tactical Repertoires." *Sociological Forum* 2:520–33.

ERIKSSON, MIKAEL, AND PETER WALLENSTEEN. 2004. "Armed Conflict, 1989–2003." *Journal of Peace Research* 41:625–36.

ESHERICK, JOSEPH W., AND JEFFREY N. WASSERSTROM. 1990. "Acting Out Democracy: Political Theater in Modern China." *Journal of Asian Studies* 49:835–65.

ESPING-ANDERSEN, GØSTA. 1990. *The Three Worlds of Welfare Capitalism*. Princeton: Princeton University Press.

EVANS, IVAN. 1990. "The Native Affairs Department and the Reserves in the 1940s and 1950s." In Robin Cohen, Yvonne G. Muthien, Abebe Zegeye, eds., *Repression and Resistance: Insider Accounts of Apartheid*. London: Hans Zell.

FARAH, DOUGLAS. 2004. *Blood from Stones. The Secret Financial Network of Terror*. New York: Broadway Books.

FARRELL, SEAN. 2000. *Rituals and Riots: Sectarian Violence and Political Culture in Ulster, 1784–1886*. Lexington: University Press of Kentucky.

FAVRE, PIERRE, ED. 1990. *La Manifestation*. Paris: Presses de la Fondation Nationale des Sciences Politiques.

FAVRE, PIERRE, OLIVIER FILLIEULE, AND NONNA MAYER. 1997. "La fin d'une étrange lacune de la sociologie des mobilisations. L'étude par sondage des manifestants. Fondements théoriques et solutions techniques." *Revue Française de Science Politique* 47:3–28.

FEARON, JAMES D., AND DAVID D. LAITIN. 2000. "Violence and the Social Construction of Ethnic Identity." *International Organization* 54:845–77.

———. 2003. "Ethnicity, Insurgency, and Civil War," *American Political Science Review* 97:75.

FILLIEULE, OLIVIER. 1997a. *Stratégies de la rue. Les manifestations en France*. Paris: Presses de la Fondation Nationale des Sciences Politiques.

———. 1997b. "Maintien de l'ordre." Special issue of *Cahiers de la Sécurité Intérieure*.

FILLIEULE, OLIVIER, ED. 2005. *Le désengagement militant*. Paris: Belin.

FINER, S. E. 1997. *The History of Government from the Earliest Times*. Oxford: Oxford University Press. 3 vols.

FISCHER, STANLEY. 2003. "Globalization and Its Challenges." *American Economic Review Papers and Proceedings* 92:1–30.

FISH, M. STEVEN. 2005. *Democracy Derailed in Russia: The Failure of Open Politics*. Cambridge: Cambridge University Press.

FORAN, JOHN, ED. 2003. *The Future of Revolutions: Rethinking Radical Change in the Age of Globalization*. London: Zed Books.

FRANCISCO, RONALD A. 2005. "The Dictator's Dilemma." In Christian Davenport, Hank Johnston, and Carol Mueller, eds., *Repression and Mobilization*. Minneapolis: University of Minnesota Press.

FRANZOSI, ROBERTO. 1995. *The Puzzle of Strikes: Class and State Strategies in Postwar Italy*. Cambridge: Cambridge University Press.

———. 1998. "Narrative as Data: Linguistic and Statistical Tools for the Quantitative Study of Historical Events." *International Review of Social History* 43, Supplement 6: "New Methods for Social History," 81–104.

FREDRICKSON, GEORGE M. 1981. *White Supremacy: A Comparative Study in American and South African History*. Oxford: Oxford University Press.

FREY, BRUNO S., AND ALOIS STUTZER. 2002. "What Can Economists Learn from Happiness Research?" *Journal of Economic Literature* 40:402–35.

FURET, FRANCOIS, ANTOINE LINIERS, AND PHILIPPE RAYNAUD. 1985. *Terrorisme et Démocratie*. Paris: Fayard.

G8. 2003. "2003 G8 Summit." Available at www.g8.fr/evian/english, viewed July 10, 2005.

GAMBETTA, DIEGO, ED. 2005. *Making Sense of Suicide Missions*. Oxford: Oxford University Press.

GÉRARD, ALAIN. 1999. *"Par principe d'humanité...": La Terreur et la Vendée*. Paris: Fayard.

GERSTENBERGER, HEIDE. 1990. *Die subjektlose Gewalt. Theorie der Entstehung bürgerlicher Staatsgewalt*. Münster: Westfälisches Dampfboot.

GHOBARAH, HAZEM ADAM, PAUL HUTH, AND BRUCE RUSSETT. 2003. "Civil Wars Kill and Maim People—Long After the Shooting Stops." *American Political Science Review* 97:189–202.

GIUGNI, MARCO. 1995. *Entre stratégie et opportunité. Les nouveaux mouvements sociaux en Suisse*. Zürich: Seismo.

———. 2004. *Social Protest and Policy Change: Ecology, Antinuclear, and Peace Movements in Comparative Perspective*. Lanham, Md.: Rowman and Littlefield.

GIUGNI, MARCO, AND FLORENCE PASSY. 1997. *Histoires de mobilisation politique en Suisse. De la contestation à l'intégration*. Paris: L'Harmattan.

GLASIUS, MARLIES, MARY KALDOR, AND HELMUT ANHEIER. 2002. *Global Civil Society 2002*. Oxford: Oxford University Press.

GLENN, JOHN K. 2001. *Framing Democracy: Civil Society and Civic Movements in Eastern Europe*. Stanford: Stanford University Press.

GODOY, ANGELINA SNODGRASS. 2004. "When 'Justice' Is Criminal: Lynchings in Contemporary Latin America." *Theory and Society* 33:621–51.

GOLDIN, IAN. 1987. "The Reconstitution of Coloured Identity in the Western Cape." In Shula Marks and Stanley Trapido, eds., *The Politics of Race, Class and Nationalism in Twentieth-Century South Africa*. London: Longman.

GOLDSTEIN, ROBERT J. 1983. *Political Repression in 19th Century Europe*. London: Croom Helm.

GOLDSTEIN, ROBERT J., ED. *The War for the Public Mind: Political Censorship in Nineteenth-Century Europe*. Westport: Praeger.

———. *Political Repression in Modern America from 1870 to 1976*. Urbana: University of Illinois Press.

GOLDSTONE, JACK A., ED. 2003. *States, Parties, and Social Movements*. Cambridge: Cambridge University Press.

GOLDSTONE, JACK A., TED ROBERT GURR, FARROKH MOSHIRI, EDS. 1991. *Revolutions of the Late Twentieth Century*. Boulder: Westview.

GOLDSTONE, JACK A., AND CHARLES TILLY. 2001. "Threat (and Opportunity): Popular Action and State Response in the Dynamics of Contentious Action." In Ronald Aminzade et al., *Silence and Voice in Contentious Politics*. Cambridge: Cambridge University Press.

GOLDSTONE, JACK A., AND BERT USEEM. 1999. "Prison Riots as Microrevolutions: An Extension of State-Centered Theories of Revolution." *American Journal of Sociology* 104:985–1029.

GONZÁLEZ CALLEJO, EDUARDO. 2002a. *El terrorismo en Europa*. Madrid: Arco/Libros.

———. 2002b. *La Violencia en la Política. Perspectivas teóricas sobre el empleo deliberado de la fuerza en los conflictos de poder*. Madrid: Consejo de Investigaciones Científicas.

GONZÁLEZ CALLEJO, EDUARDO, ED. 2002. *Políticas del miedo. Un balance del terrorismo en Europa*. Madrid: Biblioteca Nueva.

GOODIN, ROBERT E., Bruce Headey, Ruud Muffels, and Henk-Jan Dirven. 1999. *The Real Worlds of Welfare Capitalism*. Cambridge: Cambridge University Press.

GOODWAY, DAVID. 1982. *London Chartism 1838–1848*. Cambridge: Cambridge University Press.

GOODWIN, JEFF. 2001, *No Other Way Out: States and Revolutionary Movements, 1945–1991*. Cambridge: Cambridge University Press.

———. 2005. "Revolutions and Revolutionary Movements." In Thomas Janoski, Robert R. Alford, Alexander M. Hicks, and Mildred A. Schwartz, eds., *Handbook of Political Sociology: States, Civil Societies, and Globalization*. Cambridge: Cambridge University Press.

GOODWIN, JEFF, AND JAMES M. JASPER, EDS. 2004. *Rethinking Social Movements: Structure, Meaning, and Emotion*. Lanham, Md.: Rowman and Littlefield.

GOULD, ROGER V. 2003. *Collision of Wills: How Ambiguity about Social Rank Breeds Conflict*. Chicago: University of Chicago Press.

GOWA, JOANNE. 1999. *Ballots and Bullets: The Elusive Democratic Peace*. Princeton: Princeton University Press.

GRANJON, FABIEN. 2002. "Les repertoires d'action télémathiques du néomilitantisme." *Le Mouvement Social* 200:11–32.

GREER, DONALD. 1935. *The Incidence of the Terror during the French Revolution: A Statistical Interpretation*. Cambridge: Harvard University Press.

GREIFF, MATS. 1997. " 'Marching through the Streets Singing and Shouting': Industrial Struggles and Trade Unions among Female Linen Workers in Belfast and Lurgan, 1872–1910." *Saothar* 22. *Journal of the Irish Labour History Society* 29–44.

GRIMAL, JEAN-CLAUDE. 2000. *Drogue: l'autre mondialisation*. Paris: Gallimard.

GRIMSHAW, ALLEN D. 1999. "Genocide and Democide." In Lester Kurtz, ed., *Encyclopedia of Violence, Peace, and Conflict*. San Diego: Academic Press, 2:53–74.

GUENNIFFEY, PATRICE. 2000. *La Politique de la Terreur. Essai sur la Violence Révolutionnaire, 1789–1794*. Paris: Fayard.

GURR, TED ROBERT. 2000. *Peoples versus States: Minorities at Risk in the New Century*. Washington: United States Institute of Peace Press.

HAGAN, JOE D. 1994. "Domestic Political Systems and War Proneness." *Mershon International Studies Review* 38:183–208.

HAGE, JERALD, ROBERT HANNEMAN, AND EDWARD T. GARGAN. 1989. *State Responsiveness and State Activism: An Examination of the Social Forces That Explain the Rise in Social Expenditures in Britain, France, Germany and Italy 1870–1968*. London: Unwin Hyman.

HAIMSON, LEOPOLD, AND GIULIO SAPELLI, EDS. 1992. *Strikes, Social Conflict and the First World War: An International Perspective*. Milan: Feltrinelli. Fondazione Giangiacomo Feltrinelli, *Annali* 1990/1991.

HAIMSON, LEOPOLD, AND CHARLES TILLY, EDS. 1989. *Strikes, Wars, and Revolutions in an International Perspective: Strike Waves in the Late Nineteenth and Early Twentieth Centuries*. Cambridge: Cambridge University Press.

HALLIDAY, FRED. 1999. *Revolution and World Politics: The Rise and Fall of the Sixth Great Power*. Durham: Duke University Press.

HANAGAN, MICHAEL. 1999. "Industrial versus Preindustrial Forms of Violence." In Lester Kurtz, ed., *Encyclopedia of Violence, Peace, and Conflict*. San Diego: Academic Press, 2:197–210.

HANSEN, THOMAS BLOM. 1999. *The Saffron Wave: Democracy and Hindu Nationalism in Modern India*. Princeton: Princeton University Press.

HARFF, BARBARA. 2003. "No Lessons Learned from the Holocaust? Assessing Risks of Genocide and Political Mass Murder since 1955." *American Political Science Review* 97:57–73.

HARRISON, MARK. 1988. *Crowds and History: Mass Phenomena in English Towns, 1790–1835*. Cambridge: Cambridge University Press.

HART, PETER. 1998. *The I.R.A. & Its Enemies: Violence and Community in Cork 1916–1923*. Oxford: Clarendon Press.

HAYTER, ANTHONY. 1978. *The Army and the Crowd in Mid-Georgian England*. Totowa, N.J.: Rowman and Littlefield.

HEERMA VAN VOSS, LEX, ED. 2001. "Petitions in Social History." *International Review of Social History*, Supplement 9, entire issue.

HEITMEYER, WILHELM, AND JOHN HAGAN, ED. 2003. *International Handbook of Violence Research*. Dordrecht: Kluwer.

HELD, DAVID. 1996. *Models of Democracy*. Stanford: Stanford University Press.

HELLMAN, JUDITH ADLER. 2000. "Real and Virtual Chiapas: Realism and the Left." *Socialist Register* 2000:161–86.

HENDERSON, ERROL A. 1999. "Civil Wars." In Lester Kurtz, ed., *Encyclopedia of Violence, Peace, and Conflict*. San Diego: Academic Press, 1:279–287.

HIRONAKA, ANN. 2005. *Neverending Wars: The International Community, Weak States, and the Perpetuation of Civil War*. Cambridge: Harvard University Press.

HOBSBAWM, ERIC, AND GEORGE RUDÉ. 1968. *Captain Swing: A Social History of the Great English Agricultural Uprisings of 1830*. New York: Pantheon.

HOCKE, PETER. 2002. *Massenmedien und lokaler Protest. Eine empirische Fallstudie zur Medienselektivität in einer westdeutschen Begwegungshochberg*. Wiesbaden: Westdeutscher Verlag.

HOFMEYR, ISABEL. 1987. "Building a Nation from Words: Afrikaans Language, Literature and Ethnic Identity, 1902–1924." In Shula Marks and Stanley Trapido, eds., *The Politics of Race, Class and Nationalism in Twentieth-Century South Africa*. London: Longman.

HORN, GERD-RAINER, AND PADRAIC KENNEY, EDS. 2004. *Transnational Moments of Change: Europe 1945, 1968, 1989*. Lanham, Md.: Rowman and Littlefield.

HUBER, EVELYNE, AND JOHN D. STEPHENS. 2001. *Development and Crisis of the Welfare State: Parties and Policies in Global Markets*. Chicago: University of Chicago Press.

HUG, SIMON, AND DOMINIQUE WISLER. 1998. "Correcting for Selection Bias in Social Movement Research." *Mobilization* 3:141–62.

HUMAN RIGHTS WATCH. 2002a. "Peru: Human Rights after Fujimori." Available at www.hrw.org/backgrounder/americas/peru-hr-bck-0320.htm, viewed January 22, 2005.

———. 2002b. *Human Rights Watch World Report 2002*, online ed. Available at www.hrw.org/wr2k2/asia6.html, viewed January 22, 2005.

———. 2003a. *Human Rights Watch World Report 2003*, online ed. Available at www.hrw.org/wr2k3/africa13.html, viewed January 22, 2005.

———. 2003b. *Human Rights Watch World Report 2003*, online ed. Available at www.hrw.org/wr2k3/asia6.htmal, viewed January 22, 2005.

———. 2003c. *Human Rights Watch World Report 2003*, online ed. Available at www.hrw.org/wr2k3/us.html, viewed January 23, 2005.

———. 2003d. "Abducted and Abused: Renewed Conflict in Northern Uganda." *Human Rights Watch* 15(12[A]).

———. 2004a. "Morocco: Human Rights at a Crossroads." *Human Rights Watch* 1(6[E]).

———. 2004b. "Human Rights Overview: Peru." Available at www.hrw.org/english/docs/2004/01/21/peru6988.htm, viewed January 22, 2005.

———. 2004c. "Letter Urging Jamaican Government to Protect Rights Defenders and Address Violence and Abuse Based on Sexual Orientation and HIV Status." Available at www.hrw.org/english/docs/2004/ll/30/jamaic9750_txt.htm, viewed April 5, 2005.

———. 2005. *Human Rights Watch World Report 2005: Events of 2004*. New York: Human Rights Watch.

IBARRA, PEDRO, ED. 2003. *Social Movements and Democracy*. New York: Palgrave Macmillan.

IMIG, DOUG, AND SIDNEY TARROW, EDS. 2001. *Contentious Europeans: Protest and Politics in an Emerging Polity*. Lanham, Md.: Rowman and Littlefield.

JACKMAN, MARY R. 2002. "Violence in Social Life." *Annual Review of Sociology* 28:387–415.

JANOSKI, THOMAS. 1998. *Citizenship and Civil Society: A Framework of Rights and Obligations in Liberal, Traditional, and Social Democratic Regimes*. Cambridge: Cambridge University Press.

JANOSKI, THOMAS, AND ALEXANDER M. HICKS, EDS. 1994. *The Comparative Political Economy of the Welfare State*. Cambridge: Cambridge University Press.

JARMAN, NEIL. 1997. *Material Conflicts: Parades and Visual Displays in Northern Ireland*. Oxford: Berg.

JOHNSON, GORDON. 1996. *Cultural Atlas of India*. New York: Facts on File.

JOHNSON, R. W. 2004. *South Africa: The First Man, the Last Nation*. London: Weidenfeld and Nicolson.

JONES, BRUCE. 1995. "Intervention without Borders: Humanitarian Intervention in Rwanda, 1990–1994." *Millennium: Journal of International Affairs* 24:225–49.

JOSSE, RAYMOND. 1962. "La naissance de la Résistance à Paris." *Revue d'Histoire de la Deuxième Guerre Mondiale* 12:1–32.

JUNG, COURTNEY. 2000. *Then I Was Black: South African Political Identities in Transition.* New Haven: Yale University Press.

JUNG, COURTNEY, AND IAN SHAPIRO. 1995. "South Africa's Negotiated Transition: Democracy, Opposition, and the New Constitutional Order." *Politics and Society* 23:269–308.

KAISER, ROBERT J. 1994. *The Geography of Nationalism in Russia and the USSR.* Princeton: Princeton University Press.

KAKAR, SUDHIR. 1996. *The Colors of Violence: Cultural Identities, Religion, and Conflict.* Chicago: University of Chicago Press.

KALDOR, MARY. 1999. *New & Old Wars: Organized Violence in a Global Era.* Cambridge, UK: Polity.

KALDOR, MARY, HELMUT ANHEIER, AND MARLIES GLASIUS. 2005. "Introduction" to Helmut Anheier, Marlies Glasius, Mary Kaldor, and Fiona Holland, eds., *Global Civil Society 2004/5.* London: Sage Publications.

KALYVAS, STATHIS N. 2003. "The Ontology of 'Political Violence': Action and Identity in Civil Wars." *Perspectives on Politics* 1:475–94.

KARATNYCKY, ADRIAN, ED. 2000. *Freedom in the World: The Annual Survey of Political Rights and Civil Liberties.* Piscataway, N.J.: Transaction.

KECK, MARGARET, AND KATHRYN SIKKINK. 1998. *Activists beyond Borders: Advocacy Networks in International Politics.* Ithaca: Cornell University Press.

———. 2000. "Historical Precursors to Modern Transnational Social Movements and Networks." In John A. Guidry, Michael D. Kennedy, and Mayer N. Zald, eds., *Globalizations and Social Movements: Culture, Power, and the Transnational Public Sphere.* Ann Arbor: University of Michigan Press.

KEOGH, DERMOT. 2001. "Ireland at the Turn of the Century: 1994–2001." In T. W. Moody and F. X. Martin, eds., *The Course of Irish History.* Lanham, Md.: Roberts Rinehart. 4th ed.

KERTZER, DAVID I. 1988. *Ritual, Politics, and Power.* New Haven: Yale University Press.

KOOPMANS, RUUD. 2004. "Movements and Media: Selection Processes and Evolutionary Dynamics in the Public Sphere." *Theory and Society* 33:367–91.

———. 2005. "The Missing Link between Structure and Agency: Outline of an Evolutionary Approach to Social Movements." *Mobilization* 10:19–36.

KOTEK, JOËL, AND PIERRE RIGOULOT. 2000. *Le siècle des camps. Détention, concentration, extermination. Cent ans de mal radical.* Paris: J. C. Lattès.

KOTZ, DAVID, AND FRED WEIR. 1997. *Revolution from Above: The Demise of the Soviet System.* London: Routledge.

KATZ, MARK N. 1997. *Revolutions and Revolutionary Waves.* London: Longman.

KHAZANOV, ANATOLY M. 1995. *After the USSR: Ethnicity, Nationalism, and Politics in the Commonwealth of Independent States.* Madison: University of Wisconsin Press.

KRIESI, HANSPETER. 1980. *Entscheidungsstrukturen und Entscheidungsprozesse in der Schweizer Politik.* Frankfurt: Campus.

———. 1981. *AKW-Gegner in der Schweiz. Eine Fallstudie zum Aufbau des Widerstands gegen das geplante AKW in Graben.* Diessenhofen: Verlag Rüegger.

———. 2003. "The Transformation of the National Political Space in a Globalizing World." In Pedro Ibarra, ed., *Social Movements and Democracy.* London: Palgrave.

KRIESI, HANSPETER, RUUD KOOPMANS, JAN WILLEM DUYVENDAK, AND MARCO GIUGNI. 1995. *New Social Movements in Western Europe: A Comparative Analysis.* Minneapolis: University of Minnesota Press.

KRIESI, HANSPETER, RENÉ LEVY, GILBERT GANGUILLET, AND HEINZ ZWICKY. 1981. *Politische Aktivierung in der Schweiz, 1945–1978.* Diessenhofen: Verlag Rüegger.

KRUEGER, ALAN B. 2004. "To Improve Terrorism Data, the U.S. Should Follow the Lead of Economic Statistics." *New York Times,* July 22, C2.

KRUEGER, ALAN B., AND DAVID D. LAITIN. 2004. "'Misunderestimating' Terrorism." *Foreign Affairs* 83(5):8–13.

KRUG, ETIENNE G., LINDA L. DAHLBERG, JAMES A. MERCY, ANTHONY B. ZWI, AND RAFAEL LOZANO. 2002. *World Report on Violence and Health.* Geneva: World Health Organization.

KRUGMAN, PAUL. 2004. "Errors on Terror." *New York Times,* June 25, A23.

KURTZ, LESTER, ED. 1999. *Encyclopedia of Violence, Peace, and Conflict.* San Diego: Academic Press. 3 vols.

KURZMAN, CHARLES. 2004. "Can Understanding Undermine Explanation? The Confused Experience of Revolution." *Philosophy of the Social Sciences* 34:328–51.

KUSHNER, HARVEY W., ED. 2001. "Terrorism in the 21st Century." *American Behavioral Scientist* 44(6), entire issue.

LAFARGUE, JÉRÔME. 1996. *Contestations démocratiques en Afrique. Sociologie de la protestation au Kenya et en Zambie.* Paris: Karthala.

LAITIN, DAVID D. 1999. "Somalia: Civil War and International Intervention." In Barbara F. Walter and Jack Snyder, eds., *Civil Wars, Insecurity, and Intervention.* New York: Columbia University Press.

LANGMAN, LAUREN. 2005. "From Virtual Public Spheres to Global Justice: A Critical Theory of Internetworked Social Movements." *Sociological Theory* 23: 42–74.

LAUDERDALE, PAT, AND ANNAMARIE OLIVERIO, EDS. 2005. "Roots of Terrorism: Global and Local Controversies." *International Journal of Comparative Sociology* 46:3–169.

LAVERY, BRIAN. 2001a. "Target of Attack in Belfast: Little Girls Going to School." *New York Times,* September 6, A12.

———. 2001b. "Little Children in the Middle as Adults Battle in Belfast." *New York Times,* October 14, A6.

LEDENEVA, ALENA. 1998. *Russia's Economy of Favours: Blat, Networking, and Informal Exchange.* Cambridge: Cambridge University Press.

———. 2004. "Genealogy of *krugovaya poruka*: Forced Trust as a Feature of Russian Political Culture," *Proceedings of the British Academy* 123:85–108.

LEVIN, JACK, AND GORDANA RABRENOVIC, EDS. 2001. "Hate Crimes and Ethnic Conflict: A Comparative Perspective." *American Behavioral Scientist* 45(4), entire issue.

LICHBACH, MARK IRVING, AND ALAN S. ZUCKERMAN, EDS. 1997. *Comparative Politics: Rationality, Culture, and Structure.* Cambridge: Cambridge University Press.

LICKLIDER, ROY, ED. 1993. *Stopping the Killing: How Civil Wars End.* New York: NYU Press.

LIJPHART, AREND. 1999. *Patterns of Democracy: Government Forms and Performance in Thirty-Six Countries.* New Haven: Yale University Press.

LINDBLOM, CHARLES E. 1977. *Politics and Markets: The World's Political-Economic Systems*. New York: Basic Books.
LINDENBERGER, THOMAS. 1995. *Strassenpolitik. Zur Sozialgeschichte der öffentlichen Ordnung in Berlin 1900 bis 1914*. Bonn: Dietz.
LINZ, JUAN J., AND ALFRED STEPAN. 1996. *Problems of Democratic Transition and Consolidation: Southern Europe, South America, and Post-Communist Europe*. Baltimore: Johns Hopkins University Press.
LODGE, TOM. 1996. "South Africa: Democracy and Development in a Post-apartheid Society." In Adrian Leftwich, ed., *Democracy and Development: Theory and Practice*. London: Polity Press.
———. 2001. "South African Politics and Collective Action, 1994–2000." Chapter 1 in Bert Klandermans, Marlene Roefs, and Johan Olivier, eds., *The State of the People: Citizens, Civil Society and Governance in South Africa, 1994–2000*. Pretoria: Human Sciences Research Council.
LOFLAND, JOHN, AND MICHAEL FINK. 1982. *Symbolic Sit-Ins: Protest Occupations at the California Capitol*. Washington: University Press of America.
LÜDTKE, ALF. 1992. *"Sicherheit" und "Wohlfahrt." Polizei, Gesellschaft und Herrschaft im 19. und 20. Jahrhundert*. Frankfurt: Suhrkamp.
LUPHER, MARK. 1996. *Power Restructuring in China and Russia*. Boulder: Westview.
MADAN, T. N. 1997. "Religion, Ethnicity, and Nationalism in India." In Martin E. Marty and R. Scott Appleby, eds., *Religion, Ethnicity, and Self-Identity: Nations in Turmoil*. Hanover, N.H.: University Press of New England/Salzburg Seminar.
MAHONEY, JAMES. 2001. *The Legacies of Liberalism: Path Dependence and Political Regimes in Central America*. Baltimore: Johns Hopkins University Press.
———. 2002. "Knowledge Accumulation in Comparative Historical Research: The Case of Democracy and Authoritarianism." In James Mahoney and Dietrich Rueschemeyer, eds., *Comparative Historical Analysis in the Social Sciences*. Cambridge: Cambridge University Press.
MAHONEY, JAMES, AND RICHARD SNYDER. 1999. "Rethinking Agency and Structure in the Study of Regime Change." *Studies in Comparative International Development* 34:3–32.
MAIBA, HERMANN. 2005. "Grassroots Transnational Social Movement Activism: The Case of Peoples' Global Action." *Sociological Focus* 38:41–63.
MAMDANI, MAHMOOD. 2001. *When Victims Become Killers: Colonialism, Nativism, and the Genocide in Rwanda*. Princeton: Princeton University Press.
MANDELA, NELSON. 1994. *Long Walk to Freedom: The Autobiography of Nelson Mandela*. Boston: Little, Brown.
MANN, MICHAEL. 1986. *The Sources of Social Power*. Vol. 1: *A History of Power from the Beginning to a.d. 1760*. Cambridge: Cambridge University Press.
MARKOFF, JOHN. 1996. *Waves of Democracy: Social Movements and Political Change*. Thousand Oaks, Calif.: Pine Grove Press.
MARKS, SHULA, AND STANLEY TRAPIDO. 1987. "The Politics of Race, Class and Nationalism." In Shula Marks and Stanley Trapido, eds., *The Politics of Race, Class and Nationalism in Twentieth-Century South Africa*. London: Longman.
MARSHALL, T. H. 1950. *Citizenship and Social Class*. Cambridge: Cambridge University Press.
MARTÍNEZ, ASTRID, ED. 2001. *Economía, Crimen y Conflicto*. Bogotá: Universidad Nacional de Colombia.

MARX, ANTHONY W. 1991. *Lessons of Struggle: South African Internal Opposition 1960–1990*. New York: Oxford University Press.
———. 1995. "Contested Citizenship: The Dynamics of Racial Identity and Social Movements." *International Review of Social History* 40:159–83.
———. 1998. *Making Race and Nation: A Comparison of the United States, South Africa, and Brazil*. Cambridge: Cambridge University Press.
MARX, KARL. 1964. *Pre-Capitalist Economic Formations*, ed. Eric Hobsbawm. London: Lawrence and Wishart.
MASON, T. DAVID. 2004. *Caught in the Crossfire: Revolutions, Repression, and the Rational Peasant*. Lanham, Md.: Rowman and Littlefield.
MATHIEU, LILIAN. 2004. "Des mouvements sociaux à la politique contestataire: les voies tâtonnantes d'un renouvellement de perspective." *Revue Française de Sociologie* 45:561–80.
MAYEKISO, MZWANELE. 1996. *Township Politics: Civic Struggles for a New South Africa*. New York: Monthly Review Press.
MAYER, ARNO J. 2000. *The Furies: Violence and Terror in the French and Russian Revolutions*. Princeton: Princeton University Press.
MAZOWER, MARK. 2002. "Violence and the State in the Twentieth Century." *American Historical Review* 107:1158–78.
MCADAM, DOUG, JOHN D. MCCARTHY, AND MAYER N. ZALD. 1988. "Social Movements." In Neil J. Smelser, ed., *Handbook of Sociology*. Newbury Park, Calif.: Sage Publications.
MCADAM, DOUG, SIDNEY TARROW, AND CHARLES TILLY. 2001. *Dynamics of Contention*. Cambridge: Cambridge University Press.
MCCARTHY, JOHN D., CLARK MCPHAIL, AND JOHN CRIST. 1999. "The Diffusion and Adoption of Public Order Management Systems." In Donatella della Porta, Hanspeter Kriesi, and Dieter Rucht, eds., *Social Movements in a Globalizing World*. London: Macmillan.
MCCARTHY, JOHN D., CLARK MCPHAIL, AND JACKIE SMITH. 1996. "Images of Protest: Estimating Selection Bias in Media Coverage of Washington Demonstrations 1982 and 1991." *American Sociological Review* 61:478–99.
MCCARTHY, JOHN D., JACKIE SMITH, AND MAYER N. ZALD. 1996. "Accessing Public, Media, Electoral, and Governmental Agendas." In Doug McAdam, John D. McCarthy, and Mayer N. Zald, eds., *Comparative Perspectives on Social Movements*. Cambridge: Cambridge University Press, 1996.
MCMILLAN, JOHN, AND PABLO ZOIDO. 2004. "How to Subvert Democracy: Montesinos in Peru." *Journal of Economic Perspectives* 18:69–92.
MCNEILL, WILLIAM H. 1995. *Keeping Together in Time: Dance and Drill in Human History*. Cambridge: Harvard University Press.
MCPHEE, PETER. 1988. "Les formes d'intervention populaire en Roussillon: L'exemple de Collioure, 1789–1815." In *Centre d'Histoire Contemporaine du Languedoc Méditerranéen et du Roussillon. Les pratiques politiques en province à l'époque de la Révolution française*. Montpellier: Publications de la Recherche, Université de Montpellier.
MERTES, TOM, ED. 2004. *A Movement of Movements: Is Another World Really Possible?* London: Verso.
MEYER, DAVID S. 2004. "Protest and Political Opportunities." *Annual Review of Sociology* 30:125–45.

MEYER, DAVID S., AND DEBRA C. MINKOFF. 2004. "Conceptualizing Political Opportunity." *Social Forces* 82:1457–92.

MINNAAR, ANTHONY. 1992. *Patterns of Conflict: Case Studies of Conflict in Natal.* Pretoria: Human Sciences Research Council.

MIRALA, PETRI. 2000. " 'A Large Mob, Calling Themselves Freemasons': Masonic Parades in Ulster." In Peter Jupp and Eoin Magennis, eds., *Crowds in Ireland, c. 1720–1920.* London: Macmillan.

MOMMSEN, WOLFGANG J., AND GERHARD HIRSCHFELD, EDS. 1982. *Social Protest, Violence and Terror in Nineteenth- and Twentieth-Century Europe.* New York: St. Martins.

MONJARDET, DOMINIQUE. 1996. *Ce que fait la police. Sociologie de la force publique.* Paris: La Découverte.

MOODIE, T. DUNBAR. 1975. *The Rise of Afrikanderdom: Power, Apartheid, and the Afrikaner Civil Religion.* Berkeley: University of California Press.

———. 1994. *Going for Gold: Men, Mines, and Migration.* Berkeley: University of California Press.

MOORE, BARRINGTON, JR. 1966. *Social Origins of Dictatorship and Democracy.* Boston: Beacon.

MORLINO, LEONARDO. 2003. *Democrazie e democratizzazioni.* Bologna: Il Mulino.

MUELLER, CAROL. 1997. "International Press Coverage of East German Protest Events, 1989." *American Sociological Review* 62:820–32.

———. 1999. "Escape from the GDR, 1961–1989: Hybrid Exit Repertoires in a Disintegrating Leninist Regime." *American Journal of Sociology* 105:697–735.

MUELLER, JOHN. 2000. "The Banality of 'Ethnic War.' " *International Security* 25: 42–70.

MUIR, EDWARD. 1997. *Ritual in Early Modern Europe.* Cambridge: Cambridge University Press.

MURPHY, GILLIAN H., AND STEVEN PFAFF. 2005. "Thinking Locally, Acting Globally? What the Seattle WTO Protests Tell Us about the Global Justice Movement." *Political Power and Social Theory* 17:151–78.

MURRAY, MARTIN. 1987. *South Africa: Time of Agony, Time of Destiny.* London: Verso.

NAIMARK, NORMAN M. 2001. *Fires of Hatred: Ethnic Cleansing in Twentieth-Century Europe.* Cambridge: Harvard University Press.

NATIONAL COUNTERTERRORISM CENTER. 2005. "A Chronology of Significant International Terrorism for 2004." Available at www.tkb.org/nctc (incident data), viewed May 21, 2005.

NATIONAL SECURITY ARCHIVE. 2000. " 'Fujimori's Rasputin' ": The Declassified Files on Peru's Former Intelligence Chief, Vladimiro Montesinos. NSA Electronic Briefing Book No. 37. Available at www2.gwu.edu/~nsarchiv/NSAEBB/NSAEBB37/, viewed December, 30, 2004.

OBERSCHALL, ANTHONY. 1994. "Protest Demonstrations and the End of Communist Regimes in 1989." *Research in Social Movements, Conflicts and Change* 17:1–24.

OBERSCHALL, ANTHONY, AND MICHAEL SEIDMAN. 2005. "Food Coercion in Revolution and Civil War: Who Wins and How They Do It." *Comparative Studies in Society and History* 47:372–402.

OLESON, THOMAS. 2005. The Uses and Misuses of Globalization in the Study of Social Movements." *Social Movement Studies* 4:49–64.

OLIVER, PAMELA, AND GREGORY M. MANEY. 2000. "Political Processes and Local Newspaper Coverage of Protest Events: From Selection Bias to Triadic Interactions." *American Journal of Sociology* 106:463–505.

OLIVER, PAMELA, AND DANIEL J. MYERS. 1999. "How Events Enter the Public Sphere: Conflict, Location, and Sponsorship in Local Newspaper Coverage of Public Events." *American Journal of Sociology* 105:38–87.

OLIVERIO, ANNAMARIE. 1998. *The State of Terror*. Albany: State University of New York Press.

OLIVIER, JOHAN. 1991. "State Repression and Collective Action in South Africa, 1970–84." *South African Journal of Sociology* 22:109–17.

OLZAK, SUSAN. 1989. "Analysis of Events in the Study of Collective Action." *Annual Review of Sociology* 15:119–41.

———. 2006. *The Global Dynamics of Racial and Ethnic Mobilization*. Stanford: Stanford University Press.

O'NEILL, KATE. 2004. "Transnational Protest: States, Circuses, and Conflict at the Frontline of Global Politics." *International Studies Review* 6:233–51.

OSA, MARYJANE. 2003. *Solidarity and Contention: Networks of Polish Opposition*. Minneapolis: University of Minnesota Press.

PAIGE, JEFFERY M. 2003. "Finding the Revolutionary in the Revolution: Social Science Concepts and the Future of Revolution." In John Foran, ed., *The Future of Revolutions: Rethinking Radical Change in the Age of Globalization*. London: Zed Books.

PANFICHI, ALDO. 1997. "The Authoritarian Alternative: 'Anti-politics' in the Popular Sectors of Lima." In Douglas A. Chalmers, Carlos M. Vilas, Katherine Hite, Scott B. Martin, Kerianne Piester, and Monique Sergarra, eds., *The New Politics of Inequality in Latin America: Rethinking Participation and Representation*. New York: Oxford University Press.

PAPE, ROBERT A. 2003. "The Strategic Logic of Suicide Terrorism." *American Political Science Review* 97:343–61.

PARSA, MISAGH. 2000. *States, Ideologies, and Social Revolutions: A Comparative Analysis of Iran, Nicaragua and the Philippines*. Cambridge: Cambridge University Press.

PATTERSON, ORLANDO. 2001. "The Roots of Conflict in Jamaica." *New York Times on the Web*, 23 July.

PAXTON, ROBERT O. 1995 "Leçon sur les fascismes." *Vingtième Siècle* 45:3–13.

PERROT, MICHELLE. 1974. *Les ouvriers en grève*. Paris: Mouton. 2 vols.

PIANO, AILI, AND ARCH PUDDINGTON, EDS. 2004. *Freedom in the World 2004: The Annual Survey of Political Rights and Civil Liberties*. New York: Freedom House.

PIANTA, MARIO. 2001. "Parallel Summits of Global Civil Society." In Helmut Anheier, Marlies Glasius, and Mary Kaldor, eds., *Global Civil Society 2001*. Oxford: Oxford University Press.

PICHARDO, NELSON. 1997. "New Social Movements: A Critical Review." *Annual Review of Sociology* 23:411–30.

PIGENET, MICHEL, AND DANIELLE TARTAKOWSKY, EDS. 2003. "Les marches." *Le mouvement social* 202 (January-March), entire issue.

PILLAY, NAVANETHEM. 2001. "Sexual Violence in Times of Conflict: The Jurisprudence of the International Criminal Tribunal for Rwanda." In Simon Chesterman, ed., *Civilians in War*. Boulder: Lynne Rienner.

PLOWS, ALEXANDRA, DEREK WALL, AND BRIAN DOHERTY. 2004. "Covert Repertoires: Ecotage in the U.K." *Social Movement Studies* 3:199–220.
POLLETTA, FRANCESCA. 2002. *Freedom Is an Endless Meeting: Democracy in American Social Movements*. Chicago: University of Chicago Press.
DELLA PORTA, DONATELLA. 1995. *Social Movements, Political Violence, and the State: A Comparative Analysis of Italy and Germany*. Cambridge: Cambridge University Press.
———. 2005. "Making the Polis: Social Forums and Democracy in the Global Justice Movement." *Mobilization* 10:73–94.
DELLA PORTA, DONATELLA, AND GIANFRANCO PASQUINO, EDS. 1983. *Terrorismo e violenza politica. Tre casi a confronto: Stati Uniti, Germania e Giappone*. Bologna: Il Mulino.
DELLA PORTA, DONATELLA, AND HERBERT REITER, EDS. 1998. *Policing Protest: The Control of Mass Demonstrations in Western Democracies*. Minneapolis: University of Minnesota Press.
DELLA PORTA, DONATELLA, AND SIDNEY TARROW, EDS. 2004. *Transnational Protest and Global Activism*. Lanham, Md.: Rowman and Littlefield.
PRICE, ROBERT M. 1991. *The Apartheid State in Crisis: Political Transformation in South Africa 1975–1990*. New York: Oxford University Press.
PRUNIER, GÉRARD. 1995. *The Rwanda Crisis: History of a Genocide*. New York: Columbia University Press.
———. 2001. "Genocide in Rwanda." In Daniel Chirot and Martin E. P. Seligman, eds., *Ethnopolitical Warfare: Causes, Consequences, and Possible Solutions*. Washington, D.C.: American Psychological Association.
PRZEWORSKI, ADAM, MICHAEL E. ALVAREZ, JOSÉ ANTONIO CHEIBUB, AND FERNANDO LIMONGI. 2000. *Democracy and Development: Political Institutions and Well-Being in the World, 1950–1990*. Cambridge: Cambridge University Press.
RAJAGOPAL, ARVIND. 2001. *Politics after Television: Religious Nationalism and the Reshaping of the Indian Public*. Cambridge: Cambridge University Press.
RAMIREZ, RUBEN DARIO. 2001. "On the Kidnapping Industry in Colombia." In Alex P. Schmid, ed., *Countering Terrorism through International Cooperation*. Milan: International Scientific and Professional Advisory Council of the United Nations Crime Prevention and Criminal Justice Programme.
REUTERS. 2005. "Cambodian Police Break Up Vietnam Refugee Protest." Available at http://today.reuters.com, viewed July 21, 2005.
RAPOPORT, DAVID C. 1999. "Terrorism." In Lester Kurtz, ed., *Encyclopedia of Violence, Peace, and Conflict*. San Diego: Academic Press, 3:497–510.
RAY, JAMES LEE. 1998. "Does Democracy Cause Peace?" *Annual Review of Political Science* 1:27–46.
REISS, ALBERT J., AND JEFFREY A. ROTH, EDS. 1993. *Understanding and Preventing Violence*. Washington, D.C.: National Academy Press.
REITER, DAN, AND ALLAN C. STAM. 2002. *Democracies at War*. Princeton: Princeton University Press.
RHEINGOLD, HOWARD. 2003. *Smart Mobs: The Next Social Revolution*. New York: Perseus.
ROBERT, VINCENT. 1996. *Les chemins de la manifestation, 1848–1914*. Lyon: Presses Universitaires de Lyon.

RUBY, CHARLES L. 2002. "The Definition of Terrorism." *Analyses of Social Issues and Public Policy* 2:9–14.

RUCHT, DIETER. 2004. "The Quadruple 'A': Media Strategies of Protest Movements since the 1960s." In Wim van de Donk, Brian D. Loader, Paul G. Nihon, and Dieter Rucht, eds., *Cyberprotest: New Media, Citizens and Social Movements*. London: Routledge.

RUCHT, DIETER, AND RUUD KOOPMANS, ED. 1999. "Protest Event Analysis." *Mobilization* 4(2), entire issue.

RUCHT, DIETER, RUUD KOOPMANS, AND FRIEDHELM NEIDHARDT, EDS. 1998. *Acts of Dissent: New Developments in the Study of Protest*. Berlin: Sigma Rainer Bohn Verlag.

RUESCHEMEYER, DIETRICH, EVELYNE HUBER STEPHENS, AND JOHN D. STEPHENS. 1992. *Capitalist Development and Democracy*. Chicago: University of Chicago Press.

RUFF, JULIUS R. 2001. *Violence in Early Modern Europe, 1500–1800*. Cambridge: Cambridge University Press.

RUGGIE, MARY. 1996. *Realignments in the Welfare State: Health Policy in the United States, Britain, and Canada*. New York: Columbia University Press.

RUMMEL, R. J. 1994. *Death by Government*. New Brunswick: Transaction Publishers.

RUSSELL, DIANA. 1974. *Rebellion, Revolution and Armed Force*. New York: Academic Press.

SALVATORE, RICARDO. 2001. "Repertoires of Coercion and Market Culture in Nineteenth-Century Buenos Aires Province." *International Review of Social History* 45:409–48.

SAMBANIS, NICHOLAS. 2002. "A Review of Recent Advances and Future Directions in the Quantitative Literature on Civil War." *Defence and Peace Economics* 13:215–43.

———. 2004a. "Using Case Studies to Expand Economic Models of Civil War." *Perspectives on Politics* 2:259–80.

———. 2004b. "What Is Civil War? Conceptual and Empirical Complexities of an Operational Definition." *Journal of Conflict Resolution* 48:814–58.

SANDERSON, STEPHEN K. 2005. *Revolutions: A Worldwide Introduction to Political and Social Change*. Boulder: Paradigm Publishers.

SANDOVAL, SALVADOR A. M. 1993. *Social Change and Labor Unrest in Brazil since 1945*. Boulder: Westview.

SAUL, JOHN S. 1994. "Globalism, Socialism and Democracy in the South African Transition." *Socialist Register* 1994:171–202.

SAWYER, R. KEITH. 2001. *Creating Conversations: Improvisation in Everyday Discourse*. Cresskill, N.J.: Hampton Press.

SCALMER, SEAN. 2002a. *Dissent Events: Protest, the Media and the Political Gimmick in Australia*. Sydney: University of New South Wales Press.

———. 2002b. "The Labor of Diffusion: The Peace Pledge Union and the Adaptation of the Gandhian Repertoire." *Mobilization* 7:269–85.

SCHMID, ALEX P., ED. 2001. *Countering Terrorism Through International Cooperation*. Milan: International Scientific and Professional Advisory Council of the United Nations Crime Prevention and Criminal Justice Programme.

SCHOCK, KURT. 2005. *Unarmed Insurrections: People Power Movements in Nondemocracies*. Minneapolis: University of Minnesota Press.

SCHWEDLER, JILLIAN. 2005. "Cop Rock: Protest, Identity, and Dancing Riot Police in Jordan." *Social Movement Studies* 4:155–75.
SCOTT, JAMES C. 1985. *Weapons of the Weak: Everyday Forms of Peasant Resistance.* New Haven: Yale University Press.
SEIDMAN, GAY W. 2000. "Blurred Lines: Nonviolence in South Africa." *PS. Political Science and Politics* 33:161–68.
SENECHAL DE LA ROCHE, ROBERTA, ED. 2004. "Theories of Terrorism: A Symposium." *Sociological Theory* 22:1–105.
SHAPIRO, GILBERT, AND JOHN MARKOFF. 1998. *Revolutionary Demands: A Content Analysis of the Cahiers de Doléances of 1789.* Stanford: Stanford University Press.
SHELLER, MIMI. 2000. *Democracy after Slavery: Black Publics and Peasant Radicalism in Haiti and Jamaica.* London: Macmillan.
SHORTER, EDWARD, AND CHARLES TILLY. 1974. *Strikes in France, 1830–1968.* Cambridge: Cambridge University Press.
SINGER, P. W. 2003. *Corporate Warriors: The Rise of the Privatized Military Industry.* Ithaca: Cornell University Press.
SKOCPOL, THEDA. 1979. *States and Social Revolutions: A Comparative Analysis of France, Russia, and China.* Cambridge: Cambridge University Press.
SLYOMOVICS, SUSAN. 2005. "Morocco's Justice and Reconciliation Commission." *Middle East Report Online,* April 4. Available at mailto:ctoensing@merip.org, viewed April 5, 2005.
SMELSER, NEIL J., AND FAITH MITCHELL, EDS. 2002a. *Terrorism: Perspectives from the Behavioral and Social Sciences.* Washington, D.C.: National Academies Press.
———. 2002b. *Discouraging Terrorism. Some Implications of 9/11.* Washington, D.C.: National Academies Press.
SMITH, JACKIE. 2002. "Globalizing Resistance: The Battle of Seattle and the Future of Social Movements." In Jackie Smith and Hank Johnston, eds., *Globalization and Resistance: Transnational Dimensions of Social Movements.* Lanham, Md.: Rowman and Littlefield.
———. 2004. "Exploring Connections between Global Integration and Political Mobilization." *Journal of World Systems Research* 10:255–86.
SMITH, JACKIE, AND HANK JOHNSTON, EDS. 2002. *Globalization and Resistance: Transnational Dimensions of Social Movements.* Lanham, Md.: Rowman and Littlefield.
SOLNICK, STEVEN L. 1998. *Stealing the State: Control and Collapse in Soviet Institutions.* Cambridge: Harvard University Press.
SOWELL, DAVID. 1998. "Repertoires of Contention in Urban Colombia, 1760s–1940s: An Inquiry into Latin American Social Violence." *Journal of Urban History* 24:302–36.
SPRUYT, HENDRIK. 2002. "The Origins, Development, and Possible Decline of the Modern State." *Annual Review of Political Science* 5:127–50.
STANLEY, WILLIAM. 1996. *The Protection Racket State: Elite Politics, Military Extortion, and Civil War in El Salvador.* Philadelphia: Temple University Press.
STATE. 2004a. U.S. Department of State, Office of the Coordinator for Counterterrorism, "Patterns of Global Terrorism 2003." Available at www.state.gov/s/ct/rls/pgtrpt/2003/31569.html, viewed June 20, 2004.

———. 2004b. "Correction to Global Patterns of Terrorism Will Be Issued." June 10, 2004 press statement by Richard Boucher. Available at www.state.gov/r/pa/prs/ps/soor/33433.html, viewed June 20, 2004.

———. 2004c. "The Year in Review (Revised)." Available at www.state/gov/s/ct/rls/pgtrpt/2003/33771.html.

———. 2005. U.S. Department of State, Bureau of Democracy, Human Rights, and Labor. "Country Reports on Human Rights Practices, 2004: Peru." Available at www. state.gov/g/drl/rls/hrrpt/200/41771.html, viewed March 1, 2005.

STEARNS, PETER N., ED. 2001. *The Encyclopedia of World History, Ancient, Medieval, and Modern, Chronologically Arranged.* Boston: Houghton Mifflin.

STEINBERG, MARC W. 1999. "The Talk and Back Talk of Collective Action: A Dialogic Analysis of Repertoires of Discourse among Nineteenth-Century English Cotton Spinners." *American Journal of Sociology* 105:736–80.

STEPHENS, JOHN D. 1989. "Democratic Transition and Breakdown in Western Europe, 1870–1939: A Test of the Moore Thesis." *American Journal of Sociology* 94:1019–77.

STERN, JESSICA. 2003. *Terror in the Name of God: Why Religious Militants Kill.* New York: HarperCollins.

STEVENSON, JOHN. 1992. *Popular Disturbances in England, 1700–1832.* London: Longman. 2d ed.

STINCHCOMBE, ARTHUR L. 1999. "Ending Revolutions and Building New Governments." *Annual Review of Political Science* 2:49–73.

———. "Liberalism and Collective Investments in Repertoires." *Journal of Political Philosophy* 8:1–26.

STRAND, HÅVARD, LARS WILHELMSEN, AND NILS PETTER GLEDITSCH. 2004. *Armed Conflict Dataset Codebook.* Oslo: International Peace Research Institute.

SUGIMOTO, YOSHIO. 1981. *Popular Disturbance in Postwar Japan.* Hong Kong: Asian Research Service.

SUMMERS, CRAIG, AND ERIC MARKUSEN, EDS. 1999. *Collective Violence: Harmful Behavior in Groups and Governments.* Lanham, Md.: Rowman and Littlefield.

SURI, JEREMI. 2003. *Power and Protest: Global Revolution and the Rise of Détente.* Cambridge: Harvard University Press.

SZABÓ, MÁTÉ. 1996. "Repertoires of Contention in Post-Communist Protest Cultures: An East Central European Comparative Survey." *Social Research* 63:1155–82.

TAMBIAH, STANLEY J. 1996. *Leveling Crowds: Ethnonationalist Conflicts and Collective Violence in South Asia.* Berkeley: University of California Press.

TARROW, SIDNEY. 1989. *Democracy and Disorder: Social Conflict, Political Protest and Democracy in Italy, 1965–1975.* New York: Oxford University Press.

———. 1998. *Power in Movement.* New York: Cambridge University Press. 2d ed.

———. 2005. *The New Transnational Activism.* Cambridge: Cambridge University Press.

TARTAKOWSKY, DANIELLE. 1997. *Les Manifestations de rue en France, 1918–1968.* Paris: Publications de la Sorbonne.

———. 1999. *Nous irons chanter sur vos tombes. Le Père-Lachaise, XIXe–XXe siècle.* Paris: Aubier.

———. 2004. *La Manif en éclats.* Paris: La Dispute.

TAYLOR, CHRISTOPHER C. 1999. *Sacrifice as Terror: The Rwandan Genocide of 1994*. Oxford: Berg.

TAYLOR, RUPERT. 1990. "South Africa: Consociation or Democracy?" *Telos* 85: 17–32.

TERREBLANCHE, SAMPIE. 2002. *A History of Inequality in South Africa, 1652–2002*. Pietermaritzburg: University of Natal Press.

THOMPSON, DOROTHY. 1984. *The Chartists: Popular Politics in the Industrial Revolution*. New York: Pantheon.

THOMPSON, LEONARD. 2000. *A History of South Africa*. New Haven: Yale University Press. 3d ed.

THORNTON, PATRICIA M. 2002. "Insinuation, Insult, and Invective: The Threshold of Power and Protest in Modern China." *Comparative Studies in Society and History* 44:597–619.

TILLY, CHARLES. 1985. "War Making and State Making as Organized Crime." In Peter Evans, Dietrich Rueschemeyer, and Theda Skocpol, eds., *Bringing the State Back*. Cambridge: Cambridge University Press.

———. 1986. *The Contentious French*. Cambridge: Harvard University Press.

———. 1992. *Coercion, Capital, and European States, AD 990–1992*. Oxford: Blackwell.

———. 1993. *European Revolutions, 1492–1992*. Oxford: Blackwell. Rev. ed.

———. 1995a. *Popular Contention in Great Britain, 1758–1834*. Cambridge: Harvard University Press.

———. 1995b. "To Explain Political Processes." *American Journal of Sociology* 100:1594–1610.

———. 1997a. "Parliamentarization of Popular Contention in Great Britain, 1758–1834." *Theory and Society* 26:245–73.

———. 1997b. "Means and Ends of Comparison in Macrosociology." *Comparative Social Research* 16:43–53.

———. 1998. *Durable Inequality*. Berkeley: University of California Press.

———. 2001. "Mechanisms in Political Processes." *Annual Review of Political Science* 4:21–41.

———. 2002a. "Event Catalogs as Theories." *Sociological Theory* 20:248–54.

———. 2002b. "Violence, Terror, and Politics as Usual." *Boston Review* 27(3–4): 21–24.

———. 2003. *The Politics of Collective Violence*. Cambridge: Cambridge University Press.

———. 2004a. *Social Movements, 1768–2004*. Boulder: Paradigm Press.

———. 2004b. *Contention and Democracy in Europe, 1650–2000*. Cambridge: Cambridge University Press.

———. 2004c. "Terror, Terrorism, Terrorists." *Sociological Theory* 22:5–13.

———. 2005a. "Regimes and Contention." In Thomas Janoski, Robert R. Alford, Alexander M. Hicks, and Mildred A. Schwartz, eds., *The Handbook of Political Sociology: States, Civil Societies, and Globalization*. Cambridge: Cambridge University Press.

———. 2005b. "Repression, Mobilization, and Explanation." In Christian Davenport, Hank Johnston, and Carol Mueller, eds., *Repression and Mobilization*. Minneapolis: University of Minnesota Press.

———. 2005c. *Trust and Rule*. Cambridge: Cambridge University Press.

———. 2005d. *Identities, Boundaries, and Social Ties*. Boulder: Paradigm Press.
TILLY, CHARLES, LOUISE TILLY, AND RICHARD TILLY. 1975. *The Rebellious Century, 1830–1930*. Cambridge: Harvard University Press.
TISHKOV, VALERY. 1997. *Ethnicity, Nationalism and Conflict in and after the Soviet Union: The Mind Aflame*. London: Sage.
———. 1999. "Ethnic Conflicts in the Former USSR: The Use and Misuse of Typologies and Data." *Journal of Peace Research* 36:571–91.
———. 2001. "The Culture of Hostage Taking in Chechnya." In Alex P. Schmid, ed., *Countering Terrorism through International Cooperation*. Milan: International Scientific and Professional Advisory Council of the United Nations Crime Prevention and Criminal Justice Programme.
———. 2004. *Chechnya: Life in a War-Torn Society*. Berkeley: University of California Press.
TITARENKO, LARISSA, JOHN D. MCCARTHY, CLARK MCPHAIL, AND BOGUSLAW AUGUSTYN. 2001. "The Interaction of State Repression, Protest Form and Protest Sponsor Strength during the Transition from Communism in Minsk, Belarus, 1990–1995." *Mobilization* 6:129–50.
TOFT, MONICA DUFFY. 2003. *The Geography of Ethnic Violence: Identity, Interests, and the Indivisibility of Territory*. Princeton: Princeton University Press.
TRAUGOTT, MARK, ED. 1995. *Repertoires and Cycles of Collective Action*. Durham: Duke University Press.
TRECHSEL, ALEXANDER. 2000. *Feuerwerk Volksrechte. Die Volksabstimmungen in den scheizerischen Kantonen 1970–1996*. Basel: Helbing and Lichtenhahn.
TRIMBERGER, ELLEN KAY. 1978. *Revolution from Above: Military Bureaucrats and Development in Japan, Turkey, Egypt, and Peru*. New Brunswick: Transaction.
TURK, AUSTIN T. 2004. "Sociology of Terrorism." *Annual Review of Sociology* 30: 271–86.
TURNER, BRYAN S. 1997. "Citizenship Studies: A General Theory." *Citizenship Studies* 1:5–18.
UVIN, PETER. 1998. *Aiding Violence: The Development Enterprise in Rwanda*. West Hartford: Kumarian Press.
———. 2001. "Reading the Rwandan Genocide." *International Studies Review* 3:75–99.
———. 2002. "On Counting, Categorizing, and Violence in Burundi and Rwanda." In David I. Kertzer and Dominique Arel, eds., *Census and Identity: The Politics of Race, Ethnicity, and Language in National Censuses*. Cambridge: Cambridge University Press.
VANHANEN, TATU. 1997. *Prospects of Democracy: A Study of 172 Countries*. London: Routledge.
VARGAS LLOSA, MARIO. 1994. *A Fish in the Water: A Memoir*. New York: Farrar Straus Giroux.
VARSHNEY, ASHUTOSH. 2002. *Ethnic Conflict and Civic Life: Hindus and Muslims in India*. New Haven: Yale University Press.
VAN DER VEER, PETER. 1996. "Riots and Rituals: The Construction of Violence and Public Space in Hindu Nationalism." In Paul R. Brass, ed., *Riots and Pogroms*. New York: New York University Press.
VINCIGUERRA, THOMAS. 2005. "The Revolution Will Be Colorized." *New York Times*, March 13.

VOLKOV, VADIM. 2002. *Violent Entrepreneurs: The Use of Force in the Making of Russian Capitalism*. Ithaca: Cornell University Press.
DE WAAL, ALEX. 1997. *Famine Crimes: Politics & the Disaster Relief Industry in Africa*. Oxford: James Currey.
WAINRIGHT, HILARY. 2005. "Civil Society, Democracy and Power: Global Connections." In Helmut Anheier, Marlies Glasius, Mary Kaldor, and Fiona Holland, eds., *Global Civil Society 2004/5*. London: Sage Publications.
WALTER, BARBARA F., AND JACK SNYDER, EDS. 1999. *Civil Wars, Insecurity, and Intervention*. New York: Columbia University Press.
WEISMAN, STEVEN R. 2004. "State Department Report Shows Increase in Terrorism." *New York Times*, June 23, A12.
WIKTOROWICZ, QUINTAN, ED. 2003. *Islamic Activism: A Social Movement Theory Approach*. Bloomington: Indiana University Press.
WILSON, RICHARD ASHBY, ED. 2003. "Political Violence and Language." Special issue of *Anthropological Theory* 3(3).
WIMMER, ANDREAS. 2002. *Nationalist Exclusion and Ethnic Conflict: Shadows of Modernity*. Cambridge: Cambridge University Press.
WOLOCH, ISSER. 1994. *The New Regime: Transformations of the French Civic Order, 1789–1820s*. New York: Norton.
WOOD, LESLEY J. 2004. "Breaking the Bank and Taking to the Streets: How Protesters Target Neoliberalism." *Journal of World Systems Research* 10:69–89.
WORLD BANK. 2004. *World Development Report 2005. A Better Investment Climate for Everyone*. New York: Oxford University Press.
YASHAR, DEBORAH J. 1997. *Demanding Democracy: Reform and Reaction in Costa Rica and Guatemala, 1870s–1950s*. Stanford: Stanford University Press.
ZELIKOW, PHILIP. 2005. "Remarks on Release of 'Country Reports on Terrorism' for 2004." Available at www.state.gov/s/ct/rls/rm/45279.htm, viewed May 21, 2005.
ZHAO, DINGXIN. 2001. *The Power of Tienanmen: State–Society Relations and the 1989 Beijung Student Movement*. Chicago: University of Chicago Press.
ZOLBERG, ARISTIDE. 1978. "Belgium." In Raymond Grew, ed., *Crises of Political Development in Europe and the United States*. Princeton: Princeton University Press.
ZUERN, ELKE. 2001. "South Africa's Civics in Transition: Agents of Change or Structures of Constraint?" *Politikon* 28:5–20.
———. 2002. "Fighting for Democracy: Popular Organizations and Postapartheid Government in South Africa." *African Studies Review* 45:77–102.

INDEX >>

Page numbers in italics refer to figures.

Abbas, Mahmoud, 31, 42–43
action: autonomous, 54–55, 112; bifurcated, 52; collective, 192–95; cosmopolitan, 54–55, 112; forms of, 50–51, 51–52; freedom of, 128; mass, 100; modular, 54–55, 112; parochial, 51; particular, 51–52; rational, 40–41; revolutionary, 55, 162
actors: claim-making forms, 214; coordination among, 123, 126, 127; demobilization, 111; description, 19; networks, 127; openness to, 75; revolutionary situations and, 160, 165; uncertainties, 131; violent, 123, *124*, 127. *See also* performances
Advani, Lal, 68–70
Afghanistan, 140, 148
African National Congress (ANC), 92, 100, 101
Afrikaner culture, 95
agreements, enforcement of, 131
Akaev, Askar, 204
al-Aqsa Martyrs Brigade, 139
al-Mutayri, Sami, 139
al-Qaeda, 32, 138, 139
Albania, 169
Alexandra, South Africa, 103–9, *106–7*
alignments, instability of, 44
"All Purpose Revolution Finder," 159, 165
alliances, control over, 126
allies, availability of, 44, 75, 213
Alvaradok, Juan Velasco, 1
Amnesty International (AI): investigations, 119; on Jamaica, 85; on Morocco, 64, 65; reports, 81; on the U.S.A., 88–89
Andaman Islands, India, 31
Angola, 163–64
Annan, Kofi, 179
Annual Register: advantages, 62–63; data from, 49, 50, 60, 61; on Peru, 63; on Richard Cheney, 74; on terror incidents, 143, 145
apartheid, 95, 96. *See also* South Africa
Archaeological Survey of India (ASI), 69
aristocracy, 8–9
Aristotle, 8–10, 77
armed conflicts, types of, 133, *133*
Armenia, 202, 203
Armitage, Richard, 141
Ashforth, Adam, 91
assembly, right to, 58
association, right to, 58
attorneys, access to, 88

243

authoritarian regimes, 12, 26, 74, 126. *See also specific regimes*
autonomous repertoires, 54–55, 112
autonomy, claims for, 131
Ayodhya, Uttar Pradesh mosque, 67, 119–20, 187
Azerbaijan, 203

Babri Masjid mosque, 67, 69
Bagosora, Théoneste, 152
Balkans, 169, 170, 172
bargaining: citizens and rulers, 213; forms of, 22; mass citizenship and, 58; resources and, 23
Bastille, attack on, 37
Baudoin, René, 38
Beissinger, Mark, 201, 203
Belarus, 204
Belgium: collective actions, 192–95; colonization of Rwanda, 151; demonstrations, *194*; levels of collective violence in, 129; regime type, 27
Berlusconi, Silvio, 179
Bharatiya Janata Party (BJP), 68–69, 87
bifurcated actions, 52
bifurcated claim making, 116
Bihari, Atal, 87
Biko, Steve, 92
Black, J. Cofer, 142
Black Consciousness movement, 92
Blair, Tony, 179
Boer War, 93
Boers, 95
Bolivia, 144
Bophuthatswana homeland, 96
Bosnia-Herzegovina, 169
Botha, P. W., 92, 99, 110
boundaries, 127, 129–32
boycotts, organization of, 91
Bozzoli, Belinda, 103–9
Brazil, 207
Brennan, John O., 142
British Isles, revolutionary situations, 172. *See also* England; Great Britain
Burke, Edmund, 60–61

Bush, George H. W., 73–74
Bush, George W., 88–89, 179
Buthelezi, M. G., 98, 100, 101

Cambodia, 205
campaigns, definition, 53
Canada, 208
capacity-democracy space, 22, 23–25
capital, 20, 73
capitalism, 2–3, 58
capitalization, 52
Casablanca, Morocco, 65
castes, 67, 68, 87
causal coherence: collective violence and, 125; definition, 48; distinguished from symbolic coherence, 48; of performances, 47–49; revolutions and, 156–57
causes, categories of, 42
centers of power, 44, 75, 213
Central Intelligence Agency (CIA), 5, 141
challengers: definition of, 19; demobilization of, 44–45; flexible repertoires of, 44
Chartists, 190
Chechnya, 134, 138
Cheney, Richard, 74
Chiapas, Mexico, 42
Chile, 31, 32, 34
China, 11, 27, 62, 129, 207
Chirac, Jacques, 179, 180, 187
Chrétien, Jean, 179
church (priesthood), 14, 15
Ciskei homeland, 96
citizens: consent of, 212; consultation with, 24–25, 71–72; probability of being heard, 130; protection of, 24–25; revolutions and, 161; rulers and, 213
citizenship: bargaining and, 58; governmental capacity and, 26; rights and obligations of, 24; South African, 93; totalitarian regimes and, 24
city-states, 28
civic organizations, 109

civil liberties: Freedom House checklist, 79–80; ratings of, 77–80, 78, 188; threats to regimes and, 98; in the USSR, 200

civil wars: associated factors, 135; causes, 132; coercion by military forces, 146–47; collective violence and, 33, 132; revolutions *versus*, 163; since WWII, 133–34; terror and, 140, 158

claim making: categories of performances, 75; by citizens, 130; claim recipients and, 52; collective, 33, 49, 50, 187, 213; collective violence and, 121; commitment and, 162; conferences, 206; control over, 211–12; discontinuous, 49; facilitation of, 75; forbidden, 75; Great Britain, 1750–1830's, 49–58; influences on, 22; international forums, 206; nonviolent, 72, 123; performances and, 22; political opportunity structures and, 44; prescribed, 75; public, 49; repetition of routines, 41; repression of, 75; revolutionary action and, 162; ruler's point of view, 73; social organization and, 42; threats by, 111; tolerated, 75; uncertainty of outcomes, 127; WUNC displays and, 189–90. *See also* performances

claim-making repertoires, 149, 186

claimant-object pairs, 35, 186

claimants, influence over, 126

claims: receiving, 49; types of, 32, 182. *See also* claim making

class, 67, 161, 166–67

coalitions: European, 170–73; revolutions and, 160, 165–66; for social movements, 183

Coca Cola boycott, 207

coercion: definition, 19; by military forces, 146–47; organization, 19; ruler's point of view, 73; Uganda, 82–83

coherence: lack of, 215; of performances, 47–49

Cold War, 132

collaboration, 183

collective violence, 118–50; coordination of, 121; definition, 118; lessons, 215–16; low-capacity, democratic regimes, 210; salience–coordination scheme, 121, 125, 127; terror and, 137–50; types of, 122–26

Collier, Paul, 135, 136

Colombia: competition for power, 34; global civil society events, 207; January 1, 2005, 31; terror incidents, 138, 139, 144, 148

colonization, 92–93

"Colored" category, in South Africa, 95

commitments: definition, 20; idioms, 54; ruler's point of view, 73

communal coalitions, 164–65

communication, 183

Communist Manifesto (Marx), 11

communities of taste, 20

compliance, enforced, 146

computers, wearable, 42

"Comrade Generation," 104

conferences, claim-making, 206

Congo, 27, 148

Congress of South African Trade Unions (COSATU), 98

Congress Party, India, 67

consequential claims, 20, 21

Conservative Party, 99

conspiratorial terror, 123, 138

constitutional government, 8–9

contenders, stagecraft, 52

contention: bases of, 58; causal links, 113; definition, 20; in Finer's accounts, 14–15; performances and, 16–17; regime change and, 113–17, 214–15; repertoires of, 30–59, 48–49

contentious gatherings (CGs), 49–58

INDEX ‹ 245

contentious politics: collective violence and, 121; definition, 21; internal mutations, 214; on January 1, 2005, 31; observation of, 45–47; regime change and, 2–3; repertoires and, 22, 41–43; ruler's approach to, 116, 211–12; social movements and, 72; symbolic coherence, 48
contentious repertoires, 73, 80–81
contestation, Dahl on, 13
control: advantages of, 8; of crowds, 57; distance and, 83; of military forces, 65; over alliances, 126; over claim making, 126, 211–12; violence and, 126
coordination: among violent actors, 123, 127; brokerage of, 127; causes of, 126–29; costs of connection and, 128
coordination-salience space, 132
cosmopolitan claim making, 116
cosmopolitan repertoires, 54–55, 112
Costa Rica, 26
countersummits, 206
coups d'etat, 3
criminal activities, 66
criticism of authorities, 58
Croatia, 169
crowds: anticipatory control of, 57; irrationality of, 40–41; smart mobs, 42. *See also* demonstrations
Cyprus, 169

Dahl, Robert, 12–15, *13*, 73
Dalindyebo, Sabata, 97
Dallaire, Roméo, 151, 154, 155
de Klerk, F. W., 99–100
death penalties, 88
decolonization, 177
defections, 161, 162
demagogues, 9
demobilization, 108, 203
democracy: Aristotle on, 8–9; British regimes in S.A., *115*; citizen consent and, 212; citizenship and, 24; civil liberties and, 78; conditions for, 2; Dahl on, 12–13; definition, 21; degrees of, 12; Freedom House ratings, 77–80, *78*; governmental capacity and, 23–25, *26*, *27*, 72; prescribed performances, 76; regime mapping, 16; social movements and, 2; South African regimes, *109*; Western-style, 62
Democratic Alliance, South Africa, 108
democratic regimes. *See* democracy
democratization: demonstrations and, 197; military specialists and, 212; political processes and, 116; social movements and, 182; South African regimes, 111
demonstrations: collapse of the USSR and, 201–4, *202*; definitions, 189; democratization and, 197; French, 195–97, *196*; frequency of, 205; function, 205; at the G8 Summit, 180–81; political rights and, 191–95; ruler's point of view, 75; social movements and, 188–91
Deneckere, Gita, 192–93
Department of Defense, U. S., 141
Department of Homeland Security, 141
Des Forges, Alison, 153
despotic power, 23
destructiveness, 123–24, 125
detention centers, 85
Diradeng, Michael, 103
direct rule, history of, 28
dissidents, 33, 82, 148
Doherty, John, 57
Duyvendak, Jan-Willem, 195
dynastic coalitions, 167

economic inequalities, 94
Economist, 60
Egypt, 207
Eiselen, W. M., 95
elections: para-parliamentary politics and, 56; sovereign people and, 56
electoral campaigns, 53, 67, 84
elites, democracy and, 2

Emigrant Thembuland, 97
empires, management, 28
Encyclopedia of Violence, Peace and Conflict, 122
energy: demobilization and, 111; investment of, 48
England, 207
episodes, symbolic coherence, 22
Estonia, 202, 203
Estrada, Joseph, 42
ethnic divisions: civil wars and, 135; collapse of the USSR and, 200–201; commitment and, 20; identities, 98; political edges, 62
ethnos theory, 95
Europe: revolutionary coalitions, 170–73; revolutionary situations, 164–70, *171. See also specific countries*
events: contentious, 49–51; observation of, 46
Evian-les-Bains, 179–81, 185, 207
exploitation, means of, 93
extrasystemic armed conflict, 133

facilitation, choice of, 73, 74
fascism, Principle and, 10
Fearon, James, 135, 136, 175
Federal Bureau of Investigation (FBI), 141
feudal rebellions, 164
Fillieule, Olivier, 195
Finer, Samuel, 12–15
First Asian Social Forum, Hyderabad, 87
Fish in the Water (Vargas Llosa), 4
forbidden claim making, 75–76, 81–87, 111, 128, 213–14
forum (representatives of populace), 14, 15
France: civil war, 35–37, 38–39; demonstrations, 195–97, *196*; German occupation, 37–38, 39; police, 212–13; revolutionary situations, 172. *See also* French Revolution

Freedom House: checklist, 79–80; on India, 87, 119; on Jamaica, 85; ratings by, 77–80, 188; reports, 81
French Revolution: Belgian reaction to, 193; as model, 172; regime change and, 158–59. *See also* France
Fujimori, Alberto: background, 4–7; media coverage, 84; Montesinos and, 120; use of capital, 20; views of, 73

G8 summits, 179–81, 185
Gandhi, Mohandas, 70
Gandhi, Rajiv, 67, 73
gangs: armed, 66; attacks on gays, 86; salience promoted by, 127; wars, 122
García, Alan, 2, 4, 6–7, 20, 63, 73
gays, 86, 88, 119. *See also* sexual preferences
Gazankulu homeland, 96
General Directorate for the Surveillance of the Territory (DGST), 85
genocide, 151–56, 158
Gentleman's Magazine, 50
George I, King of England, 46
Georgia, 203
Germany, 27, 129, 151
Gingrich, Newt, 74
Gladkova, Inna, 205
glasnost (openness), 61, 198
global civil society, 181, 206, 207–8
globalization, 180–81
Gorbachev, Mikhail, 61, 198, 200, 201
Gordon, George, 57
government: advantages of control, 8; collective violence and, 33; description of, 18
government agents: citizens and, 24; collective violence and, 129; description of, 18; involvement of, 129; police as, 57; totalitarian regimes and, 24

governmental capacity: British regimes in S.A., 115; definition, 21, 22, 23; democracy and, 72; despotic power and, 23; regime types and, 26–29, 27; resources and, 76; rewards and, 198; rights and, 23; South African regimes, 109; totalitarian regimes and, 24; variation in regimes, 26
grassroots organizations, 109
Great Britain, 49–58, 212
Greece, 207
Guantánamo Bay, Cuba, 88–89
Guzmán, Abimael, 1–2

habit, innovation and, 41
Habyarimana, Juvénal, 151–56, 154
Hansard's Parliamentary Debates, 50
Hansen, Thomas Blom, 69
Hardy, Siméon-Prosper, 36, 37
Hassan II, King of Morocco, 64, 73
Higenyi, Jimmy, 82
high-capacity democratic regimes, 81, 86–87, 128, 129, 148–49
high-capacity nondemocratic regimes, 81, 128, 129, 148–49, 210
Hindu–Muslim strife, 67–70; destructiveness, 125; Gujarat massacre, 124; regime change and, 214–15; report on, 119; social movements and, 187
history, public politics and, 10–12
History of Government (Finer), 14
Hoeffler, Anke, 135, 136
"Holy Spirit" rebels, 64
homelands, South Africa, 96
Honduras, 207
Humala, Antauro, 33
human rights: INGOs, 206; public inquiries into, 84–85; reports, 119–20. *See also specific rights*
Human Rights Watch (HRW), 65; human rights reports, 119; on Morocco, 75, 85; reports, 81; on Toledo regime, 121
Hungary, 169, 170, 172
Hunt, Orator, 57

Hutu Power activists, 153, 154
Hutus, 130, 151–56

Iberia, 170–72, 172
identities: boundaries and, 129–32; ethnic, 98; internal conflicts and, 145–46; labels and, 47–49; repertoires and, 42; street demonstrations and, 62; tribal, 98; uncertainties and, 131; us/them boundaries, 127
identity claims, 32; description, 184; nonviolent presentation, 72; political, 195; social movements and, 182
Ilal-Amam movement, 64–65
inclusive hegemonies, 13
independence: claims for, 131; revolution and, 163
India: democracy in, 67–70; Freedom House report, 119; global civil society events, 207; governmental capacity, 72; levels of collective violence in, 129; military forces in, 34; Pakistan and, 87; performances, 86–87; regime type, 72; trajectory of, 212–13
Indian National Congress (INC), 188
Indians, South African, 94
industrial conflicts, 2–3
inequalities, regime's influence on, 14
Informal Anarchic Federation, 144
information costs, 41
informers, violence against, 91
infrastructural power, 23
Inkatha Freedom Party, 98, 100, 101–3
innovation: change and, 43, 112; in claim-making performances, 116; repertoires and, 41–43; in routines, 41; technological, 41–42
insurgencies, 87, 136
Interahamwe militia, 152, 153, 154
interest-based coalitions, 166–68
internal armed conflicts, 133
international courts of justice, 88
international forums, 206

International Labor Organization, interventions, 177
International Monetary Fund, 4, 204
international nongovernmental organizations (INGOs), 204, 206
International Working Men's Association, 194
internationalized internal armed conflicts, 133
Internet, 207
interpersonal violence, 123
interstate wars, 125, 133
Iran, 27, 72, 129
Iraq, 31, 34, 144, 148, 197
Israel, 139
Italian city-states, 14–15
izimpimpi (informers), 91, 104

Jacqueries, 164
Jamaica, 27, 65–66, 72, 85–86, 129
Jamaica Labour Party (JLP), 65, 66
Jamaican Constabulary Force (JCD), 86
Janmabhoomi, Ram, 67
Japan, 27, 129
Jarrin, Mercado, 5
Joint Expeditionary Digital Information (JEDI) program, 42
Josse, Raymond, 37–38
journalists, attacks on, 121, 139. *See also* media

Kagame, Paul, 152, 153, 154, 155–56, 163
Kaitouni, Mohamed Idrissi, 65
Kampala, Uganda, 82
KaNgwane homeland, 96
Kashmir, India: Pakistan and, 32; rally in, 87; terror incidents, 139, 140, 143, 144, 145
Kathmandu, Nepal, 31, 43
Kazakhstan independence, 203
kidnappings, 138, 140
King, Martin Luther, 62
Kingston, Jamaica, 66
Köhler, Horst, 179
Koizumi, Junichiro, 179

Kony, Joseph, 32, 64
Kosovo, 134
Ku Klux Klan, 62
Kuchma, Leonid, 204
Kuwait, 139
KwaNdebele homeland, 96
KwaZulu homeland, 100, 101–3
Kyrgysztan, 204

labeling of performances, 47–49
labor, compromises with, 2–3
Laden, Osama bin (aka Usama bin Ladin), 32, 139
Laitin, David, 135, 136, 175
Lakwena, Alice, 64
Land Warrior experiment, 42
Langevin, Paul, 37
Latvia, 202
Le Pen, Jean-Marie, 197
learning, effects of, 41
legal inequalities, 94
Léman Social Forum, 181
Lemkin, Raphael, 158
Liberation of the Cabinda Enclave (FLEC), 163–64
Liberia, 148
local assemblies, 38, 39
London Chronicle, 50
L'Opinion newspaper, 65
Lords Resistance Army, 31, 32, 83
Louis XVI, King of France, 37
low-capacity democratic regimes, 77, 81, 128, 129
low-capacity nondemocratic regimes, 81–83, 135, 148, 178, 210
Low Countries, Europe, 171
loyalty, activation of, 73

Macedonia, 169
Mahabharata, 68
Mahdi, Aideed, 137
Mahdi, Ali, 137
Mandela, Nelson, 99–100, 102, 215
manhood suffrage, 193
Mann, Michael, 23
"March 23 Group," 64
Marcos, Ferdinand, 176

Marshall, T. H., 12
martial law, 63
Marx, Karl, 11, 166–67
mass actions, 100
mass killings, 130
Mayekiso, Moses (Moss), 103–4, 105
Mayekiso, Mzwanele, 103, 105
McNeill, William H., 189
media: attention to violence, 33; claimant-object pairs and, 186; contentious politics in, 31; coverage of Fujimori, 84; importance of, 7; reports of terrorism in, 141; in Rwandan conflict, 154, 156. *See also* journalists
members, definition of, 19
Mexico, 208
migration, 56
military coalitions, 167, 171
military forces: Aristotle on, 9–10; autonomous, 72; civil wars and, 132; civilian rule and, 34; control of, 65; costs of, 56; coups d'etat and, 3; dissident, 135; insurgency, 136; insurgents and, 83; investment in, 71–72; loss of support, 164; Peruvian, 33; rebellions and, 105; salience promoted by, 127; satellite links, 42; subordination of, 174; terror applied by, 140; threats by, 146–47
military specialists, 212
militias: French, 38, 39; salience promoted by, 127; threats by, 146–47
Milles Collines radio-TV, 154, 156
Milner, Lord, 94
Milosevic, Slobodan, 203
Ming China, 11
Mirror of Parliament, 50
mobilization: based on identities, 98; peaceful, 87; of populations, 57; rapid intervention in, 206; Soviet collapse and, 203
models: emulation of, 48–49; for social movements, 183
Modi, Narendra, 119
modular claim making, 116

modular repertoires, 54–55, 112
Mogano, Piet, 105
Mohammed VI, King of Morocco, 65
monarchies: Aristotle on, 8–9; citizenship and, 24
Montagnards, 205
Montesinos, Vladimiro, 5, 120
Montesinos Torres, Vladimiro Ilyich, 5–7, 20, 33
Moore, Barrington, 11
Morning Chronicle, 50
Moroccan Association of Human Rights, 84
Morocco: contentious politics in, 64–65; Freedom House ratings, 80; governmental capacity, 72; levels of collective violence in, 129; performances, 84–85
Morote, Osman, 2
Movement for Homosexual Integration and Liberation, 31
Muhammad IV, King of Morocco, 84–85
Museveni, Yoweri, 31, 63, 73, 82–83
Musharraf, Pervez, 32
myths, drama and, 105

Namibia, 99, 114
naming, of phenomena, 46
Natal, South Africa, 101–3
national coalitions, 164, 168
National Commission on Terrorist Attacks, 142
National Counterterrorism Center (NCTC), 142, 144–45
National Forum, South Africa, 92
National Liberation Army (ELN), 139
National Party, 92, 98, 99
National Resistance Movement, Uganda, 82–83
nationalism, 131, 203
Native Affairs Department (NAD), 97
Necker, Jacques, 37
Nepal, 34
netwar, 42
networks of actors, 127
Newton, Huey P., 62

Nguni, 96
nobility (privileged class), 14, 15
nongovernmental organizations (NGOs), 84, 204, 205, 206
Norway, 72
Ntaryamira, Cyprien, 152
Ntawutagiripfa, Jean, 153
numbers, idioms, 54

O'Connell, Daniel, 57
O'Connor, Feargus, 57
oligarchies, 8–10, 14, 24
opponents, intimidation of, 148
opportunism, 199
opportunities: demobilization and, 112; shifting, 44
Opus Dei, 31, 33
Opus Gay, 33
"orange revolution," 204
organizational forms, 42
organizing arguments, 22
Other Backward Classes, 68
Ottoman Empire, 169, 170
outsiders, definition of, 19
Oxford English Dictionary (OED), 189

Paige, Jeffrey, 156
Pakistan, 31, 32, 87, 139
palace (monarch and following), 14, 15
Palerma, Ricardo, 31
Panitchpakidi, Supachai, 179
para-parliamentary politics, 56
parliamentary democracies, 3
parochial action, 51
parochial claim making, 116
Parsa, Misagh, 157, 175–76
particular action, 51–52
particular claim making, 116
path-dependency, 116
patron-client coalitions, 166
Patterson, Orlando, 65–66
peacekeeping forces, 154
Pentagon, attack on, 122, 138
People's National Party, Jamaica, 65
perestroika, 198

Pérez de Cuellar, Javier, 6
performances: description of, 35; labeling, 47–49; myths and, 105; repertoires and, 34–41, 214; routines, 41–42; ruler's point of view, 75; symbolic coherence, 22; Uganda, 82–83. *See also* actors; claim making
Peru: *Annual Register* on, 63; capital, 20; collective violence, 120–21; democracy type, 72; government, 18, 33; government agents, 18; governmental capacity, 72; history, 1–2, 4–8; January 1, 2005, 31; major political actors, 19; performances, 83–84; political resources, 19; regime space, 26; regimes, 19, 72; standing claim, 32; support for military, 164; truth commission, 209–10
Peruvian Truth and Reconciliation Commission, 83–84
petitions, 57, 58
polarization: identities and, 130–31
police: action by, 57, 62; armed, 212–13; demonstrations and, 180–81; force used by, 121; killing of, 85; powers of, 98; salience promoted by, 127; shootings by, 86
political actors: claim-making forms, 214; coordination of, 127; description, 19; revolutionary situations and, 165. *See also* actors; performances
political alignments, 75
political liberties, 200
political opportunity structures (POS): changes in, 187; regime change and, 110, 114; regimes and, 43–44; ruler's point of view, 75; social movements and, 204
Political Organizations Law, Uganda, 82–83
political resources, 19, 73
political rights: demonstrations and, 191–95; Freedom House checklist, 79; ratings of, 77–80, 77, 188

politics, forms of, 16
Politics (Aristotle), 10
polyarchies, 14, 73
population growth, 56
Portugal, 207
postwar reconstruction, 177
Powell, Colin, 141–42
power: access to, 76; advantages of, 8; centers within regimes, 44, 75, 213; despotic, 23; forcible transfer of, 159–60; of gangs, 66; independent centers of, 213; international networks, 206; national structure of, 55; predators and, 23; of rulers, 173; sharing of, 100
power holders, 19, 44, 52. *See also* ruler-citizen relations; rulers
predators, 23
prescribed claim making, 75–76, 81–87, 111, 213–14
Prevention of Terrorism Act, India, 88
Principle–History continuum, 10–12, 12–15
prioritization of observations, 46
prisons, conditions, 121
privacy, rights to, 58
Prodi, Romano, 179
program claims, 32; control over, 126; demonstrations and, 195; description, 184; nonviolent presentation, 72; social movements and, 182; street demonstrations and, 62
proletarianization, 57
Promotion of Bantu Self-Government Act, 96
public gathering permits, 84
public policies, 20–21
Putin, Vladimir, 179

QwaQwa homeland, 96

racial divisions, 62, 93–96
racial modernism, 104
Ramaphosa, Cyril, 100
Ramayana, 68
Rand Corporation, 5
Rashtriya Swayamsevak Sangh (RSS), 68
rational action, crowds and, 40–41
Reagan, Ronald, 73
reformist coalitions, 171
regime change, 14, 158–59, 214–15. *See also* revolution
regime space, 25–29, 26, 70–73
regimes: Aristotle on, 8–10; capacity-democracy space, 211–12; civil wars and, 134; classification of, 10–12, 13, 14, 15; definition, 19; description, 1–17; failed suppression of claims, 163; Freedom House ratings, 77–80; function, 18–29; map of, 16; member defections, 161; public policies, 20–21; regime space and, 70–73; repertoires and, 60–89; social movements and, 186–88; territorial dimensions, 14; trajectories of, 212–13; transitions, 2; types, 27
regional divisions, 67
religion: commitment and, 20; divisions, 67–70; Hindu–Muslim strife, 67–70; liberties, 200; right to practice, 120; violence and, 125
repertoires: autonomous, 54–55, 112; changes, 108, 175; changing, 51–55; of contention, 30–59; cosmopolitan, 54–55, 112; definition, vii; flexibility of, 39–41; incremental changes in, 45; modular, 54–55, 112; performances and, 22, 34–41, 214; reasons for change, 56–59; regimes and, 60–89, 186; revolutions and, 161–62; symbolic coherence, 22; types of, 40; variation in, 43–45
repression, 73–74, 176
resistance, 108, 162
resources, 23, 134
retaliation, 131
revolution, 151–78; "all-purpose finder," 159, 165; analysis of, 122; background to, 161–64; coalitions

and, 166–68; collective violence and, 33; definition, 156–57, 160–61, 175–76; directness of relations and, 166; European situations, 164–70; identification of, 156–61; non-European, 175–78; outcomes, 160, 162–63, 174–75, 177; political processes and, 116; proximate conditions, 159
Revolutionary Armed Forces of Columbia (FARC), 31, 139, 144
Rheingold, Howard, 42
Richelieu, Cardinal, 35
rights: British acquisition of, 58; bundles of, 13–14; citizenship and, 24; national security and, 72. *See also specific rights*
Riot Act, English law, 46–47
Robert, Vincent, 195
Robles, Cirilo, 210
ruler-citizen relations, 214
rulers: citizens and, 213; excessive demands of, 173; limits to power of, 182; means of violence and, 126; power of, 173; views of, 73–77, 116; of weak governments, 134
Russia/Poland, 171
Rwanda, 130, 157–61
Rwandan Patriotic Front (RPF), 154

Saakashvili, Mikhail, 203
Sabha, Lok, 67
salience: causes of, 126–29; freedom of action and, 128; levels of violence and, 131; of short-run damage, 123
salience-coordination topology, 137–41
Sambanis, Nicholas, 136
Sanchez, Luis Alberto, 63
Saudi Arabia, 31
Savimbi, Jonas, 163
Schock, Kurt, 163
Schröder, Gerhard, 179
Seaga, Edward, 66, 73
Sebola, Albert, 105, 107
Second War of Freedom, 93

sedition charges, 86, 105
self-representations, 54
Sendero Luminoso (Shining Path): coercion by, 19; commitment, 20; offenses, 83; in Peru, 1–2; violence against civilians, 120
separatists, 97
September 11, 2001, 122, 138
Servicio de Inteligencia Nacional (SIN), 5, 7
settings, importance of, 50–51, 183
sexual preferences, 130. *See also gays*
Shake Hands with the Devil (Dallaire), 151
Shangaan-Tsonga, 96
Shangaans, 96
Shevardnadze, Eduard, 203
short-run damage, 123, *124*
Sierra Leone, 148
signaling systems, 42
Simitis, Konstantinos, 179
Sinhalese forces, 140
Six Day War, Alexandra, South Africa, 103–9
Slovo, Joe, 100–101
smart mobs, 42
social life, 42
social-movement repertoire, 53, 162, 175
social movements, 179–208; claims, 182; collective violence and, 211; contentious politics and, 72; distinctions of, 181–83; elements of, 183–86; labeling, 48–49; parliamentary democracies and, 2; parliaorganizational mentary democracies and, 3; political processes and, 116; political resources and, 19; regimes and, 186–88; trajectories, 182; transnational, 204–8
social relations, commitments and, 20
social ties, repertoires and, 42
social transformation, 174

solidarity, redefinition of, 56
Somalia, 27, 129, 136–37
Sotho, 96
South Africa, 93, 103–9, *109*, 136
South West Africa. *See* Namibia
Southern Ndebele, 96
Southern Sotho, 96
Soviet Communist Party, 198
Soviet Union: breakup, 169, 198–201; demonstrations, *202*; levels of violence, 128–29; weakening authority, 131
Soweto, 91
Spain, 148
standing claims, 32–33; description, 184; nonviolent presentation, 72; social movements and, 182; street demonstrations and, 62
State Department, U.S., 119, 138, 140, 147–48
state socialism, 10
street courts, 104
street politics, 112
strikes, 191, 194, *194*
Sudan, 83, 129, 148
suicide bombings, 65, 137–38
supporters: availability of, 44, 75; changing, 131
Suppression of Terrorism Bill, Uganda, 82–83
Swazi, 96
Switzerland, 129
symbolic coherence: claim making and, 22; collective violence and, 125; definition, 48; distinguished from causal coherence, 48; political impact and, 215; revolutions and, 156–57
Syria, 207

tactical advantages, 43
Tamil forces, 140
Tarrow, Sidney, 206
Tartakowsky, Danielle, 195, 197
technological determinism, 41–42
Tembuland (Dalindeybo region), 97

territorial coalitions, 166–68
territorial reserves, 95
territoriality, 14, 71–72
terror: definition of, 146; by national armies, 140; violence and, 137–41
terrorism: annual reports, 119; definition, 140, 147–48; domestic targets of, 147; incidents in January 2003, 139–40; international attacks, *145*; reported deaths from, 146
Terrorist Threat Integration Center, 141, 142
Thirty Years War, 35
threats: compliance enforced by, 146; demobilization and, 112; to rights, 52; ruler's point of view, 73; shifting, 44
Tiananmen Square, Beijing, 61, 62
time periods, events and, 50
Times, 50
Tokugawa, Japan, 11
Toledo, Alejandro, 6–7, 31, 32, 84, 120, 209–10
tolerated claim making, 75–76, 81–87, 111, 127, 213–14
Tomlinson Commission, 96
totalitarian regimes, 24
Tower, John, 74
trade, 178
trade union activity, 53, 98
trading times, 20
Transkei homeland, 96
transnational corporations, 204
treason, charges of, 82
Truth and Reconciliation Commission: Peruvian, 120; South Africa, 103, 105
Tsonga, 96
Tswana, 96
"tulip revolution," 204
Tupac Amaru Revolutionary Movement (MRTA), 2, 20, 63, 72, 120
Turki-Cypriot war, 169
turnouts, definition, 193

Tutsi, 151–56, 152
Tutsi Rwanda Patriotic Front (RPF), 152
tyranny, 8, 26, 98
tyrants, power to, 210

Uganda: competition for power, 34; contention in, 32; Freedom House ratings, 80; governmental capacity, 71, 72; January 1, 2005, 31; performances, 82–83; regime type, 63–64, 72; terror in, 148; Tutsi military forces in, 152
Uganda's People's Congress (UPC), 82
Ukraine, 203, 204
unarmed insurrections, 163
Union of South Africa, 93
United Democratic Front (UDF), 98, 101
United Democratic Movement, South Africa, 108
United Jihad Council, 145
United Kingdom, 144
United Nations: High Commissioner for Refugees (UNHCR), 205; interventions, 177; peacekeeping forces, 154; political environments and, 204; in Rwanda, 152
United States: global civil society events, 207; governmental capacity, 72; levels of collective violence in, 129; regime type, 72; terrorist attacks in, 148; trajectory of, 212–13; War on Terror, 88–89
unity, idioms, 54
Universal Declaration of Human Rights, 84
urbanization, 56
Uttar Pradesh, India, 67–70
Uwilingiyimana, Agathe, 152

Vargas Llosa, Mario, 4, 20
Venda homeland, 96
vengeance, 109
vigilantes, 101
Villanueva del Campo, Armando, 63
Villeneuve, conflict of May 1440, 38–39
Vinciguerra, Thomas, 204
violence: bargaining and, 213; boundaries and, 129–32; coercion and, 19; control of means of, 126; coordination of, *124*; ethnopolitical, 131–32; by gangs, 66; in India, 86–87; interpersonal, 123, *124*; media attention, 33; penalties for, 75; regime transitions and, 2; salience-coordination space, 124, *124*; specialists in, 137; strategy of terror, 138; Uganda, 82–83; virtuous, 68. *See also* collective violence
violence specialists, 127, 148
"Vladivideos," 7
Votes and Proceedings of Parliament, 50
voting rights, 58

War on Terror, 88–89
warlords, 101
Warsaw Pact, 131
Waxman, Henry, 141
welfare paternalism, 104
welfare states, 12
Wenceslas Square, Prague, 61
Who is Controlling Whom? (U.S. Army Intelligence), 6
Wilkes, John, 57
Wolfensohn, James, 179
work-generated solidarities, 20
workers, proletarianization, 57
World Bank, 177, 204
World Health Organization, 122
World Social Forum, 181
World Trade Center attack, 122, 138
World Trade Organization (WTO), 42, 181, 204, 207
worthiness, idioms, 54

WUNC displays: definition, 53, 54; demonstrations and, 189–90; performances integrated with, 70; prescribed, 213; social movements and, 183–86, 197

Xhosa, 96

Yeltsin, Boris, 199, 201
Yugoslavia, 131, 169, 203
Yushchenko, Victor, 204

Zapatista movement, 42
Zelikow, Philip, 142
Zwane, Ashwell, 103, 105